# THE DEVIL'S TOY BOX

# THE DEVIL'S TOY BOX

*Exposing and Defusing Promethean Terrorists*

ANDREW FOX

Potomac Books

*An imprint of the University of Nebraska Press*

All rights reserved. Potomac Books is an imprint of the
University of Nebraska Press.
Manufactured in the United States of America.

∞

Library of Congress Cataloging-in-Publication Data
Names: Fox, Andrew J., author.
Title: The devil's toy box: exposing and defusing Promethean
terrorists / Andrew Fox.
Description: Lincoln: Potomac Books, an imprint of the
University of Nebraska Press, [2022] | Includes bibliographical
references and index.
Identifiers: LCCN 2021043988
ISBN 9781640124790 (hardback)
ISBN 9781640125360 (epub)
ISBN 9781640125377 (pdf)
Subjects: LCSH: Terrorism—Prevention. | Security, Interna-
tional. | BISAC: POLITICAL SCIENCE / Security (National &
International) | POLITICAL SCIENCE / Terrorism
Classification: LCC HV6431 .F677 2022 | DDC 363.325—dc23/
eng/20220114
LC record available at https://lccn.loc.gov/2021043988

Set in Arno Pro by Mikala R. Kolander.

The views expressed in this book are my own and do not
necessarily reflect those of the SIGMA organization.

For Dara,
who managed the house and kids while I was in
Monterey, who put up with my stacks of research
materials in our bedroom, and who formatted my
big, fat thesis

# Contents

# Illustrations

# Tables

# Acknowledgments

I WOULD LIKE TO thank the U.S. Department of Homeland Security (DHS) and its Federal Emergency Management Agency (FEMA), the entities that founded and continue to fund the Center for Homeland Defense and Security (CHDS), the education institute housed on the campus of the Naval Postgraduate School in Monterey, California. FEMA's financial support and my home agency's allotment of work time for study time allowed me to attend the CHDS master's degree program, a combined classroom–distance learning program, from September 2016 to March 2018 and to conduct a large portion of the research that informs this book. Classes led by Dr. Christopher Bellavita, Richard Bergin, Dr. David Brannan, Dr. Rodrigo Nieto-Gómez, and Dr. Anders Strindberg were especially helpful as I grappled with the issues raised in this book and formulated my master's thesis. Rodrigo, along with Kathleen Kiernan, also served as my thesis adviser. They provided invaluable suggestions and support while I was building my thesis, and neither of them, thankfully, gave me hell about it running way, way long (I understand it will forever hold the record of the longest master's thesis ever accepted at the CHDS). I'd also like to thank the marvelous support staff at the CHDS who performed yeoman work in ensuring we students had the knowledge and resources we needed to succeed. My educational experience at the CHDS would not have been half as rich without the engagement provided by my fellow students in my cohort, nearly thirty homeland security professionals from federal, state, and local agencies across the country in fields ranging from law enforcement to public health. I loved hearing stories about life in the U.S. Coast Guard and the Secret

Service, and I appreciate that no one scoffed at my ideas regarding the dangers of solar weather events and the usefulness of science fiction writers for homeland security.

I owe thanks to Dr. Arlan Andrews, the founder of SIGMA, the science fiction think tank, for championing the ideas first set forth in my thesis, both with his organization and then in meetings with homeland security officials. I am honored now to be a part of SIGMA. I'd like to commemorate the recent passing of three individuals, each notable for their contributions to science fiction and to SIGMA: Dr. Jerry Pournelle, Kathleen Goonan, and Dr. Ben Bova. Also, thank you, Catherine Asaro, for being so gracious and forthcoming in sharing with me your experiences in SIGMA when I asked.

Peter Rubie of FinePrint Literary Management has been a stalwart champion of this book and provided a worthy sounding board as this project went through multiple iterations. Thanks to my editor at Potomac Books, Tom Swanson, for giving me my head regarding this book rather than imposing his own vision at the outset.

Finally, I must thank my family for their patience during my eighteen months with the CHDS. Not only did they have to deal with my two-week-long absences every three months, but they also bore the brunt of my being continually distracted by the conflicting demands of concurrent work and school and the stress of completing my 420-page thesis, a self-inflicted Sisyphean mountain, in time to graduate. Special thanks are due my wife, Dara, who volunteered to format that Moby Dick of a document according to the CHDS's standards and who never once threatened to claw out my eyes when Microsoft Word made her blood boil.

# THE DEVIL'S TOY BOX

# Prologue

## *The Parable of the Devil's Toy Box*

THE DEVIL HAS A toy box. It contains many toys, and the devil loves them all, although he loves some more than others. The devil plays rough. He uses his toys to incite fear, to sow mayhem and distrust, and to destroy and kill. The devil has his favorite playthings, things he likes to play with again and again. However, like a child with a short attention span, he frequently becomes bored with his old, familiar toys and goes looking for new things to play with. So in addition to storing his old toys in the toy box, the devil also fills it with smaller boxes, gestation boxes. Inside these smaller boxes, strange new toys grow and take their forms.

The devil's victims don't like how the devil plays. They don't like his toys. They spend a lot of time and effort thinking up ways to defend themselves. But the toy box poses a seemingly insurmountable problem. The defenders can't tell which toy or what type the devil will pull from his box next. Occasionally, a spy is able to peer inside the toy box but not often. The defenders figure, reasonably, that the devil will most often choose to play with his favorite toys. They've come up with ways to protect themselves from those toys, even though their defenses don't always work. The devil still wins sometimes, even with the old toys, thanks to his stealth and craftiness.

The old toys are bad enough. But what robs the defenders of their sleep is the thought of what possible new toys are growing in the inner recesses of the toy box. Unknown, unpredictable threats are the most frightening. The element of surprise is among the devil's strongest weapons, and those new toys will best enable him to create surprise. The devil is a crafty alchemist; this is his greatest strength.

He excels in taking ordinary things, seemingly harmless things, and combining them into deadly toys no one expects.

The defenders have a harder job than their enemy does. The devil can get lucky just once and claim victory. But the defenders must be lucky *always*. The defenders know they can't exclusively rely upon luck to win. They must prepare. They have to guess what kinds of toys the devil will pull from his toy box and create appropriate shields to fend off each one. But manufacturing shields is expensive, time consuming, and resource intensive. The overstretched defenders can't possibly make shields to foil every conceivable new toy that might emerge from the box. If they tried, they would spend every penny in the treasury. So the defenders need to predict two things—which new toys are most *likely* to emerge from the devil's toy box and which will be the most *dangerous* ones.

The defenders need a crystal ball. Only a working crystal ball can tell them what they will need to defend against five to ten years in the future. Only a working crystal ball can give the weaponsmiths at the forgery enough time to create the needed shields. But crystal balls are expensive, finicky, and unreliable. They can give wrong predictions and lead users down blind alleys. Yet the alternatives to using one are either *impossible* (trying to defend against every conceivable new toy) or *immoral* (not making any shields at all and simply accepting the potentially terrible consequences).

Like it or not, the defenders need to use a crystal ball, even an imperfect one. Yet they must insist on a few essential qualities: the crystal ball must not be so expensive that procuring it will empty the treasury, it must give comparable readings over many uses, and it must allow the defenders to recalibrate and improve it over time. What is the best crystal ball the defenders can hope for? One that will provide enough foresight that its cost and inconvenience are outweighed by the costs of whatever destruction the devil's new toys would have caused in the absence of any forecasting at all.

THE PACE OF TECHNOLOGICAL change is accelerating. The prospects can make you giddy. But they should also make you afraid.

The shadow of Prometheus looms more and more darkly in our future.

In Greek mythology, Prometheus is the rebellious Titan who steals fire from the gods and grants it to mankind. But the gift proves to be a two-edged sword: fire can be used to cook and to warm, but it can also be used to destroy and kill. In other words, every benefit we derive from Prometheus's gift of fire is mirrored by the many ways fire can utterly destroy us.

The modern equivalents of Prometheus's gift of fire are such innovations as nanotechnology, gene manipulation, and artificial intelligence, to mention but three examples—all of which are all paving the way for exponential growth in our ability to modify and improve ourselves and our world, and create safe habitats for us deep in the ocean and in the frigid vastness of outer space. Powers that were once limited to governments and their armed forces can now be at the fingertips of anyone determined enough to master technical tools. But the fabulous benefits these new technologies bring are counterbalanced by their dark potential. Home gene-splicing kits can be used to make airborne pathogens (consider what the effects of a half dozen consecutive COVID-19 equivalents in a period of a few years might be). Three-dimensional (3D) home printers will let terrorists—domestic as well as foreign—create surface-to-air missiles and other weapons in a cloak of privacy. Hobbyist drones will let anyone launch deadly attacks from sheltered locations miles from their victims. The new worlds of virtual reality, when combined with a worldwide communications web and the skills of malicious hackers, open fresh conduits for targeted or indiscriminate murder.

These emerging technologies are increasingly affordable and accessible, and oftentimes they're no more complicated to operate than a satellite TV's control box or a smart phone. We're entering a world where anyone with a grudge will be able to fabricate in their basement weapons whose destructive power dwarfs that of the crude improvised explosive devices (IEDs) terrorists have used until now. The criminal hacking organization DarkSide obtained a suite of hacking tools on a dark web marketplace that enabled it to successfully carry out a ransomware attack on the Colonial Pipeline that resulted in severe gasoline shortages along the Eastern Seaboard of the United States in May 2021. Had this denial-of-service attack been coordinated with similar hacking attacks on other critical infrastructure choke points, food deliveries to wholesalers and retail grocery stores all up the Eastern Seaboard could have been disrupted, emptying shelves, causing widespread panic and looting, and possibly ending in the deaths by starvation of hundreds of thousands of people.

This is the stuff of nightmares. Frightened? If so, you're right to be apprehensive. But the more we know about these dangers, the more we can pressure our leaders to be prepared. They must not bury their heads in the sand. They need to be ready to act to keep us safe. Neither they nor we can afford to remain passive and allow threats to accumulate. What can be done?

Passivity in the face of developing threats is not the only option. We *can* prepare. Society's antagonists are unpredictable, creative, and adaptable. They range from neo-Nazis seeking to "defend white civilization" to anarchists wanting to "smash capitalism," from Islamists striving to violently impose sharia law to misogynist incels expressing their furious resentment against women. New variations of resentful and aggrieved misanthropes are bound to arise, eager to act out their hatreds in violence. All the while evading culpability, unfriendly governments, such as those of Russia, China, North Korea, or Iran, can weaponize supposedly independent criminal organizations to carry out cyberattacks or kinetic attacks.

Strategic surprise will always remain a possibility. But we *don't* have to wait passively for the hammer to fall, telling ourselves we will come up with countermeasures once we know the parameters of actualized threats.

We can be *proactive*; we can deter the worst threats from happening. We can use the Promethean "Spyglass." This procedure, which is described step-by-step in chapter 7, is based on best practices from seven decades of forecasting efforts. The Promethean Spyglass is a roadmap for conducting a thorough analysis of the devil's toy box. It can help homeland security leaders think (and act) productively to identify and tackle the threats of tomorrow *before* they wreak havoc and show up as gory pictures on our screens and newspapers.

How can we rank and prioritize threats that we haven't yet encountered and that, at present, are just fearsome ideas? We build on the past seventy years of developments in the techniques of forecasting and the elicitation and amalgamation of expert opinion. Since the end of World War II, philosophers, social scientists, statisticians, mathematicians, and computer scientists have developed a wide range of forecasting methods for predicting developments in science and technology, political events, and social trends. Futures studies, red teaming, and predictions markets all provide pieces of the puzzle, or best practices that forecasters and futurists have selected through decades of practice.

In the United States, the federal and state governments spend hundreds of billions of dollars each year on homeland security. Most of those dollars are spent preparing for, responding to, and mitigating habitual, familiar threats. Yet we as taxpayers have a right to expect that our homeland security establishment also takes measures to protect us from the unexpected. Our defenders shouldn't regularly resort to "closing the barn doors after the cows have fled." They shouldn't wait to invent new countermeasures only after innovative terror attacks are attempted. Every time spokespersons for our homeland security agencies claim that "there was no way we could have foreseen this," the public loses a bit more confidence in its defenders. A series of events equivalent to DarkSide's ransomware attack on the Colonial Pipeline, the results of which were not only highly publicized but also directly impinged upon the lives of millions of people, could easily result in a collapse of the public's trust in the competency of its governmental agencies and providers of essential infrastructure.

Again, we as a society *can* prepare. Given that society's antagonists are unpredictable, creative, adaptable human beings, we can never perfectly prepare. But we don't need to wait passively for the blows to fall and then helplessly watch the carnage on the evening news. The Promethean Spyglass, an imperfect but essential crystal ball, can help the homeland security community think (and act) productively about the threats lurking beyond the horizon.

*The Devil's Toy Box* introduces a terrifying set of emerging nightmares that most Americans have not yet begun to worry about. I'm not aiming to induce a reaction of learned helplessness, however—far from it. Resigned fatalism is the worst reaction. It leads people to cower in their beds and cover their eyes and ears, trying to ignore the dangers because they think no one can avert them. This book, however, says otherwise.

So let us now begin thinking about tomorrow, both the good possibilities and the bad. And let us do so not with an anticipative cringe but with confidence and hope.

# ONE

## Future Shock Visits the Subway

*The 1995 Aum Shinrikyo Sarin Gas Assault as
a Prototypical Promethean Terror Strike*

IMAGINE YOURSELF A RIDER on the Tokyo Metropolitan Subway system. It is a cool spring morning, March 20, 1995. You have a full day's work ahead of you. Maybe you're preoccupied with the plans you've made with coworkers to go drinking after office hours or with your fiancé(e) that evening to discuss your upcoming wedding. The stations' platforms are packed with bodies. Personal space is nonexistent. The Tokyo subway system is one of the world's most congested mass transit systems, but thanks to the social mores of the Japanese, it is also one of the world's most cordial and efficient. Unlike transit riders in American cities, such as Chicago or Oakland, you don't give a second thought to possibly becoming a crime victim on your journey. Pickpockets? Assaults? They're so rare they're not worth worrying about in Japan.

Then imagine the almost inconceivable levels of shock you and your fellow riders experience that spring morning when you begin struggling for breath. You look around you and see dozens of people foaming at the mouth or fainting. Some passed-out travelers are held upright simply by the press of bodies. Imagine the confusion and terror as hundreds of passengers on several trains rapidly sicken due to an invisible cause. Then picture the wild panic when nearly a dozen people die, and thousands are injured in the ensuing stampedes to the exits.

Members of the Aum Shinrikyo cult released sarin gas on trains of the Chiyoda, Marunouchi, and Hibiya lines of the Tokyo Metropolitan Subway during the morning rush hour of March 20, 1995.[1] The cult's chemical weapons experts had prepared plastic bags, similar to IV drip bags, filled with liquid sarin. The cult members assigned to carry out the attacks were instructed to wrap the bags of sarin in newspapers and place them on the trains' floors. They were issued umbrellas with specially sharpened tips and trained to stab the wrapped plastic bags multiple times to release the liquid, which would swiftly evaporate into a gas. Having covered their mouths and noses with gauze surgical masks, they would set off the gas, quickly exit their trains, and meet with a getaway driver.[2]

Sarin is a gaseous organophosphate. Its properties are similar to those of solid phosphates used in fertilizers. Sarin poisoning prevents the body from utilizing cholinesterase, an enzyme produced in the liver that causes contracted muscles to relax. In the absence of effective cholinesterase, muscles remain in their contracted state. In extreme cases, this leads to paralysis. The immediate impacts of sarin gas poisoning are extreme pupil contraction, resulting in a loss of vision, and paralysis of the lungs, which can lead to oxygen deprivation, loss of consciousness, and coma. In the worst cases, it kills through asphyxiation and heart stoppage.[3]

The spilled sarin had a strong, distinctive odor. One victim reported it was powerfully sweet, like coconut.[4] Another victim thought it smelled like acid.[5] A station attendant who attempted mopping up a spill stated it smelled like a dead rat or a corpse being cremated.[6] One passenger said the spilled liquid in his car on the Marunouchi line looked like beer, but he realized it wasn't beer when he witnessed three fellow passengers sitting near the spill faint or collapse almost simultaneously.[7]

Station attendants know they have precious few minutes to clean up spills inside trains or on platforms between arrivals and departures, before passengers rush aboard and some possibly slip and fall. On the Chiyoda line, attendants thought they spotted a spill of paraffin or a similar substance. Not having mops immediately on hand, they tried sopping up the spill with newspapers, then looked for plastic bags to deposit the wet newspapers in. In the meantime, the sarin-soaked newspapers sat on the platform. Two staffers who had attempted to clean the spillage died, and a third survived with serious injuries.[8]

Some victims reported a steady shrinkage in their field of vision, until they found themselves nearly blind.[9] Others noted a tightness in their chest and an inability to draw any air into their lungs.[10] A thirty-one-year-old woman suffered brain damage, endured a lengthy coma, and emerged partially paralyzed, unable to speak more than a few words, and bereft of all memories prior to her injuries.[11] Doctors, nurses, and other personnel at the hospitals deluged with patients were not immediately aware that the injuries they were trying to treat had been caused by sarin gas poisoning. Many of the victims' clothes were soaked with sarin, and the health-care workers themselves became secondary victims of the gas.[12]

The Tokyo subway attack was the culmination of earlier terror attempts. In April 1990, following the sect's humiliating repudiation in Japan's parliamentary elections, Shoko Asahara directed his bio-chemical warfare team to spray poisonous botulin on the grounds of the U.S. naval base located in Yokosuka, home of the navy's Seventh Fleet. The botulin turned out to have been defective. Only this fortunate happenstance prevented massive deaths among U.S. military personnel.[13] On June 27, 1994, cult member Hideo Murai spearheaded a sarin gas attack on the home and neighborhood of three judges who were about to issue a ruling on a land rights case involving Aum Shinrikyo. This resulted in seven fatalities and more than 150 nonfatal poisonings. It was a practice run for the Tokyo subway attack.[14]

The March 20, 1995, coordinated sarin gas assault carried out on the Tokyo subway system represented the first-ever successful use of a weapon of mass destruction by a terror organization. Had the formulation of sarin used been more potent or had the delivery system been more effective, thousands of deaths could have resulted. Even with so many factors degrading the attacks' lethality, they still resulted in eleven fatalities, dozens of serious injuries, and several thousand more minor injuries and illnesses.

Who was behind all this carnage? What motivated him? Shoko Asahara (real name: Chizuo Matsumoto), Aum Shinrikyo's charis-matic leader who commanded the five perpetrators to carry out the assaults, fervently believed that a coming apocalypse would destroy much of Japan. Bitterly disappointed by the failure of his organization to achieve legitimate election to Japan's government, Asahara decided to precipitate this apocalypse himself, thus proving to the world that he was the prophet he'd claimed to be. His acolytes, eager to see Asahara's status as a seer made unassailable, worked hard to actualize his dire predictions.[15]

Asahara's background reads as though it were in a novel written by a twentieth-century Charles Dickens. The victim of infantile glaucoma, he lost the use of one eye and retained only partial vision in the other. His impoverished parents sent him to a government-run school for the blind. There, due to his limited but invaluable remaining sight, he came to exercise great informal authority over the totally blind students. Taking advantage of this sensory superiority, he bullied his peers into paying him for guiding them and for providing other services. He managed to earn several thousand dollars that way prior to graduation.

He subsequently opened his own acupuncture clinic. Asahara achieved financial success as a businessman. But he also became known for his megalomaniac ambitions of getting elected as Japan's prime minister. He was more secretive regarding a more outré goal, that of becoming supreme lord of a kingdom entirely populated by robots. Asahara's proclivities for fighting and for becoming involved in scams and crime overwhelmed his business sense, and his acupuncture business failed, as did a subsequent business. He took the national college entrance exams and flunked. Seeking to fill empty hours, he taught himself Chinese and immersed himself in studying Eastern religions and the political philosophy of Mao Zedong. In 1984 he founded a yoga center, Aum Inc. Within a few years, the center attracted three thousand followers, proof of his overwhelming charisma. This success encouraged Asahara to begin portraying himself as a holy man. He embarked on a spiritual odyssey through the Himalayas. When he returned to his followers, he claimed to have achieved spiritual bliss and to have developed extraordinary mystical abilities. In 1987 he renamed his network of yoga centers, which had previously been secular in their orientation, Aum Supreme Truth (Aum Shinri Kyo). He fashioned himself the center of a new personality cult.[16]

The newly developed organization, Aum Shinrikyo, adopted trappings and conceptual underpinnings from a number of sources familiar to fans of science fiction, including Japanese anime, computer games, and cyberpunk fiction. Isaac Asimov's classic series of science fiction novels from the 1940s, the Foundation trilogy, provided the core of the cult's ideology. Asimov's series centers on Hari Seldon, a mathematician who discovers the new science of psychohistory, which allows for accurate forecasts of future events. Seldon foresees a coming apocalypse that will result in the fall of humanity. To preserve civilization from this disaster, he forms the Foundation, a secret society that combines scientific and religious precepts. Then he recruits the greatest minds of his time to become its founding cadre of scientist-priests. Seldon intends for the Foundation to go underground during the ravages of the civilizational disaster, after which it will rise from the ruins and lead mankind in rebuilding and perfecting its societies.

Asahara saw himself as a real-life Hari Seldon. Like Seldon, he claimed the ability to see the future. His Aum Shinrikyo mirrored the Foundation in that it sought to recruit Japan's (and later Russia's) finest scientific minds, acquire advanced technological resources and capabilities, and prepare for a coming apocalypse. Asahara convinced his followers that they would survive this apocalypse and that their holy organization would rise from the ashes as a world-dominating authority.[17]

A rational observer would probably think Asahara delusional to expect he could recruit large numbers of scientists and technologists to Aum Shinrikyo. What could such highly educated people find attractive in a cult of personality based on an esoteric mishmash of Buddhism, Hinduism, Taoism, tantric yoga, science fiction, and Maoism? Yet Asahara succeeded. The résumés of his most prominent disciples, those who killed for him or who developed his weapons of mass destruction programs, are crammed with impressive science and technology credentials.

The list of Asahara's key followers is both long and strange. Seiichi Endo, who served as Aum's minister of health and welfare, had carried out genetic engineering experiments in his graduate biology studies at Kyoto University. Given control of Aum's biolab, he researched biological warfare (biowar) uses of botulism and the Ebola virus. Asahara assigned him the task of creating the sarin nerve gas that was used in the 1995 Tokyo subway attack. Kiyohide Hayakawa, Aum's second in command, held a master of science degree in environmental planning and sought assistance in Russia for the sect's seismological and nuclear weapons programs. Dr. Ikuo Hayashi, a respected physician before joining Aum, had graduated from one of Japan's top medical schools. As Asahara's minister of healing, he perverted medical science as egregiously as the Nazi doctors in the death camps had, making use of esoteric drugs and electroshock treatments to erase the memories of dissident cult members or to torture and kill.

Fumihiro Joyu, Aum's foreign affairs minister, had studied artificial intelligence. He quit his position at the National Space Development Agency to become more involved in Asahara's sect and was Aum's primary recruiter of Russian acolytes. Masami Tsuchiya, who served as the leader of Asahara's chemical warfare team, had been enrolled in Tsukuba University's doctoral program in chemistry and organic physics. His professors described him as brilliant. Tsuchiya traveled to Russia to study Russian biowar techniques and not only created Aum's stockpile of sarin gas based on a Russian formula but also developed a supply of vx chemical warfare agent for the sect. The previously mentioned Hideo Murai, Asahara's science and technology minister, studied astrophysics and computer programming at Osaka University's Physics Department. Attracted to Aum Shinrikyo after reading one of Asahara's books, he developed several pseudoscientific inventions, including an astral teleporter and an electroshock cap called the Perfect Salvation Initiation hat, that sold widely to sect followers and netted Asahara millions of dollars. He was the mastermind behind the Tokyo subway attack.[18]

This is not a list of characters from a Robert Ludlum thriller. These men were members of Japan's technical and scientific elite. They enjoyed all the perks and career and social opportunities that came with such status. Yet they opted to devote their lives and skills to a mystical megalomaniac. They willingly followed his commands to rain terror down on the heads of their fellow countrymen.

What might an American version of Aum Shinrikyo look and act like? From what sort of social milieu might it arise? What targets would it mark for mayhem and death? The following scenario suggests some possible answers.

### Scenario 1: The Happiest Place on Earth

Jonah Sebold looked down upon the Magic Kingdom Theme Park from the summit of the tallest spire crowning Cinderella's Castle. He looked down upon a slaughter that had been going on for hours, a massacre that he had set into motion through years of planning and effort. He looked down the carnage, his creation, his drowning of light in darkness, and said, "This is good."

Before igniting the sack of fireworks shells he had dragged up the maintenance stairway, Jonah recalled other nights watching fireworks blossom over the Magic Kingdom, evenings a decade ago, when he and Eric Vogel and Hampton Dawes and Lonnie Hacken would hang out in the parking lot of a 7-Eleven on International Drive on weekend nights. They were teens who'd lived their whole lives in Orlando, Florida, without ever being taken to visit Walt Disney World, the juicy seed in the heart of the Big Orange. Their parents couldn't spare the hundreds of dollars it cost to have their offspring attend Grad Night in the Magic Kingdom, that last hurrah before leaving high school. They were the boys who'd watched the fireworks every weekend from miles away, beneath a billboard that tauntingly advertised special Disney package deals for Florida residents. The glowing, pink spires of Cinderella's Castle mocked Jonah and his friends with their magnificence and inaccessibility and flaunting of delights that would never be theirs. They were as cruel and haughty as any high school beauty queen could be to young men who were derided as poor white trash.

Little wonder their dreams revolved around the park's giant roller coasters: Space Mountain, Expedition Everest, and Seven Dwarfs Mine Train. But in their dreams, they were not riding them but steering the cars, packed with Grad Night celebrants, off their tracks and sending them soaring through the damp Florida night at eighty deadly miles an hour to crush the Hall of Presidents or It's a Small World.

JONAH SEBOLD GOT HIS coveted post-graduation job at Disney. It wasn't much—just picking up litter from the sidewalks on Main Street USA—but it got him inside his hated target. He proved to be a dutiful employee, impressing his supervisors with his evident hunger to learn all aspects of park management and maintenance. From day 1, he asked constant questions of his many coworkers, particularly those who worked the more technical jobs. Jonah soon earned the reputation of a "comer," a young man whose dedication and hard work served to inspire those less motivated.

His supervisors accepted Jonah's recommendations for new hires with interest and gratitude. Nine months after his own hiring, Jonah's friends Eric, Hampton, and Lonnie joined the Disney "family" as maintenance custodians. They were far from the last of Jonah's circle to hire on with the Mouse.

"SO NOW WE'RE ALL in the belly of the beast," Jonah said to his close friends and coworkers. He had gathered the group at Caverns and Creatures Gaming and Collectibles, a shop owned by Lonnie's uncle, in a rear room they had claimed as their informal club house. "The belly of Big Mouse."

"Don't you mean the belly of the *whale, Jonah*?" Hampton said, snickering at his own joke. He popped open a can of Milwaukee's Best.

No one else laughed. Jonah glared witheringly at him. "Put the goddamn beer away, Hampton." He wouldn't forget the slight. Nobody interrupted *him. Nobody.*

He stared into the faces of the dozen young men. "Things have gotten *real* now. Understand? No more talking bullshit and getting blitzed. No one here is a loser—not anymore. You're part of a crusade against an evil empire, an insidious empire of media and thought control that has spent nearly a century colonizing and exploiting youthful imagination, that has turned imaginations meant by Nature to be free and willful into barren mental deserts of conformity.

"They've been eating their competitors. Disney's been like the Borg, absorbing and assimilating anything that might pose a threat to them. First it was Jim Henson Studios. Then Lucasfilm and Star Wars. Then Marvel Studios. Then they swallowed Fox and Sony, so they could get their hands on the rest of the Marvel characters. Their latest acquisition? Time-Warner. So now they've got Superman, Batman, and Wonder Woman too. Soon, there won't be anything for the young outside of Disney. They refuse to allow room for a single competitor. Because they know that if you can colonize the minds of the young, you own the Future.

"We, the young, must protect the Future. Because if we don't—if we sit back and let the Mouse have his way—the Future becomes a yellow Mouse boot stomping on all the faces of humanity, forever."

He watched them shudder at his vision of the Disneyfied Future. He felt the magma of his visceral loathing emerge from his chest, then whip across the room like heat lightning. He had them. They were his partners and pawns, his anti-Mouse crusaders.

Jonah continued, "We must learn the enemy's ways if we are to succeed in taking him down. Some of you will need to become experts in Disney's command and control protocols, particularly automated protocols. Others will need to learn computer animation or robotics or virtual reality programming. We're all eligible for Pell grants. Use them. I'm signed up for Microsoft coding camp and two sessions of hackers' boot camp run through Orlando Community College. Each of you needs to do something similar. Forget working on an associate's or bachelor's degree—it's just a waste of time. Certifications will get you where you need to go faster, technical certifications from Microsoft, Oracle, and IBM. Get them online, if you can; it's cheaper.

"The Disney corporation's been getting slain in the media for firing American-born coders and replacing them with cheap, imported labor from India. They're risking the false image they built up as an all-American, mother-and-apple-pie company. So now they're trying to turn the narrative around by launching initiatives to train and promote local IT talent. We can take advantage of that."

"Uh, I don't know about this," Tom Strondstadt said. Tom had never been a member of Jonah's inner circle. His doubting tone didn't raise his stock. "Working Disney during my gap year is okay, I guess. But my dad's on me to get an accounting degree. He said he'd help me buy a car and insure it if I enrolled in an accounting major and kept up at least a B average . . ."

"Tom," Jonah said, "you've got a choice to make." He paused for nearly half a minute, letting the quiet steeliness of his voice achieve its maximum impact. "You can be part of a crusade against one of the most insidious forces our country has ever faced. You can be a fucking *hero*, Tom. Or you can do what your dad wants and become an accountant and drive a nice little Honda Civic. You can be a faceless nobody, watching cable TV in your one-bedroom apartment, and maybe get married someday and maybe enjoy a blow job on your birthday . . . if you're lucky. And you'll make as much difference to the fate of the world as a slime mold on a piece of stale bread.

"Your choice, Tom. Hero? Or slime mold?"

The other young men stared at Tom as though he were already a fungus, one whose spores they would do anything to avoid inhaling. Jonah watched him wither under their combined gaze, as uncompromising and judgmental as that of the sternest Inquisition accuser.

"I'm—I'm in," Tom said. "I'll, uh, find some way to break it to my dad. I mean, it's not like software coding's a *bad* field . . ."

"Good choice," Jonah said.

SEVERAL YEARS PASSED. The cultural hegemony of the Walt Disney Company grew. But so did the technical brilliance of Jonah Sebold and his acolytes. And their influence metastasized within the nerve center of the Magic Kingdom like a hidden cancer.

The night of his twenty-fourth birthday, Jonah attended a celebration with his work team in a banquet hall inside Cinderella's Castle. He had just been awarded one of the Disney Company's most coveted accolades, Young Imagineer of the Year. He'd also been promoted to lead a team of forty-five young coders, computer engineers, roboticists, and virtual reality specialists, and he had a big announcement to make.

"Thank you all for being here tonight," he said. He held his award high above his head. "This plaque for Young Imagineer of the Year may have my name on it, but it really honors all of you. I could not have accomplished what I have without your support, without your passion, without your devotion to providing the finest in entertainment to every one of the millions of guests who visit our Magic Kingdom. The higher-ups have given me a plaque, but they've given our team a far more impressive award, a real vote of confidence." He paused. "Project Immersion is a *go*!"

The room erupted with whoops and cheers.

"All your prep work paid off. Today represents a new dawn for Walt Disney Parks, Experiences, and Consumer Products. As of today, we won't be taking a back seat to *anyone* when it comes to fully immersive entertainment experiences—not Universal, not Caesar's, not Six Flags. The naysayers have been wagging their tongues for far too long, claiming Disney's lost its mojo, that we're stuck in the past, prisoners of our fabled history, unable to innovate. To such ignorant pundits, I have three words to say: *Eat our dust.*"

More cheers.

"We're going to build on the incredible success of Disney Interactive's *Damnation Nation* film and home video game franchise. Mickey and Minnie and Donald and Goofy are going to have some dark, scary company in the Magic Kingdom. Our *Damnation Nation* Experience will provide more thrills than *Army of Darkness*, more chills than *The Walking Dead*, more suspense than *Predator*, and more guts and gore than all the *Saw* and *Halloween* and *Nightmare on Elm Street* films put together. And it will be a *lived experience.* Our guests will leave our park remembering that *they* were the ones who defeated the alien invasion, *they* were the ones who drove the hordes of demons back to their eleven hells, *they* were the ones who saved their families from rape and defilement and evisceration.

Adventure-hungry young men from all over the world are going to line up for a night of the *Damnation Nation* Experience, something they can't get anywhere else. And the Walt Disney Company will win back an audience segment that had been increasingly shunning the corporation's offerings.

"By the end of this fiscal year," Jonah continued, "we will beta test a pilot version of the *Damnation Nation* Experience with a live audience of park guests. I realize that's only ten months away. It's a huge ask. It'll require monumental efforts on the part of each and every one of you. By announcing this as our goal, we're taking on tremendous risk. But nothing of great value has ever been accomplished by setting goals too low. This is our Manhattan Project. This is our moonshot.

"I believe in this team. I look around this room, and I see nothing but go-getters, strivers, overachievers . . . *champions*. Working as a team, as the fingers of a single fist, we can accomplish *anything*.

"So enjoy your meals. Drink up! Relax and have fun . . . just for tonight. Because as of tomorrow morning, you are going to be working harder than you ever thought possible. And I'll be down in the trenches with you. A word of warning: I only sleep four hours a night, so anyone who intends to keep up with me had better start brewing their pots of coffee right now.

"Thank you for your passion. I know we will win, and our victory will change the face of world entertainment . . . forever."

AFTERWARD, JONAH HELD A private meeting with his inner circle, his oldest and most trusted acolytes: Eric, Lonnie, Hampton, and Tom, as well as Rick Angleton and Chance Zimple. "You realize, of course," Jonah said, "you're about to take on double the work of the rest of the team. During the day, you'll be imagineering with the rest of your coworkers. At night, you'll be doing *our* work. I trust that each of you has gotten proficient with your home CRISPR setups?"

All six men nodded.

"I've gotta admit, I kinda jumped the gun a little," Chance said. He was the group's best amateur chemist, having studied biochemistry in college before dropping out to join Jonah's group full time. "I've already been experimenting with mushroom extracts." He grinned sheepishly. "I've been combining them with other types of hallucinogens and stimulants, both natural and synthetics. I haven't hit pay dirt yet, but then again, I haven't been trying all that long."

"That's exactly the kind of initiative I want to hear," Jonah said. "Thomas Edison had to try three thousand different substances for his light bulb filament before he found one that worked. That's three thousand failures and one success. The world only remembers the one success."

IT TOOK THEM SEVEN MONTHS. The winning rage-inducing synthetic hallucinogen turned out to be a collaboration between Chance, the self-taught expert in the genetic structure of psilocybin "magic" mushrooms, and Hampton, who'd developed a deep fascination for South American venom-spitting toads. They invited Jonah to watch them repeat a test run of the new substance with a group of white mice.

Jonah stared down into the large terrarium that housed five of the rodents. They looked docile, even cute. He reached inside the glass container to stroke one's head with his index finger. "Why did you shave off a patch of fur from each mouse?" he asked.

"The drug gets absorbed through the skin," Chance said. "We've prepared it in a gel base, so it's spreadable, like a cream."

"How long does it take before it kicks in?"

"Anywhere between eight and ten minutes," Chance said. "After about five minutes, the mice start getting agitated. Twitchy, and they'll bite if you put a finger near their mouths. Then, anywhere from three to five minutes later, it's like a switch gets thrown or a turbo-booster spins up. They just *explode* into ultra-violent activity."

Chance donned a pair of thick latex gloves, then applied with a swab a small dab of the drug-infused cream to each mouse's patch of shaved skin. The three men watched and waited. Initially, the mice gathered in a corner of the terrarium. Then, one by one, they began twitching. Each mouse scurried to a separate part of the terrarium, as though it could no longer tolerate the proximity of its fellows.

Then, nine minutes after the application of the drug, they leaped at each other. Jonah watched, fascinated. The mice seemed supercharged by fury. In their attempts to gut one another, they hurled themselves with such force that when they hit the sides of the terrarium, the heavy glass enclosure shook. Within ninety seconds, blood coated the walls. Entrails plus severed paws, tails, and legs littered the wood shavings lining the terrarium's floor.

"Incredible," Jonah said. "Have any of the mice ever survived long enough for you to see whether they eventually emerge from their psychosis?"

"None have yet," Hampton said. He looked drunk. Drunk on violence.

THE MEN BOUGHT A pair of monkeys from an exotic pet shop. They dosed one monkey and left the other untreated. Ten minutes later, they watched the drugged monkey savagely kick the undrugged monkey's severed head into the side of the cage, again and again, as though it were a soccer player practicing foul kicks.

Their final step would be to test the drug on a human subject in conjunction with the virtual reality programming. The *Damnation Nation* Experience imagineering team had perfected a prototype virtual reality helmet and bodysuit, both fully ruggedized, weeks ahead of schedule. Thanks to his status as team lead, Jonah would be able to "borrow" the prototypes without raising any alarms. The software's entertainment content hadn't yet been developed beyond the rudimentary stage, but this didn't matter to Jonah. He needed to see how the drug and the equipment interacted.

Jonah ordered Tom to recruit a homeless man from the downtown tenderloin district. Tom got the man to agree to accompany him to the food refrigeration warehouse, east of downtown, where Tom's father worked as a refrigeration mechanic. Tom promised him a meal from Church's Chicken as well as drugs. That much was true. The man insisted on bringing his dog along.

Tom "borrowed" the facility's keys and alarm code from his father. He brought the homeless man to the warehouse, which was devoid of employees at 1 a.m. and silent apart from the omnipresent hum of the coolers. They met Jonah, Chance, and Hampton in the parking lot. Once inside, Chance and Hampton helped the homeless man, who told them his name was Blaine, don the virtual reality gear. Hampton had smeared the drug cream inside the helmet, concentrating on places where it would rub against the wearer's neck and cheeks. The dog, named Bucky, remained beside his master, nuzzling his hand and staring warily at the two strangers.

Tom locked the pair inside a meat cooler. Then he, Hampton, and Chance went outside to join Jonah in a parked van, where they could watch the remote feed on Jonah's laptop. Hampton had hacked into the cooler's security camera so they could get a view from above in addition to seeing whatever Blaine's VR helmet pointed at. They didn't have the equipment that was needed to see what Blaine would be seeing, the images of invading demons and aliens; all those interfaces remained locked in the Disney labs. But Jonah considered what was available good enough for tonight's test.

They watched Blaine wander inside the meat locker. He tugged at a small, jutting flap of meat until he managed to pull it loose, then he offered it to his dog. Bucky accepted it gratefully, tail wagging.

Eight minutes after the homeless man had donned the drug-slathered helmet, Blaine started twitching. "Takes a little longer with a human," Chase said. "Greater body mass, I guess."

"Turn on the VR feed," Jonah ordered. "Let's see how he reacts to that."

Blaine's initial startle reaction was as clear as mountain spring water. He glanced wildly around him. Then he began punching and kicking at phantom antagonists. A stray kick clipped Bucky on the side of his head. The dog scurried to a far corner, whimpering.

Blaine began running, fleeing unreal monsters. He grabbed a meat hook, a six-foot-long pole with a sharp steel hook at its end and swung it all around him. The four observers watched Blaine circle the meat cooler five times, running full out, shrieking for help. Then, apparently exhausted, he sank to his knees and huddled into a trembling, twitching ball.

"This isn't what I want, goddamn it," Jonah said.

"Wait, just *wait*, Jonah," Chase said, fear making his voice crack. "Give it a little time. He—he hasn't reached the explosive stage yet. Remember, everything's slowed down with a human subject . . ."

They waited. Four and a half minutes later, Blaine suddenly sprang to his feet. Screaming obscenities, he launched himself at the nearest hanging beef carcass. He savaged it, tearing at with his fingernails, kneeing it in its imagined groin. He scampered to the meat hook he'd abandoned earlier and used it to batter one hanging meat carcass after another, swinging it wildly, stabbing its sharp hook into the fatty slabs.

This went on for thirty-eight minutes. At last Blaine collapsed, gasping, apparently at the limits of his endurance. Yet the drug was not yet done with him. Four minutes later, he sprang to his feet again, newly charged with psychotic fury, and renewed his assault.

The cycle repeated three more times. Each time, Blaine's endurance decreased. "It's a lack of calories," Chance said. "That chicken meal Tom bought him wasn't enough to sustain him."

"That shouldn't be a problem in the Magic Kingdom," Hampton said. "There's loads of high-calorie snacks everywhere, free for the pillaging. Popcorn, hot dogs, ice cream sandwiches. Plenty of fuel . . ."

Finally, an hour and thirty-seven minutes after he'd been locked in the cooler, Blaine appeared done in. He lay on his back, loudly gasping, arms weakly flailing. He began sobbing. His dog pattered cautiously across the floor to his side.

"I think he might be coming out of it," Chance said.

Jonah glanced at the van's clock. "Just under two hours. Not nearly long enough. I need it to last an entire night. Do you think we could do a timed release of the drug? Rig up something inside the helmet or suit that would reapply a fresh dose every two hours?"

"I'll check with Rick," Chance said.

Blaine's final spurt of psychotic violence, before Hampton switched off the vr feed and Tom and Chance removed the near-comatose homeless man from the meat cooler, was to break Bucky's neck.

THE BIG NIGHT ARRIVED. Grad Night. The locus of everything Jonah Sebold hated.

Both his teams, his official team of Disney Imagineers and his covert team of acolytes, had performed splendidly over the prior ten months. All was in readiness.

Jonah sat in front of his bank of monitors in his underground operations center. He felt like Dr. No or Lex Luthor or Thanos—their original, *nasty* versions, before Disney had gotten their hands on them and softened and emasculated them. Tonight, he'd make all the supervillains from his childhood look pathetic.

Some of his monitors displayed the Magic Kingdom's different "lands"—Fantasyland, Tomorrowland, Adventureland, Frontierland, Main Street USA—all currently empty, awaiting the hordes of high school guests to come. Other monitors showed the Magic Kingdom's entrance turnstiles, where tens of thousands of high school students from Florida and other states, plus their teachers and chaperones, streamed through the gates.

He watched the girls, many of them buxom and enticing, bounce with excitement as they laughed with their friends. Their breasts jiggled within sweatshirts emblazoned with the licensed likenesses of Disney Princesses: Ariel, the little mermaid; Aurora, the sleeping beauty; Belle, the French maiden; Jasmine, the sultan's daughter. He also watched the boys. He especially looked for the ones with red tickets in hand. Those foil badges signified they were among the incredibly lucky three hundred selected to be the initial "beta testers" for Disney's newest and wildest adult-themed attraction, the *Damnation Nation* Experience.

Jonah glanced at another set of monitors. Those four units showed a quartet of large halls, filled with rows of oversized seats that held VR helmets and suits, awaiting the three hundred testers. The four large halls, all part of the Magic Kingdom's network of subterranean control and monitoring facilities, each rested beneath a different land. Jonah had pushed hard for this dispersal, telling management these various test facilities could eventually be repurposed as attractions offering various VR experiences, with each individualized for the theme of a different land. Actually, he wanted to make sure that, come Grad Night, bands of berserkers would emerge from all points of the compass, trapping tens of thousands of guests between them.

The walls of the VR rooms had been lined with weapons: edged weapons, projectile weapons, and firearms, either human, alien, or demonic in origin. The Magic Kingdom's talented team of set constructors had created these deadly-looking facsimiles as decorations. Little did they realize that members of Jonah's inner circle had been busily manufacturing lethal versions of the facsimiles on their home 3D printers, then smuggling them onsite, and replacing the facsimiles with their own creations.

Other monitors, dozens of them, remained dark. But they wouldn't remain so for long. Soon, once the beta testers were outfitted with the VR equipment, those screens would display what the players were seeing: the hordes of invading aliens and demons, the masses of claws and tentacles and endless dagger-like teeth, the laser cannons and flying raptor drones and their ravenous outpourings of hellfire. Jonah would be able to switch to the viewpoints of any of the three hundred participants. With a few rapid keystrokes, he could view, side by side, what a "player" *thought* he was seeing—what was being projected into his brain by the Disney VR systems—and what was actually in his field of vision.

The first of the three hundred testers entered the four VR rooms. Jonah watched as smartly uniformed Disney Imagineers, all dressed as human soldiers from *Damnation Nation*, led the guests to their chairs and assisted them with donning the suits and helmets. *They know not what they do*, he thought. *They don't realize it, but they're giving me the Grad Night I never had.*

One by one, the screens in Jonah's control room that transmitted what the testers were seeing in their virtual reality world brightened. All the helmets and suits were networked, so the participants, who would be allowed to move about within their rooms, could "see" each other and one another's play. The first few minutes of the *Damnation Nation* Experience set up the world and its scenario. Participants were mustered into the ragtag Earth Defense Force as Minutemen, emergency soldiers called up after a worldwide series of coordinated sneak attacks by the combined alien and demon invasion forces. The players' commanding officers gave them their assignment: defend to their last breaths the scientific citadel in Lucerne, Switzerland, where a last-ditch superweapon was being developed, Earth's final hope to turn back the invading hordes.

To grant the coming virtual battles greater verisimilitude, the Imagineers also distributed to the players those weapons that had been mounted on the walls. The game's original props had been chipped so they would appear to have outrageous destructive power: rifles that could shoot plasma beams capable of melting steel girders, scimitars with molecule-thin cutting edges that could decapitate the most heavily armored gargoyles, laser-guided crossbows that could slay enemies a mile away, and shoulder-launched rockets that could topple an alien battle tripod. The genuine weapons, which the excited Disney employees now unwittingly distributed, had been similarly chipped by Jonah's acolytes. Unlike the originals, however, these items' lethality would not be confined to the world inside the game.

Jonah counted down the eight minutes until the first players began twitching convulsively inside their VR gear. He watched as concerned Imagineers rushed to the sides of the afflicted guests and tried to remove the players' helmets. All the affected players refused to be removed from the game, shoving the Imagineers aside.

More and more players displayed signs of neurological distress. The Imagineers, realizing something had gone terribly wrong, tried shutting the VR sessions down. Jonah overrode their control inputs. The game would last all night long. He would make sure of that.

He adjusted the VR feeds so that the players saw the Imagineers as hideous demons raping Earth women and feasting on the entrails of the women's male kinfolk. *So long, Mickey Mouse Club*, Jonah thought. Players in the vanguard of a tidal wave of rage gutted the Imagineers with their broadswords, hacked at them with their axes, and shot them at point-blank range.

Jonah remotely opened the doors that led from the subterranean testing halls to the various lands, all of which now teemed with teen-agers and their chaperones. He watched, feeling giddy, intoxicated, as four separate mobs of enraged, well-armed boys surged out into the Magic Kingdom. He remotely closed and locked the park's gates. The most athletic and desperate of the tens of thousands of guests might be able to climb out to safety. But for the rest, there would be no escape.

He arranged his screens for dual vision, so he could simultaneously view what the murderous players believed they were seeing and what was actually in front of their masked faces. One intrepid lad believed he pursued a fleeing alien soldier, its tentacles and pseudopods flap-ping wildly in its desperation to escape. He caught up to it, shoved it to the ground, and smashed its misshapen skull with his ax. In reality, his bloodied victim was a pudgy boy whose jacket had been pinned with a ribbon that indicated he was a mentally challenged guest who should be ushered to the front of rides' lines. Another Earth warrior chased after an eight-foot-tall demon, who turned to belch flame at him. The young Minuteman ducked behind a trash receptacle, took careful aim with his techno-pistol, and fired a series of shots. His bullets punctured the spine and lungs of a middle-aged art teacher, knocking the screaming woman onto a brick path.

There was so much to see, Jonah had difficulty making choices ...

Alien general = blonde senior girl wearing a Sun Devils hoodie, shot in the buttocks.

Quill-studded demon = the White Rabbit from *Alice in Wonder-land*, a hapless costumed Imagineer hunted down with barbed pikes.

Three-headed, acid-spewing demon = white-bearded man in a Hawaiian shirt, beheaded with a broadsword.

Alien phalanx = a group of All-State Honors Chorale members, boys and girls, herded into a cul-de-sac and hacked to pieces.

Young guests cowered behind food carts and benches, training their cell phone cameras on the mayhem. Jonah had known this would happen; this generation recorded and broadcast *everything*. Some of his acolytes had suggested disabling the park's Wi-Fi system so that guests under siege could not transmit video or call 911. Jonah overruled them. He wanted word to get out. He wanted thousands of amateur newscasts to be uploaded to YouTube and Instagram and Snapchat. He needed the entire planet to have a front-row seat for the evisceration of the Disney Empire.

The Magic Kingdom's private security force tried containing the violence. But it was like trying to drain the ocean with a thimble. The mayhem was too spread out, too intense. The park's security guards had trained to break up fights between two rowdy customers, a handful, at most. They hadn't trained to quell a park-wide riot, especially not one involving rioters far better armed than they were. They were quickly overwhelmed, added to the swelling ranks of the dead and dying.

Police units began arriving. Their cruisers sped across acres of parking lots. Jonah alerted Hampton. His acolyte activated the Magic Kingdom's fleet of automated trams, the long, snaking vehicles the park used to transport its guests from their parked vehicles to the entrance gates. Rather than avoiding collisions, the robot trams now used their banks of cameras and motion sensors to seek out collisions. Dozens of them rammed into speeding police cruisers. Others mowed down police officers who had managed to crawl out of their demolished vehicles.

An hour passed without a single officer reaching the entrance gates. Jonah knew that SWAT teams would eventually arrive with armored vehicles, ex-military equipment whose machine guns could blow apart the rampaging trams. And they would bring helicopters with drop ladders to infiltrate heavily armed police into the killing zone.

But by then, it would be too late. The Disney Empire's corporate image would be indelibly defiled—forever.

He waited in the monitor room until ninety minutes before sunrise. His final act required darkness. His acolytes would escape, thanks to their knowledge of the Magic Kingdom's network of tunnels. Jonah, however, had no intention of leaving. Ever. He wanted to go out with a bang.

JONAH SEBOLD LOOKED DOWN upon all his works, and he judged them good.

Main Street USA was Massacre Street USA. Fantasyland had become Nightmare Land. Tomorrowland was now No Tomorrows Land.

In the pre-dawn, a trio of news helicopters flitted and hovered like fat, noisy versions of Tinkerbell. As the eastern sky purpled like an immense bruise, Jonah switched on his own phone camera, then recited his manifesto through a bullhorn electronically hooked into the park's public address system. He enumerated the sins of the Walt Disney Company. He praised himself for freeing the minds of future generations of youngsters from mental colonization by the Mouse.

He closed with his Princess incantation, the most succinct summation of his philosophy:

> Cinderella! Grow fat and gross like a rotting pumpkin!
> Belle! May the Beast's giant hairy dick impale you from cunt to chin!
> Fuck you, Ariel, and all your fucking fish!
> Snow White, be raped by your goddamn dwarves forever and ever!

Then he ignited the shell fireworks for his grand finale.

Burning bits of Jonah Sebold glowed as bright as the tip of the Fairy Godmother's magic wand as they drifted down over the shattered spires of Cinderella's Castle, where they would be forever infused with the rubble of the Fall of the House of Mouse.

# TWO

## Made in Japan?

*Or "Overeducated and Underemployed"?*

UNLIKE THE JAPANESE SHOKO ASAHARA, the American Jonah Sebold is not an actual person, only an imagined one. So was Aum Shinrikyo a purely Japanese phenomenon, something those of us who live in different societies needn't to worry about? Or are there elements of the Aum experience that would allow the cult's brand of apocalyptic extremism, or something horribly similar, to take root in many other countries?

Some observers claim that Aum Shinrikyo was very much a "made in Japan" phenomenon. Researchers have suggested that Japan's daunting, rigid expectations of its young people—that they should excel academically and then devote their lives to whichever corporation hires them—leads some to rebel. Japanese culture's focus on the well-being of the community and of economic collectives such as corporations, as opposed to the self-actualization of individuals, may have made the countercultural aspects of Asahara's cult particularly attractive to would-be rebels. Aum's fusion of many different religious traditions, its elevation of "low culture" products such as anime and science fiction, its leader's claims to having vast supernatural powers, and its promise to its followers that as members of a select group, they would survive a coming apocalypse—all these qualities proved irresistible to those young, educated, alienated Japanese wanting to take a stand against social conformity.[1]

Yet intellectually cordoning off Aum Shinrikyo and its like as a peculiarly Japanese phenomenon would be a mistake. Prior to the Tokyo subway attack, Aum Shinrikyo's leadership claimed to have thirty thousand followers in Russia, or three times the number of their

Japanese acolytes.[2] Even if this number were overstated by a factor
of five, this figure is still impressive. Russian society differs greatly
from that of Japan. Russian youths were not subjected to the same
intense pressure to excel academically and to devote themselves to a
corporation as their Japanese peers were, yet Aum Shinrikyo achieved
notable success in crossing over to a different national culture.

What might account for this? Sociologist James Dingley's "overeducated and underemployed" thesis could provide an explanation for
the cross-cultural allure of Aum Shinrikyo in 1990s Russia. Dingley's
notions expanded upon ideas first formulated by historian Lenore
O'Boyle. O'Boyle's study, "The Problem of an Excess of Educated
Men in Western Europe, 1800–1850," offered an explanation for the
sociopolitical unrest and revolutions endemic in Europe during the
first half of the nineteenth century. O'Boyle pointed out that the
transition from an agrarian to an industrial society required ambitious
young men to seek more formal education than previous generations
had if they hoped to enter the newly expanded middle class. Yet
various European economies and societies failed to offer sufficient
opportunities for this new mass of educated young men to achieve
gainful employment in their fields of study, leading to widespread
frustration with the existing social order. This discontent, in turn,
led to the growth of various revolutionary movements.[3]

Dingley used O'Boyle's insights to develop a new theory of the
causes of terrorism. He pointed out that nineteenth-century revo-
lutionaries and twentieth-century terrorists have a lot in common.
The former were predominately highly educated professionals in
nontechnical, nonscientific fields; demographic surveys indicated that
twentieth-century terrorists were predominately college-educated
as well, with degrees mainly in the social sciences or humanities.
Dingley's "anarcho-ideological terrorists" are overeducated, underemployed would-be cosmopolitans who want to change their societies
and are willing to use violence if necessary. Their goal? To bring
about a new order that will properly reward the talents of persons
like themselves.[4]

Russia, prior to the dissolution of the Soviet Union in 1991, was a highly educated society, boasting many talented, well-trained scientists and engineers, many of whom had worked in the defense and space sectors. Following the abolition of communism and a tumultuous, cronyism-plagued transition to a partially market-based system, the Russian economy painfully contracted. Funding for national defense, the space program, and all associated research and development (R&D) efforts was slashed. This economic contraction put many Russian scientists and engineers out of work and halved others' salaries or at least made their continued employment naggingly tenuous. It also dashed the career hopes of tens of thousands of Russian students then in the science, technology, engineering, and mathematics (STEM) higher education pipeline.

Dingley's theory suggests that being overeducated and underemployed made it much more likely that economically battered Russians would find a malignly countercultural group such as Aum Shinrikyo perversely attractive due to both the opportunities it provided them to strike back at their society and to feel the ego-soothing balm of being told they were members of an elect group. While Japanese and Russian STEM graduates had greatly differing motivations for signing up with Aum Shinrikyo, they demonstrated similar levels of willingness to join the cult.

Could a group like Aum Shinrikyo attract large numbers of adherents in the United States? Naysayers point out that the cult's effort to recruit American acolytes in the early 1990s failed miserably; Aum only won over a few dozen followers in the New York City metropolitan area.[5] They may also highlight the enviable successful record of the Federal Bureau of Investigation (FBI) in infiltrating and dismantling or minimizing various groups of violent extremists, including left-wing and Marxist terror groups in the 1960s and 1970s and right-wing, racist terror groups during subsequent decades.

Yet let's not dismiss this possibility too quickly. A powerful, wealthy, and influential American analogue to Aum Shinrikyo has existed since the 1950s—the Church of Scientology, founded by the science fiction writer L. Ron Hubbard. Had Hubbard, an Asahara-like figure in many ways, been more interested in forcing an apocalypse than in amassing wealth and infiltrating the motion picture industry, his Scientologists might now be better known for their use of weapons of mass destruction than for the on-screen heroics of acolyte Tom Cruise.

Could Dingley's overeducated and underemployed thesis prove as applicable to the present-day United States as it did to 1990s Russia? You bet it could. A 2014 study found that rates of underemployment (the study defined "underemployment" for college graduates as working in a job or occupation for which fewer than half the occupants hold at least a bachelor's degree) for both American college graduates as a whole (those aged twenty-two to sixty-five) and for recent college graduates (those aged twenty-two to twenty-seven) rose steadily from 2003 to 2014. As of 2014, the underemployment rate for graduates as a whole was 34 percent. The rate for recent graduates stood at 46 percent.[6]

Job prospects for college graduates stand to be further undermined by advances in machine learning, artificial intelligence, and robotics. In March 2017 the global advisory firm PwC estimated the shares of employment in various UK sectors that will be at risk of being automated by the early 2030s. The projections are daunting. For administrative and support services, the percentage of jobs placed at risk was pegged at 37.4 percent. For professional, scientific, and technical jobs, the corresponding figure was 25.6 percent; for public administration and defense jobs, 32.1 percent; for information and communications jobs, 27.3 percent; and for financial and insurance jobs, 32.2 percent. The report's overall figure for jobs at risk from automation, including blue-collar and manufacturing jobs, was estimated to be 30 percent. The report's author estimated that an even larger overall percentage of jobs in the United States was at risk.[7]

Venture capitalist Fred Destin estimated that advances in machine intelligence and automation will eventually obliterate up to 70 percent of white-collar jobs.[8] The heavily indebted financial status of a majority of American college graduates will assuredly make the impact of such dismal employment prospects far worse. As of 2017, approximately 70 percent of college graduates exited school carrying student debt. How much debt? About 44 million Americans collectively owe more than $1.4 trillion in student loans. Sixty percent of these graduates do not expect to be able to finish paying off their loans until they have reached their forties.[9]

As gainful employment prospects dim for many young people, including those with college educations, proposals such as 2020 Democratic presidential primary candidate Andrew Yang's for a guaranteed minimum income will gain in salience and mass appeal. If granted enough money monthly by the government to live on, will unemployed college graduates devote themselves to artistic or intellectual pursuits, or serve as volunteers to improve their communities? This is the hope, certainly. Yet the reality is likely to fall far short of this somewhat utopian vision. The experiences of an earlier cohort of widely unemployed Americans does not inspire optimism. Sociologist Charles Murray, in his 2012 book *Coming Apart: The State of White America, 1960–2010*, describes what he sees as a bifurcation among white Americans into a new upper class and a new lower class. Members of the former maintain orderly lives characterized by stable marriages, religious observance, a solid work ethic, and a high degree of formal education. Members of the new lower class, whose parents and grandparents were employed in factories or on farms, tend to have unstable relationships, bear children out of wedlock, have spotty employment histories, tend to forgo organized religious observance or involvement in community fellowships, and are far more likely to abuse both legal and illegal drugs. The people in the latter group have been dying "deaths of despair" over the past decade from suicides or from drug overdoses involving either prescription pain killers or illegal opioids such as heroin and illicit fentanyl. Many earn a kind of guaranteed minimum income from Social Security disability benefits, yet they do not spend their free hours painting landscapes or writing family memoirs. They devote their waking hours to playing video games, watching streaming television shows, drinking, taking drugs, and at times plaguing their communities with crimes committed to support their drug use.

Won't Dingley's overeducated and underemployed cohort at least exhibit better, less destructive personal habits due to their extended exposure to the formative influences of university culture? Perhaps. Perhaps not. At one time, the role of universities was widely seen as inculcating the young with the accumulated wisdom of Western civilization so that their graduates could become productive and thoughtful citizens, well prepared to engage in their civic responsibilities. This has not generally been the case since the late 1960s. Many observers have documented a multigenerational shift in how universities perceive their role, moving away from being the prime buttresses of Western civilization and toward becoming the intellectual centers of opposition to traditional aspects of Western societies. French theories of deconstructionism became fashionable in American colleges and universities in the 1970s through the 1990s, with professors advocating the deconstruction of traditional family life, gender roles, sexuality, and capitalism, as well as emphasizing that all societal constructs, even language, are based on unequal distributions of power and exploitative relationships between dominating elites and those they dominate. The civil rights movement of Black Americans was soon emulated by Native Americans, Latinos, gays and lesbians, women, and members of other ethnic and cultural groups who felt they had been kept out of the ranks of the American elite. These various social liberation movements resulted in the establishment of hundreds of "studies" departments on American campuses (some as spoils won from cowed administrators), academic redoubts of "resistance" to the status quo within which the theories of deconstructionism, Marxism, and anti-colonialism found fervent adherents.

The latest popular spawn of deconstructionism is critical race theory, a cornerstone of the mass movement popularly called wokeness or variously referred to as cultural Marxism, campus culture, or the "Successor Ideology." Opinion writer Wesley Yang coined the latter term in 2019 to refer to an amalgamation of intersectionality, identity politics, oppression studies, and anti-racism into a quasi-religious set of dogmas that is encroaching on the predominance of traditional American liberal ideals of individualism, free speech, open debate, pluralism, economic liberty, freedoms of conscience and of association, and distrust of too much centralized power. Columnist Matthew Yglesias has named the rise of this Successor Ideology "the Great Awokening," an ironic reference to earlier "Great Awakenings" in American history, periods of sustained and passionate religious revival.[10] A number of commentators have noted the close similarity of many elements of secular critical race theory and white fragility to Christian doctrines: in particular, Original Sin (all white persons are indelibly imbued with racism at birth and cannot ever completely overcome this mark of Cain; any denials on the part of a white person that they are not racist are, in fact, proof of their innate racism), a future paradise on Earth (an "end of days" time when all inequity, colonialism, oppression, and power differentials will be abolished), and the evil, depravity, and damned nature of nonbelievers (all conservatives and Republicans are evil racists, and so-called moderates falsely believe they are not racist). A key difference between critical race theory and Christianity is that the former lacks any doctrine of salvation; white people are irrevocably stained by racism and cannot wash themselves clean of it, no matter how hard they may try to be allies to the oppressed. James Lindsay, a scholar of the psychology of religion, has noted that wokeness, similar to cults and various forms of fundamentalist religion, attracts adherents by using doctrine as a tool to ameliorate the pain associated with emotional vulnerabilities. He states that both cults and wokeness operate in an unhealthy fashion, exploiting emotional weak points (in the case of converts to wokeness, a pervasive sense of guilt over unearned racial privilege) to more completely indoctrinate their converts.[11]

The present generation of young Americans contains the highest percentage of college graduates and college attendees of any generation in U.S. history. Perhaps it is no coincidence that members of this generation exhibit the lowest degree of pride in their country of any age cohort. A June 2020 Gallup poll regarding patriotism and pride in one's country indicated that among young adults aged eighteen to twenty-nine years old, only 20 percent claim to be "extremely proud" of the United States, a decline of 23 percent from 2017. By way of contrast, 48 percent of respondents aged fifty to sixty-four years old expressed "extreme pride" in their country. The negative correlation between college graduation and pride in country was borne out in the difference between the 46 percent of all those without college degrees who reported feeling "extreme pride" in America and the 34 percent of all college graduates who reported the same, the latter figure representing a decline of 10 percent since 2017.[12]

Making for a toxic, potentially explosive brew among wide swaths of the young is the combination of these factors: extreme indebtedness; boredom and disillusionment caused by unemployment or chronic underemployment; dashed hopes of joining the American economic and social elite (or at least the comfortable middle class); a lack of trust in and affection for U.S. institutions; a growing certainty that America's foundations are unsalvageably racist, exploitive, and genocidal; and a gnawing suspicion that their unsatisfying lives are the result of the machinations of selfish profiteers. The summer-long sequence of unruly protests in 2020—many marred by looting, arson, vandalism, and violence, kicked off by the killing of Black Minneapolis resident George Floyd by white and Asian police officers during his arrest for possibly passing off a counterfeit twenty-dollar bill—certainly reflects this. The anarchist elements behind much of the property destruction, arson, and interpersonal violence of the riots were foreshadowed by the anti-capitalist Occupy movement of 2011–12 and a series of anti-globalism actions going back to the 1999 protest against the meeting of the World Trade Organization in Seattle, Washington. The anarchists, many loosely affiliated with the anti-fascist movement, have been able to spread their "tear it all down" campaigns from leftist redoubts such as Seattle and Portland, Oregon, to dozens of cities around the United States in 2020, including Minneapolis, Boston, Los Angeles, New York City, Philadelphia, Louisville, Chicago, Atlanta, Dallas, Houston, Phoenix, Richmond, and Washington DC.

These social dynamics are not isolated to the woke or the anarchists. Identity politics have spread like an algae bloom far beyond their spawning grounds on the left and on university campuses. Victimhood has become, especially among the young, a badge of honor and righteousness, as well as a potent glue to hold members of affinity groups together. Some young whites, resenting their demonization by their woke peers, have found new salience in primarily identifying with a manufactured, synthetic white identity, sometimes having cultish Christian religious elements. Some young people, often socially awkward heterosexual males, feeling demonized by feminists and the LGBTQ communities and rejected by the women they yearn for, have banded together under the invented identity of "incels," or involuntary celibates.

The following scenario illustrates how such a subset of Dingley's radicalized overeducated and underemployed, made even more extreme by their self-perceived victimization and marginal group identity, might take their revenge against society in general and women in particular in a not very distant future.

### Scenario 2: Where the Boys Are

"Can I hit the button yet? Can I hit it?"

Damien Johnson sighed with pent-up irritation. "No. Not yet. The plan is to set the three devices off simultaneously at eight o'clock. Check your watch. It's seven fifty-seven. Three more minutes, Brian. Patience."

Had he done the right thing, throwing in with this lot? They'd seemed so much more impressive when he'd only known them from their posts in 4chan forums and message boards on the dark web. The Incel Nation, aka the Jolly Rodger's Army.

Now that he'd met many of them face-to-face, though, and now that they'd taken advantage of his technical skills and offered such *mediocrity* in trade, Damien had his doubts. He couldn't help but wonder whether self-labeled incels such as Brian Habbert didn't *deserve* to be involuntarily celibate for the rest of their misbegotten lives. Wouldn't it do America's gene pool a favor?

He bit his lower lip. *Stop it. Stop that insidious, corrosive self-talk right now. You're defeating yourself before you've even begun to fight.* His private contempt for his comrades deeply shamed him. He'd internalized it, hadn't he? The years of corrosive contempt he'd been forced to swallow from the "Chads and Stacys" of the world, contempt that had twisted him inside until he could hardly tell the difference between enemies and allies. Men like Brian were his *brothers*, he reminded himself, fellow sufferers of the sex drought, fellow victims of the feminazi conspiracy, the evil cabal dedicated to denying most members of the male population their rightful share of soul-salving sexual intercourse. Wasn't sex, holy *sex*, one of man's basic needs, as necessary for male thriving as air, food, water, and sleep?

Damien watched the parade of Chads and Stacys head for the beach, then stared out from the alleyway where he and Brian guarded one of the three electromagnetic pulse generators Damien had built. The Chads and Stacys—the lucky few, the sexual elite—motored toward their bonfires and drunken luaus, soon to be afloat on clouds of pot smoke and pre-hookup foreplay, their reward for having put in a few desultory hours in their classes at the University of California–Santa Barbara. He watched them drive south on Ocean Road toward the sea, an endless procession of pretty-boy alpha males (the Chads) in their brand-new BMW convertibles and open-top Camaros, and the Stacys, their blond hair flowing behind them in the coastal breeze, driving Daddy's gift of a Tesla or a Mercedes roadster. Bad as the Chads were, the Stacys were worse. They were *sadists*, arrogantly boasting of their chastity and virtue to any non-Chad male, yet happily spreading their suntanned thighs for the alphas.

No wonder Elliot Rodger had hated them so. Saint Elliot of the Incels. No wonder the mere sight of a clump of them holding a picnic next to their parked convertibles had compelled him to buy a Super Soaker water gun at a nearby convenience store, fill it with orange juice, and then slowly drive by the picnic, soaking his tormentors' two-hundred-dollar jeans with the pulpy juice of his fury. A mere rehearsal, that had been, for the main event on May 23, 2014—Incel Independence Day, today's anniversary. The day when Elliot Rodger said, "*Enough*." When he'd stated so presciently in his final YouTube manifesto, "One day incels will realize their true strength and numbers and will overthrow this oppressive feminist system. . . . Start envisioning a world where WOMEN FEAR YOU."

He'd certainly made them fear him that day. He'd replaced his Super Soaker with three semiautomatic pistols—a Glock 34 Long Slide and two Sig Sauer P226s. He'd stalked Isla Vista's student bars and sorority row like the Angel of Death in his black BMW, killing six and wounding eight before terminating his own tormented, virginal existence.

Just a few more seconds to go . . .

*You won't have died in vain, Elliot. Your words were heard. We who share your pain and humiliation will finish the work you valiantly started. After tonight, no one will laugh at us ever again.*

"Brian, press the button."

*Lights out, bitches . . .*

The EMP wave couldn't be heard or felt. But its silent, intangible invisibility did not detract from its immediacy or effectiveness. Every electric motor within a half-mile radius ceased working. Every integrated circuit within the cursed circle turned to slag, with micro-etched silicon wafers rendered as useless as sand.

This section of Isla Vista was instantly thrown back into the nineteenth century. *The Victorian era,* Damien thought. *Not that any of those sex-crazed morons could appreciate the irony . . .*

Shouts of dismay and confusion erupted from drivers on Ocean Road as their engines and headlights died in unison along with every streetlight and store sign. Electric power steering failed, as did power brakes, turning automobiles into uncontrollable billiard balls. Cries of confusion quickly turned to screams of horror. Then those screams were overwhelmed by the grinding screech of metal on metal and brutal smashings in the dark. Damien saw an Audi convertible flip onto its roll bars, brutally scattering unbelted Stacys across the asphalt.

Brian gibbered and bounced like an overstimulated chimpanzee. "Isn't this fun? Isn't this frickin' *fun*?"

"It's just the beginning," Damien said. He stared north, then northwest, trying to determine how far the zone of sudden and complete darkness extended. Had the more crucial electromagnetic pulses, the ones that targeted the Ellwood Power Plant on Las Armas Road and the Goleta Valley Cottage Hospital, been properly triggered? Had his other two EMP generators worked as designed?

He had to know. The group's plans, simpleminded and limited though they might be (he had argued for a more realistic and worthwhile set of goals, but he'd been outvoted by his intellectual inferiors), all hinged on killing the power plant and ensuring that no backup generators at the hospital would kick in.

He didn't trust his partners' competence. He had to go see for himself.

"I'm heading for the hospital," he said.

"And miss all the *fun*?" Brian said. "I'm getting a woody, listening to all those Stacys screaming out there . . ."

"Then I'll leave you alone to enjoy your pleasures. But don't get too preoccupied. If you hear anything mechanical approaching—any cars, police cruisers, fire engines, or helicopters—you press that button again, you understand?"

"Nothing gets past *me*, brother. *Nothing*."


THE HOSPITAL LOOMED AS dark as a mausoleum at midnight. *That much went right, at least,* Damien told himself.

He recognized Fred MacKenzie, the gun-toting sentry posted at the entrance. Before he could be challenged, Damien recited the pass phrase: "Jolly Rodger lives on in us."

"Brother Damien?"

"That's right."

"How did things go near the campus?"

"As good as we'd hoped. Everything going according to plan here?"

Fred lit a cigarette. Bathed in its dim glow, he smiled. "We've got this place shut down tight. I had to get rough with a rent-a-cop. None of the doctors or nurses have tried playing hero."

"Good. Where did Conor set up his command post?"

"The cafeteria. Third floor. It was too noisy in the emergency room. Too many patients hyperventilating and shit. The crew's got most of the employees herded together in the cafeteria. The ones who didn't fit got locked in the basement."

"Thanks," Damien said. "Keep an eye out, in case any cops make it through the outer cordon on foot."

He entered the building's main lobby. No emergency generators hummed; his EMP generator had ensured that. A ray of moonlight entered through a window. There'd be no moonlight in the stairwell; he'd have to use his flashlight. Ascending the stairs, listening to his footfalls echo, he wondered whether he'd ever get to enjoy the purported reward for his labors—the submissive, fawn-like former Stacy that Conor had promised each member of the Incel Nation. Even the modest utopia that Conor envisioned for his followers, an expatriate existence in St. Petersburg or Moscow with a former-Stacy servant-wife and multiple Russian mistresses, seemed fantastically far-fetched to Damien. Conor's pronouncements were daydreams with no more weight than a helium-filled balloon. Unicorns, chimeras.

But he hadn't joined the movement for the promised rewards. He'd yoked his talents to this rickety cart to make a statement. To show the world that incels like himself would not go gently into that dying of the light, the zombie half-life of unending frustration and torment imposed upon them.

He exited the stairwell, then scanned the hallway's walls with his flashlight beam until he found signage directing him to the cafeteria. Walking closer, he heard a jumble of voices, male and female, interspersed with weeping.

He opened the door. One voice stood out among all the others. Conor's voice. The leader of the Incel Nation stood near the cafeteria's windows overlooking the darkened streets of Goleta, hunched over in his peculiar fashion, holding an old-fashioned slimline telephone, connected by a long cord to a landline port in a wall. Damien had bought the phone at a garage sale, knowing his EMP generators would render all cell phones and even landline phones with electronic features useless.

"These are our demands," Conor said, speaking into the phone. His voice was unusually high-pitched, almost like an adolescent girl's; Damien had overheard some group members make cutting jokes about it in private. Conor Smythe was one of those leaders best encountered online. "We demand one hundred UCSB or Santa Barbara City College women student volunteers for us to choose from. They must be totally submissive and absolutely willing to become the wives of any of us who will deign to have them. No women with handicaps or deformities, nobody with body mass indexes that would put them in the overweight or obese categories. So no uglies, no fatties. That's for starters.

"No—stop giving me arguments! Are you taking this all down, every word? Look, every second you waste trying to obstruct me, more patients here at the hospital are going to sicken and die. There's not a spark of power here. All the medical machinery, it's all turned OFF.

"That's right. People are dying, you stupid cuck.

"Let me get back to our list of demands. A jumbo jet, a 747 or equivalent, topped off with fuel, ready to fly across the ocean. A pilot to fly the plane. Twenty million unmarked dollars on the plane. And safe passage for all my people and our new future wives from this hospital to the airport. You got that? We're giving you twelve hours to pull all that together. Twelve hours.

"No, I'm *not* threatening to start shooting hostages if we don't get what I said. Mother Nature will do our dirty work for us . . ."

Damien heard the *thup-thup-thup-thup* of an approaching helicopter. He scanned the sky beyond the windows. Sure enough, there were blinking lights less than a mile away, heading toward the hospital. Damien couldn't tell whether it was a news or a police helicopter. It didn't matter. He was glad. He could show the world the power he'd amassed with his brilliance—the power to make all power vanish.

"Brother Conor," he said, "hold the phone up to the window." Damien pushed aside the two group members who'd been guarding the EMP generator. He spoke loudly enough that the negotiators on the other end of the line would clearly hear him. "You cops, you hear that sound? That's a helicopter flying toward the hospital. I don't know whether it's one of yours or some TV news station's. I want you to keep listening, so you'll hear what you're up against."

He pressed the generator's button. The safety lights on the nearing helicopter blinked out. The *thup-thup-thup-thup* slowed, then stopped. Seconds later, a blinding flash made Damien's pupils defensively contract. The boom of the explosion, then the clattery sounds of pieces of the aircraft striking surrounding buildings, reached his ears less than a second later.

"Did you hear that?" he said. "That was the helicopter crashing. *I* did that. I did it by pressing *one* button. We're not a bunch of dumb, sex-starved teenagers, no matter what the fake news media says. We are *serious* people with serious weaponry. Hundreds of people will die if we don't get what we're demanding. There are patients here on oxygen feeds who aren't getting that anymore, who are slowly asphyxiating. Others on antibiotic IV drips whose infections are now running wild. Blood transfusions got halted halfway. You hear that weeping in the background? Those are the doctors and nurses.

"Nobody's leaving. Nobody's getting in. And not just this hospital—this whole damn *town.* Food's going to run out, or it's going to spoil. It'll be on *you,* on *your* consciences, when people start dying. When they start fighting each other for cans of food out there on the streets. You can save Isla Vista and Golenta. Or not. We're prepared to sit here in the dark for as long as it takes. Your choice."

He motioned for Conor to hang up the phone.

LESS THAN AN HOUR remained before the deadline was to expire. Four patients had already died. Conor had ordered hospital employees to place the bodies in one of the rapidly warming walk-in freezers in the basement.

Damien helped guard those hospital staff who had begged to distribute food to the surviving patients. He'd escorted them through the hospital's dark halls and chambers with his flashlight. Now the sun's earliest light began flowing through the windows.

A quavery, weak voice called to him from one of the intensive care recovery rooms. "You—you're one of *them,* aren't you? The ones who turned off the power?"

Damien motioned for another incel to take over his guard duties. He entered the woman's room. He saw that she might've been attractive, once. Now her skin had a grayish tinge, her hair was matted like a stray dog's, and her reeking sheets were soaked through with sweat. Bandages that should've been changed hours ago, discolored with greenish-yellow puss, covered the place on her chest where her left breast had been.

"What do you want?" Damien said. The room's atrocious odor made him want to leave immediately.

"To talk with you. Is that allowed? To talk with one of my own murderers?"

"You aren't dead yet. And I'm not your murderer. If you die, that'll be due to the authorities not giving us what we deserve."

The woman surprised him by laughing, weakly. "What you *deserve*? And what would *that* be? Apart from life in prison?" Her voice somehow gathered strength. "I'm anti-death penalty, just so you know."

"What do we deserve? We deserve what men used to have. What men have always had, until this screwed-up century. Women to make homes for us. To bear our children. To give us pleasure and affection in exchange for safety and sustenance."

"And what *keeps* you from having that, exactly? I'm just asking."

"Feminism, political correctness, hatred of masculinity and men."

"What's your name? Or am I not allowed to ask that?"

"Damien. What's yours?"

"Won't that risk humanizing me? Knowing my name?"

"Tell me."

"Karen."

"Did you have breast cancer?"

"How observant of you. I thought I'd just be having a lumpectomy. The docs told me they'd only be removing a piece of me the size of a gumball. But when I woke up, I was sans breast. And here I am. Here we are."

He nearly said he was sorry. But he stopped himself.

"I do technical writing for a living, write magazine articles on the side," she said. "So I'm fond of words, neologisms. But I can't say I've warmed to 'incel.' Couldn't you guys have come up with something snappier? Maybe the ss? Short for 'Sexually Starved'?"

"We're not a joke."

"I didn't say you were. I heard something from one of the nurses. You and your group are demanding your pick of UC–Santa Barbara students, right? As chattel wives? Like mail-order brides in the Old West?"

Her choice of words—"chattel," "mail-order brides"—excited him in a way he didn't find pleasing. "That's right."

"That's why I'm lying here, dying? You all want sex *that* badly?"

He didn't say anything. She would only laugh in that weak but superior way of hers.

"I have a proposition for you," she said. "Actually, I'm *propositioning* you. You're a virgin, aren't you? Well, fuck me. Rape me. Do whatever you want. I'm giving you permission. Go ahead. I may be down to one breast, but there's nothing wrong between my legs. Have at it, Damien."

He couldn't believe what he was hearing. "What . . . ?"

"Stick it in me. If you don't know where, I'll show you. Hurry it up, before the last of my pain meds give out. I'm hot. Really, *really* hot. Burning up. Isn't that what you boys want, a hot pussy?"

"That . . . that isn't what I want . . ."

"Isn't it? Come *on*, Damien . . . be honest. Isn't what you want to humiliate women? To put us in our places? To get *revenge* for years of rejection? I should *turn you on* like nobody else. Look at me. How much more *humiliated* and *debased* can I get? I lost a *breast*. I'm completely, utterly at your mercy. Doesn't that *excite* you? A woman who used to be quite lovely, now reduced to *this*?"

He pictured a UCSB Stacy lying in Karen's bed, weak as a newborn kitten, having been robbed of one of her precious, oh-so-desirable breasts. He felt himself stiffening in his pants.

But when he looked at the woman who was really there in front of him, his burgeoning erection went flaccid.

She was . . . a real person. Someone he had gotten to know a little.

"This . . . isn't what I want."

"What *do* you want, then?" she asked.

"For this to be over."

"HEY, WHERE WERE YOU?" Conor asked. "Look, there've been some changes."

Damien didn't like the sound of this. "What kind of changes?"

"In our negotiating position."

He couldn't stop himself from reacting badly. "Oh, *Christ*, Conor . . ." His emotions were just spilling out of him now.

"It's nothing bad, okay?"

"You're going to tell me you've accepted magic beans, right? After I told you to sell the cow for gold?"

Conor gave him a queer stare. "What the *fuck*, man?"

"It's from Jack and the Beanstalk. What, you don't know it?"

"No, like, *whatever*. What I'm saying is, I got us a *better deal*. Fuck those college Stacys, man. They wouldn't be good lays, anyhow. A total waste of good Trojans. The dude from the mayor's office said he'll provide fifty top-of-the-line Matsushita cybernetic sex partner dolls. From the Penthouse Collection. All the options included—warm skin, self-lubricating orifices, programmable scent, programmable orgasms, programmable personalities. I'm talking adaptive sex patter, suckable nipples that'll produce milk—the *works*. They even *breathe*. These are the kind that would set you back twenty grand a pop, top-of-the-line Japanese workmanship, can't tell 'em apart from genuine pussy. Only they're *better*. They're sending them to us on a tractor trailer. We get to inspect them before they load 'em onto our jumbo jet."

Damien wasn't listening. Mentally, he was back in Karen's room. Who gave *her* the *right* to make such judgments about him? Did the act of dying grant some supernatural ability to see into someone else's soul?

"Didn't I cut us a better deal?" Conor continued. "Why should we have to be saddled with American bitches when we're over in Russia anyhow?"

She was wrong about him. *Wrong*. Dead wrong.

"We're gonna be swimming in Russian pussy, dude," Conor said. "We're gonna be *famous*. And when we get tired of Russian pussy, we'll have our Penthouse Collection dolls waiting in the closet."

"Great, Conor," Damien said, not caring. "Great job . . ."

He headed downstairs to Karen's room. He'd let her emotionally batter him, and he didn't know why. He'd make her take back what she'd said about him.

He stormed into her room. Her bed was empty.

He found a nurse, under guard, providing water to patients. "That woman in room 237. Karen. Where is she?"

"In the basement," the nurse said, avoiding his stare.

"What . . . ? So quick? I was just talking with her . . ."

"You—you were talking to yourself. You must've seen she . . . needed to be moved."

"No, she was *alive*. I saw. I talked to her. She *argued* with me . . ."

"You were talking to yourself," she said flatly. "The patient in 237 died at least an hour before you went into her room."

He nearly struck her. How *dare* she *lie* to him? But then he realized she had no reason to lie. It only risked enraging him.

She had told him the truth.

Had he seen Karen's lips move in the morning's uncertain light? He couldn't say. Her color, that awful smell . . . But he remembered her *voice*! Her words! Where had they come from?

From inside of him?

What had he done after he'd left room 237? He hadn't gone straight to see Conor. He remembered now. He'd wandered the hallways. People had looked at him strangely. He remembered hearing the sound of his own voice.

But he *had* talked to her. He *knew* this. How else would he have learned her name?

But when? When had she told him that?

After the helicopter crash. After the explosions last night. After he'd killed multiple people by pressing a button . . .

He'd volunteered for guard duty. Anything to get him away from the cafeteria's windows, from the garish, accusatory reflections of the fires outside. He'd heard a voice from one of the rooms. Room 237. He'd gone inside with his flashlight. He remembered the flashlight's beam lighting her face. Illuminating the soiled bandages covering where her breast had been. *That's* when she'd told him her name.

So this morning . . . this morning . . .

He heard from a great way off the low whine of an approaching vehicle, the sound of a large diesel engine. He hurried to a window in one of the rooms. A huge tractor trailer rumbled along an access road to the hospital's main entrance.

The Penthouse Collection sex dolls.

*I haven't been thinking straight. When did I sleep last?*

How many dolls were supposed to be in that truck? Enough for everyone, right? Fifty? Sixty?

What had Conor said? About Stacys being a waste of Trojans . . . ?

*Trojans . . .*

The back of his throat tightened.

*A Trojan horse.*

He had to warn them. A crowd of his brothers stood outside the hospital's entrance, waiting. Waiting for their rightful reward.

He had to stop it. He had to warn them.

None of the windows would open. He couldn't make himself heard from up here. So he ran down the hallway. Took the steps in the stairwell two, three at a time, ignoring the darkness. As he burst through the front doors onto the breezeway, the truck had already pulled into the breezeway. Its rear trailer doors were open, with the Incel Nation crowding around.

Conor and Fred had already climbed into the huge trailer's cargo area. They'd begun ripping open cardboard shipping boxes as big as coffins. Neither had their rifles with them. "Look at the *tits* on that thing," he heard Conor say.

"*Conor!*" Damien shouted, struggling for breath. "Get *out* of there!"

Conor looked up and grinned. "Hey, Damien, get in *line*, man! You snooze, you *lose!*"

Other incels climbed into the trailer. They, too, began ripping into boxes like wild dogs scouring garbage cans for discarded meat.

Some of the men waiting in the breezeway had their sidearms with them. Damien, wild-eyed, grabbed Ben Lazarri's shoulder. "Shoot the boxes!" he cried. "Shoot them while you still can!"

A diminutive lad whose name Damien couldn't recall moved

farther back into the trailer, reading the shipping labels, presumably looking for his preferred set of specifications. He selected a box, ripped it open, and leaned over it, peering inside.

Naked arms reached up from the box and pulled him down. He squealed like a pig in the slaughter pen.

The lids of other shipping boxes, those near the back in the trailer, burst open. Women stood and stepped out of their hiding places. They all wore revealing lingerie or tiny bikinis, faces slathered with makeup, looking just like the dolls from the Penthouse Collection. But these women brandished guns.

Conor caught it first. The blast of a tactical shotgun hurled him out of the truck. His lifeless body slammed into the crowd of incels waiting their turns on the breezeway, knocking three of them onto the pavement.

Fred got his reward next. Then Butch. Then Alonzo.

Two dozen armed women rushed to the trailer's entrance. The barrage of detonations pounding Damien's ears made it sound as though he stood in the midst of an erupting fireworks factory. All around him, men shuddered backward, tumbled, and fell. He sensed a warm rain splatter his skin, an iron-scented cologne.

He locked eyes with a member of the SWAT team standing on the trailer's lip who towered above him. Time turned to taffy, stretching with infinite elasticity. This one, the one who'd chosen him as a target, seemed different than the others. Her costume—was it a costume?—looked archaic, something from a museum. She wielded a bow instead of a gun. She drew the bowstring back, her biceps bulging. The arrow's polished tip reflected the rays of the morning sun, dazzling him.

His vision deranged, he saw it then, and everything made sense. One of her breasts was gone. So familiar. Didn't Amazon warriors mutilate themselves that way to make themselves superior archers?

*See, Karen, I know things, I'm smart. Will you love me now?*

The muzzle flash was the last thing he would remember, and that not for very long.

# THREE

## Promethean Technologies

*Adding Accelerants to the Spreading Fire*

THE JAPANESE POLICE WERE relatively fortunate in confronting Aum Shinrikyo. The cult had to operate under the old rules for developing advanced weaponry. It needed to create its own biolab, which meant acquiring components from a network of legitimate suppliers. Aum accomplished this through various illegal and clandestine means, such as inserting followers into key companies, recruiting insiders, or setting up front corporations to buy sensitive materials. On other occasions, the organization worked through legal means, such as purchasing companies outright.[1]

However, all these activities, both legal and illicit, required the cult to engage with the outside physical world. Aum's acquisitions created paper trails. Every financial and physical transaction left potential leads for investigators to follow.

Our world is considerably different from the world of 1994. The worlds of tomorrow and the day after tomorrow will vary even more. Jonah Sebold and his friends do not require a large, sophisticated lab to produce the rage-inducing hallucinogens they force upon their victims in "Scenario 1: The Happiest Place on Earth" (chapter 1). In "Scenario 2: Where the Boys Are" (chapter 2), Damien Johnson doesn't rely upon a factory to produce his EMP wave generator; he fabricates it with consumer-grade 3D printing equipment in his basement, using schematics acquired on the dark web.

Future Aum Shinrikyos will be more "virtual" than physical in nature, more likely to gather in cyberspace than in a yoga ashram. They will not need to build research laboratories or acquire high-tech companies to produce innovative weaponry; instead, they will take advantage of new technologies that are colonizing the home consumer market. These Promethean technologies will grant "godlike" powers to "mere mortals," just as the mythical giant Prometheus offered fire, previously the provenance of the gods alone, to humanity.

A future Shoko Asahara who decides to create an apocalyptic cult will use forums on the dark web to gather hundreds or thousands of outraged, frustrated, and overeducated and underemployed acolytes. Those acolytes, dispersed around the country or around the world, acting mostly independently, will download schematics for weapons of mass destruction from the same dark web. They will use those schematics in conjunction with their 3D printers to manufacture implements of death in the shelter and privacy of their own homes. Unlike Aum Shinrikyo's Kiyohide Hayakawa or Masami Tsuchiya, they will not need to physically travel to Russia to buy expertise in weapons of mass destruction. Unlike that cult's Hideo Murai, they will not need to build an extensive laboratory installation, employing a dozen or more technicians, to fabricate their advanced weapons.

Tomorrow's techno-terror acolytes will burrow, termite-like, into the "wood" of ordinary communities. Then they will hollow out that wood from within until the seemingly placid milieu they have infested collapses into violent chaos. They will use the most effective, most efficient, least expensive, and most terror-inspiring tools they have at hand—Promethean technologies.

## What Are Promethean Technologies, and Why Should They Keep Me Up at Night?

*Promethean technologies* are any technologies that grant their possessors (persons of average resources, skills, abilities, and intelligence) capabilities that formerly had only been available to governments, military establishments, or large resource laboratories—or perhaps not even available to those institutions. (One quick note: I'll be using the term "Promethean technologies" differently from how earlier writers have. The term was first introduced by economist Nicolas Georgescu-Roegen in 1979 in his article "Energy and Matter in Mankind's Technological Circuit." Georgescu-Roegen defined

Promethean technologies as technologies that had granted mankind the ability to alter the environment. He listed two—fire and the heat engine.)[2] In particular, Promethean technologies are those that combine elements of strategic latency and emergent behavior, factors we'll discuss in chapter 4. Promethean technologies threaten to unleash strategic surprise. Their unsuspecting victims may include the nation's critical infrastructure, its significant symbols, the homeland security establishment, and the public at large.

Have there been Promethean technologies in the past? Of course there have. The Chinese invention of gunpowder led to the Promethean technology of firearms. Prior to the fielding of firearms (and, arguably, crossbows, at least before the Catholic Church outlawed them), the prime arbiter of the battlefield was the armored knight on horseback. The technological "system" of the mounted knight was very expensive and resource intensive, demanding skills in metallurgy, heraldry, and the breeding of horses to produce war horses capable of bearing enormous weights. Both its expense and the strict social restrictions on who could serve as a knight limited the actual fielding of this weapons system to the rulers of nation-states and their aristocratic vassals. Also, it took a long time—years, for most—to train a mounted knight to proficiency in the use of his weapons. The use of a firearm, however, could be taught in a matter of weeks. Although their fabrication also required sophisticated metallurgical skills, not too many decades passed before common folk could afford to purchase their own guns, weapons that were equal to those issued to soldiers serving in national armies. The results of the profusion of this early Promethean technology, for instance, were seen on many battlefields of the American Revolution. Colonial militiamen armed with their own guns were able to hold their own, when deploying guerrilla tactics, against units of one of the world's best-trained and best-equipped armies.

Events leading up to the American Revolution were powerfully influenced by another Promethean technology, the printing press. Prior to its invention, only the church and rulers of nation-states possessed the resources to inform, propagandize, and ideologically

mold an entire population, primarily through agents who disseminated proclamations face-to-face. The widespread use of printing
presses, however, allowed a band of political rebels in the American
colonies to effectively compete with the king of Great Britain and
his parliament at winning the hearts and minds of the hundreds
of thousands of colonists spread out along the Atlantic seaboard.
Without the use of this Promethean technology, the success of the
American Revolution—indeed, its very initiation—would have been
unthinkable.

The internet, the World Wide Web, and the dark web should be
seen not as new Promethean technologies but instead as extensions
of the earlier technology of the printing press. Ownership of printing
presses "stole the divine fire" of communications, propaganda, and
the shaping of public opinion from the state and the church and gave
it to private publishers of newspapers, pamphlets, broadsides, and
magazines. The internet and its offshoots have lowered the bar even
further. Ownership of a computer or mere access to one (such as at a
public library) grants anyone who can type or use speech-to-screen
software a comparable ability, at least theoretically, to influence public
opinion as that wielded by the owners and editors of the *New York
Times* or the *Economist*, now that mass communications no longer
require the burden of distributing physical media.

Thus, the rise of Promethean technologies isn't an entirely new
phenomenon. However, we are now entering an era in which they
will play a decisive role—a *Promethean Age*.

Why the shift? Zachary S. Davis, a senior fellow at Lawrence
Livermore National Laboratory's Center for Global Security Research,
offers an answer: we've reached a time when the research, development, and implementation of many key cutting-edge technologies are
no longer under the control of governments. We have left behind the
days when, for example, we could safely assume that NASA was over-
seeing and managing the development of space technology or when
the U.S. Department of Energy (and its counterparts in the Soviet
Union and Europe) oversaw all notable advancements in nuclear
power. Davis states that "potentially world-changing technologies in

biology, lasers, nanotechnology, space, and computers are essentially ungoverned," and he adds breakthrough developments in advanced materials science, robotics, and medicine to this list.[3] He describes two categories of likely challenges that Promethean technologies pose to national security: "black swan" strikes, which can take the form of innovative uses of older technologies, and unforeseen, bolt-from-the-blue uses of cutting-edge technologies. This second type of threats emerges so gradually and innocuously—hidden in plain sight—that these dangers may remain undetected by law enforcement and homeland security.[4] Fifteen years ago, who was talking about hackers using the internet to hold power grids, banking networks, schools, and hospitals hostage to their extortionary demands?

Another aspect of technology that will heighten the dangerous unpredictability of our new Promethean Age is the devil's talent for alchemy, which I highlighted in this book's introductory parable. Not only can new technologies pose dangers individually but also creative malefactors can combine the striking power of more than one new technology into a weapon no one else had foreseen. Or they can combine the destructiveness of new technologies with that of existing ones.

Analyst Bryan Arthur introduced the concept of "combinatorial evolution" of technology. He points out that technologies produce outputs that can be reconfigured and recombined in virtually endless combinations for new purposes, similar to how chemists can create new molecules from more basic elements. Rodrigo Nieto-Gómez, a professor and futurist with the Naval Postgraduate School's Center for Homeland Defense and Security, points out the salience of Arthur's concept for homeland security. He highlights that this combinatorial evolution of technologies continually opens up fresh vulnerabilities in our society, which has become increasingly dependent on technology for its most basic and essential functions. Nieto-Gómez states that "the few"—small, decentralized groups that intend to disrupt our society—are better situated to recognize and exploit those vulnerabilities than large, centralized, vertically oriented organizations, such as law enforcement agencies and homeland defense departments. He doesn't foresee this situation improving. In fact, he warns that we face a "permanently disrupted high-tech homeland security environment."[5]

## Not the Future, Already Here: CRISPR and 3D Printing

What are some examples of existing Promethean technology tools that can transform James Dingley's overeducated and underemployed into far more dangerous, super-empowered angry guys?

CRISPR, the gene-splicing kit for the home inventor and hobbyist, sits at the top of the list. Daniel M. Gerstein, the former acting undersecretary and deputy undersecretary in the Science and Technology (S&T) Directorate of the Department of Homeland Security and an analyst with the RAND Corporation, writes:

> CRISPR differs from other proliferation threats. The novelty and importance of CRISPR is not that it can enable the genetic editing of a pathogen—tools for this have been available for decades. What CRISPR does is make the technology widely available, allowing even largely untrained people to manipulate the very essence of life. CRISPR-based kits go for less than $500 in some cases, with pathogen-specific kits—West Nile virus, human coronavirus 229E, human adenovirus 35, to name a few—offered up like so many choices at a grocery store. Companies selling these kits are certainly not keeping registries of buyers or attempting to control the technology beyond the intellectual property that has been invested. The kits come with operator manuals that have only minimal warnings about containing hazardous materials and being for laboratory use only.[6]

Gerstein ponders whether the wide availability of CRISPR has made obsolete the Biological Weapons Convention, an international treaty that outlawed the development and use of biological weapons. The treaty, written and ratified in the early 1970s, clearly assumed that national governments were the only institutions with the technical ability to develop and produce biological weapons. Accordingly, the treaty's provisions revolve around controls on exports, nonproliferation regimes, and inspections of government labs and facilities. By making capabilities that were formerly available only to government, military, or academic labs easily accessible to the public for the price of a mid-range television set, CRISPR has made such provisions grossly inadequate. As Gerstein notes, "Traditional verification based on quotas for proscribed items, restrictions on use, and intrusive inspections is simply not an option for this new technology."[7]

Anthropologist Eben Kirksey, who frequently writes about the intersection between technology and art, notes that genetically modified organisms (GMOs) routinely escape from government and commercial labs. As a paradigmatic example, he offers the story of the "bio artist" Adam Zaretsky, who, while working as a visiting professor at San Francisco State University, accidentally released genetically modified fruit flies from his lab. This brought opprobrium down on his head. Seeking some form of penance, he decided to bring attention to the issue of GMOs being mistakenly released into the environment by using CRISPR to create his own GMOs and purposefully releasing them into the wild. (Don't ask me to explain his logic here.) Kirksey mentions that the evolving biohacking movement, encompassing both bio artists and pranksters, has attracted the attention of the FBI. Its agents, clad in biohazard gear, raided the Buffalo, New York, home of the cofounder of the Critical Art Ensemble. To the agents' undoubted relief, they uncovered only harmless bacteria. The FBI and homeland security agencies cannot count on this always being the case, however. Kirksey, with his artistic sensibility, may be charmed by the glowing green bunny rabbit "created" by a bio artist who made the animal luminescent by inserting jellyfish genes into its DNA. But he then describes a potentially far less benign project involving E. coli bacteria, commonly available from biological supply companies, that had been worked over by the bio artists of the Critical Art Ensemble.[8] Had their intention not been to create new forms of bio art but rather to indiscriminately sicken and kill, they could just as easily have inserted DNA from more virulent strains of E. coli—those that cause severe diarrhea, bleeding, fever, and sometimes death—into insects such as mosquitoes or stinging gnats and then unleashed an airborne swarm of pestilence carriers.

Another obvious Promethean tool that has become increasingly available over the past decade is the 3D printer. As their name implies, 3D printers compile three-dimensional shapes and objects from patterns downloaded to the printer from online schematics. Affordable 3D printers currently available for home use utilize plastic as their building material, but more advanced systems that can fabricate end products from metal are dropping in price and will soon begin showing up in the consumer market.

The first printed firearm, a single-shot plastic pistol known as the Liberator, was created in 2013. Since then, the craft of 3D-printed firearms has progressed rapidly. The next anticipated breakthrough in 3D printing will be the substitution of aluminum for plastic as a building material; this will allow for the printing of high-powered, semi-automatic rifles, such as AK-47s. The federal government forced the creator of the Liberator 3D-printed gun schematics to remove those schematics from the internet. But just as pirated music, movies, and software have proliferated despite international bans, we can expect much the same to occur regarding online schematics for toys from the devil's toy box—and not only guns.

Thus far, terror organizations have not yet made use of 3D-printed firearms, although criminal cartels have shown an interest in the technology. National security analyst Robert J. Bunker postulates that terrorists likely have not made use of 3D printing to date for the simple reason that they find it much more convenient, at present, to acquire conventional firearms on the black market. He anticipates that terrorists may become far more interested in 3D printing, however, once the confluence between firearms and computerized controls facilitates remote-controlled sniping weapons. A Texas commercial firm briefly marketed the Live-Shot system in 2005 that allowed disabled hunters to fire pre-placed deer rifles from controls on the internet. Political revulsion against the idea of video game–type hunting of deer resulted in the product being banned. However, such moral qualms aside, we can expect such internet-firearms synergistic developments to continue and improve. Bunker predicts that future terror applications of 3D printing will include remote sniping, virtual targeting presence (being able to remotely keep a weapon aimed at a target under remote surveillance), and remotely carrying out sophisticated, layered attacks involving both firearms and explosives.[9]

Other observers fear 3D-printed terror on an exponentially larger scale. The U.S. Defense Threat Reduction Agency has sponsored research to determine the likelihood of 3D printing technologies being used to subvert nuclear export ban regimes. Agency analysts worry that through 3D-printing, rogue regimes and terror organizations will acquire centrifuges and other technological implements needed for the nuclear fuel cycle.[10]

Gene-splicing home kits and advanced consumer-grade 3D printers provide obvious examples of Promethean technologies that can be subverted for violence and destruction by those who seek to provoke mayhem for political or economic gain, for religious or ideological dictates, or simply for a boost in self-esteem. But what about the seemingly more innocuous technological advancements that are making their way into our homes? What about labor-saving and efficiency-optimizing innovations, such as the Internet of Things?

The combinatorial evolution of Promethean technologies can result in some highly volatile, massively deadly combos. Young people's immersion in social media has fueled a hunger for online recognition and increased status, whether such ascension springs from fame or from infamy. The overeducated and underemployed, however, are not the only actors prone to spectacular bouts of antisocial mayhem. As the following scenario illustrates, acts of cruelty are not only born of the marriage of anger and resentment. Sometimes murder is the offspring of boredom and status anxiety. And sometimes terror is the best entertainment value money and ingenuity can buy.

### Scenario 3: Initiation Rites

*There's my puppet. Finally . . .*

Fabiana Silvio smiled. She watched Roberta Danberg stroll along the sidewalk toward the Metro station with far greater ease than any cripple should enjoy. Fabiana's grin grew wider, even though she was down to her last stick of bubble gum, and the wad currently in her mouth had lost the last vestige of its delicious raspberry flavor. It had taken her a whole lot of research to track down Roberta Danberg, the quadriplegic. Rendered paralyzed from the neck down following a brutal five-car smashup on I-95, she had been the beneficiary of one of the first human implantations of an Armstrong neural armature, a virtualized fiber-optic web that bypassed her ruined organic nerve pathways. Invented by Dr. Norman Armstrong, the artificial network facilitated transmissions of commands from Roberta's brain to the muscles in her limbs even more efficiently and effectively than the nerve network she'd been born with. It enabled her to walk, to cook, and to care for herself, as well as even to dance far more gracefully than she'd been able to before the accident.

Fabiana had read all the news articles, followed the online coverage, and even reviewed the science journal monographs. The case of Roberta Danberg had become a bit of an obsession for her and not only because Roberta lived in Owings Mills, Maryland, just twenty miles from Fabiana's family's home in Ellicott City. No, Fabiana's obsession was due to something far darker than mere proximity to celebrity. For months now, she'd been planning her campaign to compete for a prized membership with the Bolivarian League of Assassins (BLA). And she'd learned something about Roberta Danberg that would help elevate Fabiana into the winners' circle.

Dr. Armstrong had carried out his procedure on Roberta at Johns Hopkins Hospital in Baltimore. Researchers at Johns Hopkins maintained a 24-7 data link with Roberta, continually monitoring her vital signs, hormonal secretions, the operation of the neural armature, and the status of the organic-cybernetic "handshake" so vital to Roberta's independent existence. They even monitored her dreams, searching for subconscious signs of distress.

It had taken Fabiana weeks of work, but she had finally located a vulnerability in the data communications system connecting Johns Hopkins with the artificial neural web inside Roberta—a flaw she could exploit, a door left askew just enough for her to virtually squeeze through. She then learned how to pull Roberta's cybernetic "strings." Anytime she wanted, she could grasp those strings and manipulate them, overriding whatever signals Roberta's brain attempted to send through the neural armature to her muscles. Fabiana couldn't control Roberta's speech or facial expressions; the neurons and synapses controlling them remained old-style meat connections. But the rest of her, from the neck down? That was all Fabiana's personal Punch and Judy show.

Today she would prove herself, not only to her faceless BLA judges but also to her anonymous opponent, who was supposedly a hacking wizard beyond compare. Screw him and his fearsome reputation. Today she would mark herself as the worthiest of the worthies, the flashiest and maybe the youngest Bolivarian assassin on the East Coast. After today, all future contestants in the Tournament of Murder would measure themselves against her deeds. Of that, she was quite sure.

Fabiana watched Roberta walk closer to the trash receptacle where Fabiana had hidden the counterfeit Uzi submachine gun she had manufactured on her parents' home 3D printer. Fabiana double-checked the settings on her MegAphone, making sure she had retained her stealthy stranglehold on the data comms link between Johns Hopkins and Roberta's neural armature. Everything checked out. She next spun up a virtual joystick so that she'd be able to control Roberta's movements as precisely and easily as she might a radio-controlled model car. Then she pulled her sweatshirt's hood over her head and much of her face so that in case any bystander recalled seeing her standing a block away from the berserk shooter and inexplicably not fleeing, she couldn't be identified.

First things first, she had to make Roberta retrieve the Uzi from the trash can.

*Here we go!* Fabiana couldn't help but laugh when she saw the astonished, then intensely distressed expression on Roberta's face as Fabiana commanded the older woman to jerkily walk like a poorly made robot toward the trash can and then reach inside. Roberta pulled out a box a little larger than a sneaker shoebox. Then she opened it, removed the Uzi and its spare magazine, and awkwardly tossed the box behind her.

*Maybe she'll get arrested for littering,* Fabiana thought and giggled.

"Help! *Help me!*" Roberta screamed as she was forced to grasp the Uzi's trigger and swivel about like a first-person shooter in a *Call of Duty* game.

*Who gets it first?* Fabiana knew she didn't have time to dither. Roberta's screams would make everyone around her notice the gun, and they'd scatter like roaches when the kitchen light gets switched on. *That guy—he looks like a stuck-up dork, probably some government contractor for the military-industrial complex.* Fabiana forced Roberta to aim the Uzi at the man, who was wearing earbuds connected to his phone and hadn't heard her screaming. *Short burst. Don't waste ammo.* Fabiana experienced a surge of happy gratification as the slugs tore into the man's back, slamming him face-first into the sidewalk. His phone flew from his hand and landed in the gutter, where it clattered down a drain.

The staccato burst of gunfire set pedestrians to running in a way that Roberta's screams for help hadn't. Yet Fabiana was astonished to see that some people didn't react at all. Either their earbuds muffled all outside sounds or they were completely mesmerized by their music or phone conversations. *Makes life easier for me, death easier for them. More points on the board!*

She aimed Roberta at a woman in her twenties who wore a figure-flattering yellow dress and dauntingly high heels. *Probably a snob or a bitch.* Two slugs to the back and down the bitch went.

She next aimed Roberta at a group of Owings Mills High School kids, rivals to her own high school. A pudgy boy caught a bullet in the stomach. His glasses flew so high into the air, they hit the sidewalk three seconds after he did. A white girl with blue streaks in her hair ended up splattered with blood—red, white, and blue. *Salute!* A tall, skinny boy folded in half like a soggy stand-up cardboard cutout. Another girl lost her pretty knees in a shower of liquefied bone and flesh.

Fabiana heard *click-click-click.* Her puppet had emptied the Uzi's first magazine. The sudden absence of gunfire made the victims' shrieks and groans sound much louder. But loudest of all were Roberta's frenzied screams: "*It's not me! It's not ME!*"

*Of course it's not you, you silly cow,* Fabiana thought. *Now be a good girl and reload your Uzi before all my other points run away.* She commanded Roberta to detach the empty magazine and slide in the spare one.

*Is anyone filming this on their phone?* She certainly hoped so. All the news networks would air it, and the footage would clearly show Roberta had not murdered these people of her own will, backing up the assertions Fabiana would make to the BLA while claiming credit. Looking around, she saw a woman cowering in a corner of a third-story apartment balcony, clearly aiming her cell phone's camera at the carnage below. *Thanks, sweetie!* Fabiana thought. *Since you're doing me a solid, I won't have my remote-control killer cyborg blow your head off.*

She didn't need to resort to that anyway. There were still good pickings on street level, even though Fabiana had to prod Roberta into running after some of them. In the next sixty seconds, she racked up two customers fleeing a coffeehouse, an indeterminate number of schoolchildren in a passing school bus, and an old lady (*deaf?*) who'd been walking her dog. Some homeless dude who'd been sleeping on a blanket in a shoe repair shop's doorway was awakened by the noise, stumbled toward Roberta (*drunk? high? crazy?*), and asked for a handout before literally losing his head. Roberta used the clip's final bullet on the homeless dude.

Fabiana mentally kicked herself for not providing a third magazine. This had all gone so much better than she'd expected, and angry with herself now, she realized she could've marched Roberta into the Metro station and racked up dozens more points.

Well, no sense in crying over spilled milk. A garbage truck conveniently turned the corner. Having no further use for her, Fabiana commanded her puppet to leap beneath the wheels of the onrushing five tons of steel behemoth.

She could hardly wait to return home and turn on the news. What would her tally end up being?

SHE WAS A STAR. Oh, of course, nobody knew her name, but she was the subject of headlines, video crawls, and social media blasts worldwide. That woman on the balcony had been a crude but spectacularly effective citizen-journalist with her cell phone camera. She'd captured close-ups of Roberta Danberg's horrified face, her jerky, forced movements, and her agonized cries of *"It's not ME! It's NOT ME!"* Early reportage had speculated that the shooter had been a deranged sociopath, but once Roberta's identity had been released to the media, reporters swiftly made the connection to the quadriplegic who'd had the use of her limbs miraculously restored at Johns Hopkins Hospital, thanks to the experimental Armstrong neural armature. A technician at the hospital who'd been monitoring Roberta's artificial nervous system broke an FBI-imposed embargo on sharing details to the media. His leaking that the electronic linkage to Ms. Danberg's neural armature had been hacked created a media feeding frenzy. This, in turn, cascaded into conspiracy theories growing like mushrooms all over social media.

"Hello, Fabiana! I'm home! I brought you something to eat, honey."

Her mother. Home from the office. Fabiana closed the lid on her laptop. She'd been so engrossed in all the coverage, she'd forgotten to eat. She went downstairs. Her mother had put a bag of take-out food on the kitchen table. Fabiana crinkled her nose with disgust. "Oh, *Mom!*" she said. "Chick-fil-A *again*? Don't make me *puke . . .*"

"I thought you *liked* Chick-fil-A . . ."

"That was *before* I got *woke*. They're *way* too reactionary and Christian and right wing. That's what Consuela says."

Her mother frowned. "I think that Consuela has been a bad influence. Speaking of which, I got an email from your school earlier today. They said you were absent. You want to tell me where you were?"

"They're such *dummies* in the school office. They don't know *anything*. We had an away-assignment today. From history class. We had to go to the public library—"

"Doesn't the school have its own library?"

"Yeah, but the public library's *better*. I had to do research on nineteenth-century revolutions in Latin America. Really. *Honest*."

Her mother appeared unconvinced. "Fabiana, you'd better be telling me the truth . . . I couldn't bear for you to get a demerit placed on your school record. You know how much your father and I want you to get into the business program at Wharton . . ."

"*Wharton?*" Fabiana nearly spat on the floor. "That's a school for capitalist *pigs*. That's what Consuela says. I'm going to UCLA for Chicano studies, not that capitalist business crap!"

"Don't *say* such things, Fabiana! You know we arrived here with nothing, thanks to the *bastardos* who raped Venezuela. Your father and I have worked so hard to make a good life for you. Say such horrible things and you will break your father's heart . . ."

Fabiana didn't bother continuing the argument. She snatched the bag of Chick-fil-A. It might be creepy Christian and sucky, but she was hungry. She stalked back upstairs to her room and locked the door.

The latest death tally was fourteen, including Roberta Danberg. Bullets had connected with six kids on the school bus, three fatally, so there was that. Fabiana learned that twenty-three victims had been admitted to hospitals with varying degrees of injury. Five were in critical condition. Fabiana smiled; her points total might yet increase. She decided to hold off reporting her tally to BLA for another day or two, until she learned whether additional victims died.

She'd first learned of the Bolivarian League of Assassins from her best friend, Consuela. She and Consuela had been BFFs since the fifth grade. They had so much in common, it almost seemed they were twin sisters. Just like Fabiana, Consuela's favorite hobby was hacking. Just like Fabiana's parents, Consuela's had fled Venezuela during the collapse of the nation's economy under international sanctions meant to topple the Bolivarian socialist government. Fabiana and Consuela both rebelled against their parents' strident anti-socialist conservatism, especially hating the adults' constant demonization of the former president Hugo Chávez. Fabiana had expressed her defiance by furtively dressing in T-shirts emblazoned with the faces of Chávez and Che Guevarra, but Consuela had gone further than mere griping and token opposition. She had sought out a group willing to take dramatic action—not only to restore Bolivarian democracy and socialism to Venezuela but also to punish those nations that had snuffed out the movement's first flowering. The BLA wasn't a legitimate political party or social movement, and it wasn't exactly a gang like MS-13, either. In some ways a violent revolutionary vanguard, it was more like a secret guild, one with exacting standards for membership. Fabiana discovered that achieving BLA membership by winning a competition of "murder from a distance" guaranteed massive status and respect from the underground elite, social perks she came to hunger for. Consuela might not have had the *cajones* to try to become an official member, but Fabiana was determined to prove she was made of sterner stuff than her friend.

Her initial application for membership had been painfully jejune, she now realized (cutting herself no slack for having been merely fourteen years old at the time). How the lords of the BLA must have laughed at her bragging about her hacking skills, chortled at her pubescent bravado over having remotely turned off her neighbors' basement freezers through the Internet of Things so their frozen foods and meats would spoil! Yet they must have seen potential in her. They must have valued her pluck and her persistence, for they assigned her a mentor, the mysterious Comandante X, who eventually allowed Fabiana, after she had passed increasingly daunting tests of loyalty, to enroll in the Tournament of Murder.

And now she was well on her way to official membership, she told herself. Who could dislodge her from the top of the heap, after what she'd accomplished? No matter how much of an awesome hacking wizard he might be, how could her anonymous opponent possibly upstage Fabiana's creativity, originality, and daring? She was *world famous*. If he were still alive, Steven Spielberg would make a movie about her, for sure. Now it was just a matter of waiting a while for more victims to die in the hospital so she could report her final tally, and then membership was hers. The only downside was that Fabiana couldn't spill the beans to Consuela. How she'd love to see the look on her friend's face when she'd reveal that she, Fabiana Silvio, was the infamous "Marionette-Master Murderer" (so titled by the *New York Post*) and a member of the BLA! Maybe someday she could find some secure way to bring Consuela into her confidence . . . just to see the look on her face.

Fabiana's giddy sense of anticipation did not last long, however. The next day, she was appalled to see her deeds knocked from the newspapers' front pages and off CNN's Headline News by an unprecedented rash of deadly house fires throughout metropolitan Baltimore. Nothing even close to this number of fires devastating a single area, absent a wildfire, had occurred since the worst years of Detroit's Devil's Night, when vandals had competed to set the largest numbers of abandoned houses ablaze on Halloween. In her school on the outskirts of Baltimore, Fabiana heard fire engine after fire engine race past, as fire companies from hundreds of miles around sent their teams to assist the city's overwhelmed firefighters. She and her fellow students were denied outside recess for fear that exposure to the clouds of black smoke darkening the midday sun would damage their health.

Crestfallen from suddenly being denied the limelight she had worked so hard to achieve, Fabiana decided to delay no longer in reporting her activities and death tally through her dark web connection to Comandante X. That, surely, would buck up her spirits. Yet rather than receiving a warm cascade of congratulations and encouragement and an assurance that BLA membership was easily within her grasp, Fabiana suffered a virtual kick in the stomach: Comandante X revealed she was now far behind on points in the Tournament of Murder! The fires had been the work of Fabiana's opponent! The *bastardo* had pursued quantity rather than quality. Whereas Fabiana's murders had been elegant and sophisticated in conception—the work of a true *artista*—her opponent's had relied upon sheer numbers and brute chance. According to Comandante X, her opponent had used massively parallel computing—thanks to the processing power of tens of thousands of remotely purloined home computers and cell phones—and hacked many hundreds of internet-connected gas stoves and ovens throughout the Baltimore area, overriding their safety limiters and setting them all on maximum gas output in the expectation that some residents would have carelessly left flammable material sitting on or near their stove tops or, not noticing the gas odor, would light a cigarette or a fireplace. The ploy had worked well enough to overcome Fabiana's early twenty-one-point lead, in any case. Her opponent's score now stood at sixty-two, and it was climbing by the hour. Fabiana argued fruitlessly that she should at least be awarded style points. *No dice*, Comandante X had typed back.

Fabiana could not copy her opponent's tactics to pad her own points tally; the rules clearly stipulated that once a particular gambit had been utilized, it was off the table for the remainder of the tournament. She couldn't fight *fire* with *more* fire, not exactly. Nor could she afford to take months, as she had with her Roberta Danberg strike, to plan another truly creative, sophisticated attack. Rather than a scalpel, she'd have to wield a swift ax.

She overrode the navigation controls of a Tesla Model X suv and bowled it through a Memorial Day military parade in Annapolis. Sixteen points on her side of the board. Her opponent remotely grabbed the controls of an Uber Air taxi and plunged it from ten thousand feet onto the big-top tent of a Shriners' charity circus in Woodbridge, Virginia. Thirty-two points for him, including the four passengers on the air taxi.

*Damn him!* Fabiana fell further behind!

She read about an upcoming virtual reality Dungeons and Dragons tournament to take place in Chevy Chase, Maryland. Snatching control of the groups' vr helmets, she maneuvered a group out of the convention rooms the people occupied and onto the roof of the eighteen-story hotel. She marched sixteen of them off the edge, dropping them nearly a hundred feet onto the outdoor swimming pool deck. Sixteen points for her. Her opponent smashed a speedboat into a ferry crossing the Potomac River. Five were killed by the impact and a dozen more by drowning, trumping Fabiana by one point.

She just couldn't win. Every week, she found herself falling further and further behind. Every week, she plunged deeper into despair and furious resentment. Even her parents, oblivious as they were, had begun noticing the marked change in her mood. They were threatening to put her on medication. Consuela had been no source of cheer, either. The more depressed and resentful Fabiana had grown, the more reasons Consuela had found to avoid her company, as though Fabiana had the chicken pox.

There was only one thing she could think to do. The rules didn't say anything about eliminating one's opponent. If this wasn't specifically prohibited, Fabiana reasoned, that meant it was allowed. And if she found a way to identify, locate, and disable or kill her opponent, then he would stop putting points on the board—obviously, *duh*—and she would snatch the opportunity to overtake his tally.

She switched gears from hacker to dark web detective. She searched all the underground forums she knew the BLA members and their supporters frequented, looking for discussions about the ongoing Tournament of Murder. She scanned hundreds of different threads to see if any of the anonymous commentators claimed credit for any of the attacks. If she could locate one of her opponent's pseudonyms and user handles, that would give her a starting place, a set of digital footprints she could try to follow.

It didn't take long. After just a couple of days, she came across the first example of her opponent being sloppy. Bragging about crashing the air taxi into the Shriners' circus and "killing clowns with fire." *Stupid, stupid* . . . It was more childish and immature than she would've expected the "master wizard" hacker to behave. Within the week, she uncovered three more instances of such indiscreet braggadocio on dark web forums. Each time her opponent posted a different pseudonymous user handle, which actually proved useful to Fabiana, because she was able to correlate common digital fingerprints shared by each and start compiling an online profile for her hated adversary.

Armed with this fragmentary profile, she decided to pursue a hunch. What if her opponent *also* had been assigned Comandante X as his BLA handler? In that case, Fabiana would be able to triangulate her antagonist's digital fingerprints. Additionally, he might reveal personal details of himself to Comandante X. The latter might even refer to him by name . . .

Fabiana's hunch hit pay dirt. But the taste of victory was not as sweet as she'd expected . . . Actually, it tasted like *dirt*, dirt with *worms* crawling in it.

Comandante X had misled her. Fabiana's opponent wasn't a "he." Wasn't a mysterious, ten-foot-tall mastermind with a brain like a supercomputer. Wasn't even a stranger . . .

FABIANA WAITED A SAFE distance from the sweetFrog frozen yogurt shop where her hated adversary worked after school. The little strip mall that housed the shop sat in the shadow of an I-95 overpass and at the edge of an access road, convenient for the millions of commuters on the always congested stretch of highway between Baltimore and Washington DC.

On the screen of her MegAphone, Fabiana watched a blinking blip make its way south on the Waze map of I-95, drawing closer to the sweetFrog's strip mall. The blip represented an automated Walmart eighteen-wheeler transporting frozen foods. Walmart wasn't driving the truck any longer. Fabiana was. It was a big, diesel-electric hybrid pulling a heavy, fully stocked freezer trailer, and it had just taken on a fresh load of diesel fuel.

It drew close enough that she could hear it approaching at a steady sixty-five miles per hour. Then she saw it, the long trailer painted the colorful Walmart way with a cornucopia of foods even Norse gods would salivate over. *Probably just a bunch of frozen peas and fish sticks inside,* Fabiana thought. *The kind of crap Mom feeds me when she can't be bothered.*

When the Walmart truck reached the apex of the overpass and the closest spot to the sweetFrog, Fabiana spun its virtual steering wheel and brutally jackknifed the giant robot vehicle. Sudden deceleration lifted the rear of the trailer off the highway and swung it about while the tractor heeled over on its right wheels and smashed through the railings on the east side of the overpass.

She watched it soar through the air between the overpass and the strip mall, twisting and rolling like a high diver at the Summer Olympics. Then it plowed into the strip mall like a gigantic sledgehammer. It obliterated a nail salon, flattened a FedEx store, and blossomed into a blazing, screeching, sliding meteor before simultaneously enveloping the sweetFrog in burning diesel fuel and hurtling fragments of the store and its occupants across the parking lot.

*Adios, puta,* Fabiana thought. TRUCK YOU, *Consuela* . . .

# FOUR

## Endless Threats

*Promethean Technology's Mind-Bending*
*Challenge to Homeland Security*

HOW CAN WE KNOW what is in the devil's mind?

Let's return to the parable at the beginning of this book. At first glance, the defenders would appear to have many advantages over the devil: they outnumber him, they have access to more money and more resources, and they enjoy the backing and support of virtually their entire society. However, the devil possesses one enormous advantage: the devil holds the initiative. *The devil knows what is in his own mind.*

The defenders would give virtually anything to gain even partial knowledge of the devil's intentions. Sometimes they get lucky. Sometimes, thanks to the keen ears of their thousands of field agents, they learn enough of the devil's intentions early on that they can go on offense and derail their foe's plans. But the defenders know that no matter how many resources they may devote to gathering intelligence, at times the devil, with all his deadly toys, will evade their best efforts. The defenders realize that for those times when interdiction fails, defensive measures must already be in place to protect as many innocent lives as possible. Yet the devil is an alchemist, a tinkerer, an inventor. He can repurpose the fruits of other persons' genius for his own malign ends. And he acts at times and places of his own choosing.

Put yourself in the defenders' shoes. The money, time, and manpower available to you aren't infinite. Yes, in many ways you are stronger than the devil, but you are like a circus strongman trying to fend off attacks from dozens of midgets in the dark who might be armed with knives, spears, poisoned darts, even pistols. You can defend against some possible weapons but which ones?

In this new age, the varieties and conceivable combinations of weapons the devil might choose approach the incalculable. You have to winnow that almost infinite number of possibilities. You have to decide which toys the devil is most likely to create, which toys he will most enjoy using, and which toys can cause the worst destruction. You have no choice but to try using your imperfect crystal ball.

Using a crystal ball takes special skill, however. If you hope to be truly effective, you'll need to learn to think the way the devil thinks.

The key to learning to think as the devil thinks? *Imagination.*

### Strategic Latency and Failures of Imagination

The best-remembered quote from the 9/11 Commission's *Final Report of the National Commission on Terrorist Attacks upon the United States* was its conclusion that of all the mistakes and missed opportunities made by the intelligence and law enforcement sectors in the years leading up to the attacks of September 11, 2001 (9/11), "the most important failure was one of imagination."[1]

Contrarily, the perpetrators of the 9/11 attacks showed no failure of imagination. The same way a judo master can take advantage of an opponent's larger size and weight, they used our strengths against us. Their use of Western civilization's technologies—commercial airliners, skyscraper office buildings, and implements as seemingly innocuous as box cutters—has been described as a terroristic hacking of our high-tech society. Their aggressions were "a deviant result of the innovation process that also fuels progress inside our technologically dependent civilization."[2]

Such judo-like maneuvers by malign actors are increasingly likely in our new Promethean Age. Dr. Ronald Lehman, the director of the Center for Global Security Research at the Lawrence Livermore National Laboratory, characterizes this growing vulnerability as "strategic latency." He defines *strategic latency* as "a package of diverse technologies that can be deployed quickly, often in new ways, with limited visibility that could have decisive military and geopolitical implications."[3]

What makes this phenomenon so insidious is that virtually *any* technology can be dual use. Given enough imagination and will, almost all technologies can be repurposed to improve existing weapons or to destroy a target in new ways.[4] Think about the amazing skill of Hawkeye the marksman from *The Avengers* movies. His primary weapons are his bow and his endless variety of specialized arrows. But if deprived of them, he can turn virtually anything at hand—a fork, a dinner plate, even a paperclip—into a deadly projectile weapon. In Hawkeye's hands, even simple household fixtures have strategic latency.

The factor that grants strategic latency to complex technologies is what Dr. Lehman calls their *emergent behavior*, or their tendency to be used by adopters in ways completely unforeseen by those technologies' inventors.[5] Even very simple technologies can possess emergent behavior. Prior to the attacks on the World Trade Center and the Pentagon, who would've thought that the offensive capability of a box cutter was anything other than extremely limited? With its blade measuring less than two inches, it only enables an attacker to strike about six inches beyond the reach of his own arm. Yet on 9/11, the humble box cutter possessed a strategic latency and emergent behavior that far more formidable, bladed weapons did not have. Why? Unlike broadswords or rapiers or daggers, box cutters were allowed to be carried on board passenger aircraft by travelers. And however limited they might be in deadliness, the flight attendants and passengers nonetheless considered them deadly *enough* in the hands of determined terrorists to compel their passivity on the two planes that targeted the World Trade Center. Humble box cutters brought about the immediate deaths of nearly three thousand persons. Plus the deaths of tens of thousands more within the following decade, since those box cutters can be considered to have ignited the American war against the Taliban and al Qaeda in Afghanistan.

How much did those eighteen box cutters cost al Qaeda? Less than fifty dollars. A more cost-effective use of the terrorists' money could hardly be imagined. The strategic aftershocks of those box cutters' threatened use still rumble around the world.

Our commercial passenger transportation system demonstrated both strategic latency and emergent behavior on September 11, 2001.

In little more than half a century, commercial aircraft evolved from piston engine–driven, single-passenger craft weighing a few hundred pounds and with a range of less than a dozen miles to jet engine–driven behemoths that weigh hundreds of tons and cross oceans. As they grew bigger, faster, and capable of carrying increasing loads of fuel, the strategic latency of passenger aircraft gathered force. On 9/11 the world learned that the destructive power of a large passenger jetliner, when used as a missile, rivals that of the biggest nonnuclear bombs in the U.S. arsenal.

Emergent behavior also contributed to that day's toll of destruction. From the 1970s through the turn of the millennium, terror-related hijackings of commercial passenger aircraft taught governments, law enforcement agencies, and the managers and pilots of commercial airlines that the safest response on in-flight aircraft, the response most likely to avert deaths or injuries, was to give in to the terrorists' demands regarding where to fly and land the aircraft. Protocols instructed pilots to land their aircraft at the location demanded by the terrorists and to allow local law enforcement agencies to resolve the standoff. These protocols rested on two assumptions: the hijackers would issue negotiable demands, and the longer the standoff persisted, the more likely the passengers would emerge safely.[6] The 9/11 terrorists were well aware of this emergent behavior on the part of aviation authorities and shaped their plans around it. They knew the pilots and attendants would unwittingly facilitate the terrorists' use of the jetliners as guided missiles. Only the passengers and crew of Flight 93—the last of the four 9/11 airliners to take to the air—had time to learn about this terror innovation, thanks to their receiving reports of the attacks on the Twin Towers over the plane's Airfones. Only they knew enough to realize that the protocols that had preserved lives for decades were now obsolete and that to avert mass deaths on the ground, they had to fight for control of their aircraft. They, too, exhibited emergent behavior, heroic behavior that, to date, has denied terrorists the ability to replicate the tactics used on 9/11.

Dr. Lehman sums up civilized society's dilemmas in the Promethean Age: "(1) Weapons and technologies related to them are advancing and spreading widely, (2) lead times for exploitation by more actors are shrinking significantly, (3) intelligence information and awareness are fuzzy, (4) vulnerabilities exist that increase the risk of leveraged threats, (5) players with deadly motivations exploit latency, (6) challenges to timely response are significant, (7) norms and goals are unclear, (8) enforcement options may be unattractive or ineffective, (9) tipping points are approaching, and (10) consequences are strategic in that they alter international security relationships in important ways."[7]

The devil is growing more skilled at his alchemy. He is fabricating new, deadlier toys at a faster pace. Society's defenders have a shrinking amount of time in which to manufacture shields. Thanks to this escalating time pressure, they must rely on their crystal ball to predict the devil's intentions. But their crystal ball's reception is as fuzzy as an analog television set with a broken antenna.

### Homeland Security's Already Taking Care of This, Aren't They? *Aren't They?*

How much should all this worry you? Aren't we spending, at the federal, state, and local levels, trillions of dollars to protect our homeland security? Surely, with all that money being spent, those agencies will take care of the problem, won't they?

You may want to think again.

Despite having been founded in response to the most creative and devilish use ever of a David's slingshot against our American Goliath, the Department of Homeland Security spends only a tiny fraction of its considerable funding on research and development to counter emerging technological threats. The Homeland Security Advanced Research Projects Agency (HSARPA) was meant to be the department's response to such threats. HSARPA was established concurrently with DHS in 2003 as part of that department's Science and Technology Directorate. HSARPA was deliberately modeled after the Defense Advanced Research Projects Agency (DARPA), the federal government's most successful technology incubator. Congress initially allotted HSARPA many of the same acquisitional and organizational partnership flexibilities that have helped make DARPA one of the government's greatest success stories.[8] Its creators meant for HSARPA to do the sort of blue-sky, high-risk, high-reward research and development that, under DARPA's purview, had led to the creation of the internet and stealth technology—exactly the sort of R&D necessary to counter Promethean technologies.

However, HSARPA's portfolio has exhibited a far more conservative research orientation than one would expect from an innovation incubator with "advanced research" as part of its name. An internal review of the DHS S&T Directorate performed a deep dive analysis of fifty-two HSARPA projects from the FY 2014 portfolio. Analyzing this review, I determined only 8 percent of these projects were of the type—novel in conception and technically challenging—that might be expected to make up the majority of a "revolutionary" advanced research organization.[9] An April 2014 report by the Congressional Research Service complained that much of HSARPA's efforts have been conventional, incremental R&D work of only moderate risk.[10] The S&T Directorate's Strategic Plan for FY 2015–FY 2019 showed little change in HSARPA's R&D goals. It listed five visionary goals and the planned Apex programs to support those goals. As of FY 2015, eight Apex programs were underway: Screening at Speed; Real-Time Biological Threat Awareness; Next Generation First Responder; Relational, Adaptive Process of Information and Display; Cybersecurity in Critical Infrastructure; Border Situational Awareness; Border Enforcement Analytics; and Air Entry and Exit Reengineering.[11] Cutting through the jargon, with the possible exception of Cybersecurity in Critical Infrastructure, virtually all these Apex programs are responses to familiar, quotidian threats and risks—not blue-sky R&D of the DARPA sort to counter emerging Promethean technology threats.

A Homeland Security Advanced Research Agency that engages in hardly any advanced research? What could account for this? The leading culprits appear to be *habit* and *politics*.

We'll cover habit first. Rodrigo Nieto-Gómez of the Center for Homeland Defense and Security separates the responsibilities of the homeland security enterprise into two mission sets—the *systemic mission* (preparing for and responding to known threats) and the *future-shock mission* (preparing for highly uncertain or unknown threats from emerging technologies). The systemic mission includes defending against and responding to both regularly occurring natural threats (hurricanes, earthquakes, and floods) and man-made threats (purposeful attacks that rely on conventional weapons such as guns, knives, explosives, or vehicles). Nieto-Gómez characterizes the future-shock mission as "neutraliz(ing) disruptive—almost random— threats posed by the rapid pace of technological evolution."[12]

Most organizations, just like most of the people in them, prefer to do the types of work they are used to doing and have learned to do well. For homeland security, this is its systemic mission. Nieto-Gómez says that our existing homeland security apparatus handles its systemic mission very effectively due to the very nature of its bureaucracy, a system of efficient organization and management that was developed to apply standardized policies and procedures to deal with known, incremental problems and threats.[13]

However, the very qualities of homeland security bureaucracies that make them effective at performing their systemic mission make them ineffective in grappling with their future-shock mission. "Bureaucracies are good organizations for managing iterative processes that are subject to continuous improvement loops and must be executed every time in the same way. . . . They are the best solution to the problem of maintaining the same level of quality in a repetitive process," Nieto-Gómez says.[14] But the future-shock mission demands much more organizational flexibility and an entirely different mindset—namely, innovation rather than efficient repetition. He explains that "disruptive and unpredictable threats posed by the recombining nature of new technologies cannot be confronted by incremental methodologies. They are by definition outside of the feedback loop. . . . The bureaucracy might get as good as it can possibly be and still miss the next threat precisely because it has learned to be very efficient in its normal operation, thus resisting any change outside its sustaining processes."[15]

Christopher Bellavita, a colleague of Nieto-Gómez's at the Center for Homeland Defense and Security, has directed attention to another factor in HSARPA's failure to serve as homeland security's DARPA— *politics*. He points out that our homeland security establishment's most politically powerful constituency is the nation's community of first responders: firefighters, police, emergency medical technicians, and disaster response specialists. The first responders' constituency lobbies very effectively for funding for more and better equipment for the systemic mission: firefighting vehicles, police cruisers, surveillance equipment, ambulances, and stockpiles of disaster relief supplies. However, the future-shock mission, concerned with the prevention of yet unactualized, notional threats, lacks a similarly influential political constituency. Current concerns trump future worries.[16] This mindset is perfectly illustrated in the testimony of then undersecretary of the Science and Technology Directorate Jay M. Cohen on March 8, 2007, before the Emerging Threats, Cyber Security and Science and Technology Subcommittee of the House Homeland Security Committee. He promised disgruntled members of Congress that he would focus his directorate's efforts on what he termed the "four Bs—bombs, borders, bugs and business."[17] In other words, he would neglect the future-shock mission to focus on the systemic mission and the S&T Directorate's internal reorganization.

I am in no way deprecating the importance of the homeland security systemic mission and the thousands of first responders who perform that mission every day. But with all the resources we taxpayers grant them, our homeland security establishment should be capable of walking and chewing gum at the same time—that is, taking care of both mission sets simultaneously. Truth be told, the Department of Homeland Security has a steeper climb than the Department of Defense does when it comes to carrying out the future-shock mission. The Department of Defense, despite its name, is much more focused on taking the offense than the Department of Homeland Security, which, in essence, is a reactive organization. DARPA's mission is to counter strategic surprise by creating strategic surprise. This exemplary Defense Department organization seeks to keep potential adversaries off-balance by forcing them to respond to continual American innovations.[18] Thus, DARPA project managers have the initiative in selecting their R&D projects, as they are playing offense and can set the rules and pace of the competition. Meanwhile, the mission of the homeland security enterprise is essentially protective, defensive, and reactive. On nearly all occasions, the antagonist holds the initiative; that is, the devil gets to choose which toy he will select from his toy box next and where and when he will play with it. A successful HSARPA, or something like it, would have far less freedom to blue-sky its R&D priorities than DARPA does. Assuming its resources are finite, a homeland security R&D establishment focused on the future-shock mission would need to choose very judiciously which emerging Promethean technology threats it intends to attempt to counter. We'll call this deliberation over possible choices of R&D priorities a devil's toy box analysis.

Are existing, commonly used methods of threat assessment good enough to support such an analysis?

### Threat Assessment the Quick and Easy Way: Good Enough?

Let's perform a simple thought experiment. Let's imagine we are the heads of a homeland defense research and development agency focused on countering future-shock threats. We have $20 million to spend on R&D for the upcoming fiscal year, and we must spend the entire amount on a single project. The two future-shock threats we are considering developing counters for are genetic-sequencing kits and 3D printers. How should we decide between the two options? Where would we begin? What questions should we initially ask?

We may find at least some of the answers we need in the Defense Threat Reduction Agency's April 2009 monograph *Thwarting an Evil Genius*. The impetus behind the "Evil Genius" study can be found in the following commonsense observation: "There are obvious limits to the imagination that prevent us from predicting which among the endless number of nightmare scenarios an intelligent terrorist will choose. . . . The impulse to defend against every conceivable attack . . . can be self-defeating—we would simply spend ourselves to economic collapse. Nonetheless, a small number of attack scenarios, by their ease of execution and the magnitude of their effects, require extraordinary countermeasures."[19]

In selecting their Evil Genius scenarios, the authors stipulated that the scenarios must combine tremendous negative impact with relative ease of execution. Additionally, such attack modes must be plausible, innovative (the authors assigned additional points for innovation for those attacks that could likely catalyze cascading, second- and third-order consequences by pushing defenders into self-harmful overreactions), and inexpensive. The study grouped its notional attackers into three categories (while allowing that there could be many others): *jihadists*, who value casualties and negative psychological impacts above all other outcomes; *nihilists*, who may be fulfilling a desire to strike back at society or to financially enrich themselves but who lack the jihadist's desire for mass casualties; and *thrill seekers*, who primarily seek notoriety and place a high value on avoiding capture.[20]

The Evil Genius risk tool divides the *consequence* of attacks into two subcategories—*prompt effects* (which include casualties and physical damage) and *human response effects* (second- and third-order effects, including the psychological changes in the general population, the government's responses to the attack, and the economic impacts). The authors place great emphasis on the latter, pointing out both that the bulk of a terror attack's negative consequence often falls within the realm of human response effects and that government must avoid counterproductive, self-defeating responses.[21]

With the Evil Genius study to guide us, our determinative analysis would begin by answering the following questions:

What are the *prompt effects* that could result from a malign use of the identified technology/threat vector? What *magnitude of consequences* could result?

What are the *human response effects* that could result? What could be the *magnitude of consequences*?

How *accessible* to potential malign actors are the products of the identified emerging technology? How much *technical skill or training* would be required to use them? How much *manpower*? How much *planning*?

How *expensive* are the products of the identified emerging technology? How *affordable* are they for individual malign actors? For international terror groups?

Let us apply these questions to the two Promethean technologies considered in our thought experiment and see how those technologies stack up as future-shock threats, or potential toys in the devil's toy box.

Going by table 1, we analysts would likely recommend programing the $20 million toward research projects to counter gene-splicing kits such as CRISPR. Gene-splicing kits, especially when combined with the sort of "genetic manipulation for dummies" guides available online, provide a paradigm-shifting new capability to individual malign actors or terror cells, which will then have access to biological weapons that were formerly only producible by large, government- or military-sponsored labs. Even failed attempts to create a viable biological weapon, if publicized widely enough, could create very damaging human response effects with high-magnitude consequences. Fear of the unknown is a potent inciter of panics.

By contrast, the more likely usages of 3D printer technologies by malign actors would not represent a paradigm shift from the weaponry that terror and criminal groups already use. Access to homemade firearms of varying capability and the addition of remote-control features represent merely incremental improvements to the devil's toys. Human response effects will likely be very low. To members of the public, a gun is a gun is a gun.

Regarding CRISPR, public health sentinels need to be alert to the possibility of the accidental release of malign biological entities. Hobbyists may not intend to cause anyone harm, but through carelessness or error, they might produce harms no less significant than those caused by the most malign terrorists. This danger hardly exists regarding hobbyists' use of 3D printers. After all, printed firearms do not fly or crawl out of hobbyists' homes on their own.

Regarding our hypothetical risk analysis, so far, so good. Using

## Table 1. Comparison of gene-splicing kits and 3D printing tech on Evil Genius questions

| Evil Genius question | Gene-splicing kits (CRISPR) | 3D printing technologies |
|---|---|---|
| Prompt effects? | Spread of infectious diseases; could cause illnesses or deaths; if infectious agent is unknown to medical science, currently available antibiotics and cures might prove ineffective, leading to an uncontrollable outbreak, potentially an epidemic | Firearms made from plastics or other nonmetals could be easier to sneak aboard passenger aircraft or other public transportation conveyances; targeted assassinations would require less manpower, potentially less skill if computer guidance is added to the remote weapon; rogue regimes and large transnational terror organizations could potentially complete their nuclear fuel cycles and create atomic weapons |
| Magnitude of consequences for prompt effects? | Potentially very great; could cause massive resource drain in medical and public health sectors; if epidemic results, could harm the economy | Most likely consequences (use of plastic firearms or remote-controlled firearms) are low to moderate on a societal scale; less likely consequences (fabrication of parts to complete a nuclear fuel cycle) are potentially extremely high |
| Human response effects? | Knowledge of and rumors of a new, unknown pathogen and a spreading outbreak could cause widespread panic, leading to large numbers of people avoiding public places, not going to work, pulling their children out of school, not going to stores | Human response effects in the case of the more likely consequences (use of plastic firearms or remote-controlled firearms) would be low because, to the public, these home-brewed weapons would not represent a paradigm shift or even much of a noticeable change from the weaponry already used by criminals and terrorists; however, should the tech be used to complete a nuclear fuel cycle, the human response effects could be very significant, with panic spreading over terrorists' possible deployment of a deliverable nuclear weapon |

| | | |
|---|---|---|
| Magnitude of consequences for human response effects? | Potentially very great; widespread panic would adversely impact the economy, and large numbers of employees staying home from work could adversely impact other vital infrastructure sectors | In the case of mild human response effects, the magnitude of consequences would be low; in the case of very significant human response effects (panic over potential nuclear strikes), the public response could push the government and military into counterproductive overreactions |
| Accessibility to malign actors? | Highly accessible over the internet | Highly accessible over the internet |
| How much technical skill and training required? | At present, at least an undergraduate-level background in biology is required to formulate and gene splice an entirely new pathogen; creating lesser, known pathogens using genetic material from sources such as E. coli requires less educational background | High levels of technical skill are required on the part of those individuals who upload schematics of various weapons or components to be printed, but virtually no technical skill is required for the end user, who benefits from the former's intellectual efforts; this calculus changes, of course, in the case of a vastly more sophisticated project, such as the creation of a nuclear fuel cycle and the assembly of a working nuclear weapon |
| How much manpower needed? | Minimal; equipment can be operated by a single individual | To fabricate relatively simple, man-carried weapons, such as firearms, a lone individual can use a 3D printer |
| How much planning is required? | To achieve maximum terroristic effects, a relatively high level of planning is required | A relatively low level of planning is needed |
| Affordable for transnational terror groups? | Yes | Yes |
| Affordable for lone malign actors? | Yes | Low-level 3D printers are currently affordable to many individuals; higher-level 3D printers, which utilize aluminum or other metals as a feed stock, are presently only affordable for businesses or wealthy individuals |

the Evil Genius questions as a decision-making guide seems to be adequate in this case. But what if, rather than just two Promethean technologies, the Foresight and Understanding from Scientific Exposition Program (FUSE)—an automated tool for tracking technical emergence (or some system like it)—had identified *twenty* emerging technologies of concern? How useful would the Evil Genius questions be for making resource-allocation decisions then?

In such a situation, we might create a risk evaluation chart, assigning a different column to each of the Evil Genius questions and a different row to each of the emerging Promethean technologies. We could assign color values (green = low, yellow = moderate, red = high) or numeric values (1 = low, 5 = moderate, 10 = high) to the various likelihoods of negative impacts and severities of consequences, perhaps put in some weighting values to assign more significance to certain factors, run the numbers (or colors), pick the three technologies with the top three worst risk scores, and call it a day. This system has the advantages of being simple, cheap, quick, replicable, easily documentable, and any analyst with a modicum of intelligence and familiarity with the subject matter area can use it. What's not to like?

As a nonscientist and nonexpert, I made several assumptions that may or may not be accurate but that could skew the analysis. Regarding gene-splicing kits, I assumed that readily available, online technical guidance would make it comparatively simple for a malign layman or careless hobbyist to produce harmful genetically modified organisms that would be viable in the wild, ones that could cause illness, disease, and death for humans. A trained biologist or geneticist might very well make a far different and better-educated assumption than mine.

Regarding 3D printing technology, I based my risk assessment on just two possible uses—a low-consequence use, such as the printing of firearms, and a high-consequence use, such as the printing of precision-tooled parts required for completing the nuclear fuel cycle. A more expert analyst, one with a military or intelligence background, could likely vastly expand the list of the technology's possible uses. In fact, putting on my science fiction writer's hat, I realize that 3D printing tech could also "democratize" the availability of weapons systems such as lasers, ground-to-air missiles (based on modifications to commercially available hobbyist drones), electromagnetic pulse devices, and devices that could turn off or disrupt medical equipment implanted in patients, such as electronic pacemakers. I also assumed a low likelihood that detailed online schematics for a nuclear fuel cycle and weapons components would be available for download. An intelligence community analyst conversant with top secret intelligence regarding rogue nuclear engineers might very well make a far different assumption, which in turn would flip the resource-allocation decision outlined in table 1. The potential for such wrong assumptions to skew an analysis expands as the number of Promethean technologies under consideration grows.

Relying upon color-coded or ordinal, numeric ranking–based risk assessment charts to guide resource-allocation decision making poses its own set of problems. Douglas W. Hubbard, in his book *The Failure of Risk Management: Why It's Broken and How to Fix It*, describes the basic flaws inherent in these types of tools. Hubbard divides the most commonly used risk-scoring methods into two categories—additive weighted scores and multiplicative risk matrices. In his view, the following types of flaws apply to both methods: (1) skewing resulting from human cognitive distortions regarding the perception of uncertainty and risk; (2) subjective, differing interpretations of the definitions of ordinal scores (low, medium, high) among users and observers of the risk matrices, despite attempts to thoroughly define what those scores mean; and (3) errors induced by the very structure of the scoring schemes.[22]

Here's an example of the latter type of flaw, illustrating the problems with using ordinal rankings (1, 2, 3; low, medium, high). Say a risk analyst wants to assess the risks to an airport terminal. As part of the risk assessment chart, the analyst ranks the severity of possible casualties. She or he decides that low equals zero casualties, medium equals one to nine casualties, and high equals ten or more casualties. In this model, a change of just one casualty—for example, going from nine to ten—changes the casualty severity ranking of a scenario from medium to high. If the analyst is calculating a combined risk score, low may be assigned a zero; medium, one; and high, two. In terms of the risk score calculation, an 11 percent change in the casualty variable (from nine to ten) equates to a 100 percent change (from one to two) in the number that is fed into the combined risk score calculation.

This quick-and-easy method won't do for a devil's toy box analysis. Were we to stop our crystal ball development program at this point, we would be stuck with a glass globe that appeared to be infused with octopus ink. The black clouds would only occasionally recede enough for observers to see anything at all. Any intermittently revealed visions would be hazy and untrustworthy.

Making use of an emerging-technologies discovery tool such as the FUSE Program and then applying the Evil Genius questions as an analytical frame are only two *initial* steps in our analysis. Creating a perfect crystal ball with which to observe the evil toys most likely to emerge next from the devil's toy box isn't possible; perfect knowledge of future events is not attainable. What we must strive for is an *improved* crystal ball, one that will compensate for analysts' limited knowledge, incorrect assumptions, ignored or overlooked variables, and analytical errors introduced by a risk-measurement schema.

The stakes are too high for weak analysis, especially when Promethean criminals themselves are likely to be surprised by the second-order and third-order consequences of their actions. In Cologne, Germany, ransomware hackers crippled IT systems of the main hospital associated with the University of Düsseldorf. Undoubtedly, these cybercriminals were only seeking a payday, but they got more than they bargained for: they are being charged with negligent homicide in addition to violating statutes prohibiting malicious hacking. When their cyber vandalism led to the disruption of the hospital's ambulance routing system, a critically ill patient was instead rerouted to a distant hospital twenty miles away and died due to the delay in receiving treatment at the emergency room.[23]

If Promethean terrorists and criminals can overlook the possible second- and third-order impacts of their malign actions, devil's toy box analysts cannot allow themselves to make the same misjudgments when deciding which emerging threats require the most urgent attention. The following scenario vividly illustrates how one man's hate, badly aimed, can unintentionally ignite a civil conflagration in a large neighboring country, leading to hundreds of thousands of deaths and ethnic hatreds and distrust that will linger for generations to come.

### Scenario 4: More Than You Bargained For

"Jean-Louis, it's *cold*," Marla complained. She was aces at complaining; she might be the most accomplished complainer in all New York State. "This is accomplishing, like, *nothing*. I mean, these people, they won't even *look* at you. Here comes one now. Go ahead. Try your pitch on him. You'll see!"

He really wanted to tell Marla to shut the hell up. But if he got into an argument with her—and she could argue almost as well as she complained—he'd miss his chance to possibly win over an ally or at least spread some seeds of truth that might someday sprout. He told himself maybe he shouldn't be all that peeved at Marla. It *was* cold, what with the winter winds blowing off Long Island Sound, and Marla didn't have a foam-core sandwich board to protect her from the wind like he did.

*Enough about Marla. Concentrate.* Jean-Louis's potential convert ducking out of the Sashay Bar and Grill looked to be a real doozy. A queen-size faggot, judging from the hoop earrings, gaudy mascara, and sterling silver nose bolt as big as a bone some cannibal in Africa might wear. *Still, best not to judge the book by its cover*, Jean-Louis told himself. *You never know when someone might be open to listening to reason, after all.*

"Excuse me, sir," Jean-Louis said. "Would you like to learn the truth about Jews and gays? The *real* truth?"

The man refused to meet his eyes. He hurried past, not even mumbling in response.

"This could change your life!" Jean-Louis shouted after him. "The Jews have been *using* you! These Jews you see everywhere, they're not even the real Jews from the Bible! They're interlopers, *pretenders*! Listen, you don't have to be their tool anymore!"

The man hurried across the street to his car. "See?" Marla said to Jean-Louis. "What did I *tell* you?"

"Shut up, Marla," he said. He wanted to pluck her eyebrows out a hair at a time, then set the stubble on fire.

"Oh, *that's* a great counterargument, 'shut up.' Mr. *Brilliant* here."

"Nobody listened to the prophets in the Bible, either," Jean-Louis said, "until suddenly, they *did* listen. If you don't have the patience for this, why don't you just go home and save me a headache?"

"*No*," she said stubbornly, thrusting her freckled face into what he considered his personal space, one of her many obnoxious habits. "I'm not leaving you standing out here by yourself. If you can stand it, *I* can. And don't try telling me I'm not as down with the cause as *you* are. That's so *sexist*, Jean-Louis. I'm totally here to support you. I just want you to be more *effective*, y'know? Especially now that all the fake Jews are in a panic . . ."

"You think this *isn't* effective? Spreading the word online is great, but that only goes so far. You've got to *talk* with people, Marla. You've got to meet them where they are, even if it's outside a degenerate gay bar."

"No need to preach to the choir, Jean-Louis. We're just having a debate about tactics. Aren't I allowed to debate tactics?"

Jean-Louis spotted another man emerging from the Sashay Bar and Grill. This individual, a Black man dressed in an olive spandex jumpsuit, a caramel cashmere jacket, and loafers with no socks, stared Jean-Louis and Marla up and down from across the street. He pursed his lips and furrowed his brow. Then, decision apparently made, he made a determined beeline for the couple.

*I might have good luck with this guy*, Jean-Louis thought. *Some Blacks hate the Jews even more than I do.* "Would you like to learn the truth about Jews and gays? The *real* truth?"

"I saw your sign," the man said, "from inside the bar. I asked Charlie, the bartender, if you guys were for real or if this is, like, performance art. He said no, you're regulars on this here sidewalk. You're the genuine shit. So you got me curious. Just what *is* this double-dog-top-secret truth about Jews and gays?"

Jean-Louis heard the underlying tone of mockery. But an audience was an audience. "Do you and your friends smoke joints?"

"Yeah, sure, man. Who *doesn't*, nowadays?"

"How old were you when you started smoking doobies?"

"Oh, shit, I don't know . . . thirteen or fourteen, I guess."

Jean-Louis smiled in triumph. He had him. "There you go."

"There I go *what*?"

"That's about the time you discovered you were gay, right?"

"Yeah, I suppose. What, are you saying there's a *connection*?"

"Of *course* there is. Where do you think that pot came from?"

"I dunno. Mexico?"

"Maybe it was *grown* in Mexico, sure. But who was *behind* it? Who was giving the orders to have it shipped to neighborhoods all over America?"

"I dunno. Mexicans?"

"No. *Jews*."

"There are *Jews* in *Mexico*?"

"Friend, Jews are like cockroaches. They're *everywhere*."

The man crossed his arms and gave Jean-Louis a fresh appraisal. "Okay. *Now* you have my *full* attention. You *must* tell me. *Why* would Jews, in *particular*, be growing pot in Mexico?"

Jean-Louis waved his hands in protest. "Don't get hung up on the Mexico thing. Jews have secret drug-growing fields all over the planet. That's how they fund their persecution of the Palestinians. They don't want to waste their banking and diamond profits on piddly stuff like subjugating the Arabs. But marijuana, that's their specialty, see? The reason is this: Jew chemists spent decades perfecting this new chemical. When you combine it with cannabis, it turns men gay and women into lesbians. *Truth*, one hundred percent."

Jean-Louis saw the man's mouth quiver, as though he were about to either laugh or spew. But then the man pursed his lips tightly, inhaling deeply through his flaring nostrils. "So . . . what you're telling me is, I . . . am *gay* . . . because I smoked Mexican Jew marijuana when I was thirteen years old?"

Jean-Louis nodded vigorously. "Yes!"

"So what you're really *saying* is, Jews want to *create* gay and lesbian people . . ."

"Yes!"

"Because Jews love gays and lesbians and want there to be *more* of us?"

Jean-Louis shook his head. "That's only partly right. See, the Jews want there to be more *Gentile* gays and lesbians. That distinction, it means *everything*. They mean to depress Gentile birth rates all over the world. It's their revenge on everybody who's not them, on all of us they call *goyim*. Where does this whole 'gay rights' and 'gay marriage' thing come from? The *Jews*! It's a long-term plot. All the big gay organizations, the court cases that legalized gay marriage—who funded all that? Gay people on TV and in the movies—who was behind *that*? The Jews, my friend, the *Jews*.

"Haven't you ever wondered why nearly all Jews in America support the far left–liberal wing of the Democratic Party? Jews have money, right? Lots and lots of money? So why aren't they all Republicans? Because their strategy means they have to be down-the-line supporters of abortion and the so-called gay agenda, and that means supporting the loony-left wing of the Democrats.

"See how it all fits? It's a genocidal strategy, fiendish in its cleverness. They're trying to make people like you and me *extinct*."

"You and *me*, huh?" the man asked.

"Right. We're in this together."

"Well, Brother Gentile, I must beg your pardon. I have to go now. I simply *must* get home to tell my Jewish boyfriend that his fellow Jews in Mexico made us both gay with mickeyed-up dope. This has been *most* enlightening. I simply can't thank you *enough*." He nodded to Marla. "You, too, darling. Shine on, you crazy diamonds!"

He strode toward a red Mazda Miata, inserted himself in the driver's seat, put down the top, and waved to them before speeding off.

"He didn't stay long enough for me to tell him about the Jews and the slave trade," Jean-Louis said sadly.

"*Whatever*. Let's get out of here. I'm freezing my boobs off. Don't you have exams to study for? Buy me a coffee at Starbucks so we can study together?"

Uh, oh. He hadn't told Marla yet what he'd decided. This wouldn't go down well. "I withdrew from my classes."

"*What*?" She started wildly slapping his shoulder as if his shirt had caught fire. "You *dropped out*? You *dummy*! I—I mean, *we* were *counting* on you getting your bio-chem degree! What the *fuck*, Jean-Louis?"

He didn't want to tell her the real reason. "I'm just not into it anymore."

"Dude, that's, like, what you say about playing *Call of Duty* or going bowling. Not about what was supposed to be your fricking *career*. And after you went into debt buying all that CRISPR stuff. So what are you gonna do with yourself *now*?"

His next statement had a little more truth to it. "I'm thinking of going to Canada, to Quebec. Join up with the separatists. They're my people, after all . . . if you go back two or three generations. They're getting slaughtered by the Anglophones."

"That's not what *I've* been hearing. I mean, don't get pissed at me, Jean-Louis, but I think the French speakers are giving back as good as they got. If not *double*."

"Maybe for now. But they're outnumbered. And lots of them are falling sick. They're doing good now, because they've got a better cause than the Anglos, and they're fiercer fighters. But they're going to get worn down. Not so much from the Anglos. From . . . y'know, the fucking plague. Muscular-Skeletal Ebola."

The mere mention of M-SE was enough to muzzle Marla's verboseness, at least for several seconds. "Jean-Louis, are you scared you're gonna come down with it? Is *that* why you dropped out of school? To lessen your exposure?"

Admitting to this would get him off the hook. But it would also brand him a coward. "If I haven't caught it yet, it's probably not going to happen," he said. "It must mean . . . I must not be a Tay-Sachs carrier."

"You haven't gotten *tested*? Jean-Louis, that's *whack*. I mean, your mother . . ."

She had to *go* there, hadn't she? Had to bring up his mother, couldn't keep her damn mouth shut on that subject even though she *knew* that pissed him the hell off. "Don't you know *anything* about genetics, Marla? Jesus, you're so fucking *dense*. If my dad, who I don't know shit about, were a carrier, I'd have a one-in-two chance of being a carrier myself. If he were clean, I'd have a one-in-four chance. I haven't caught M-SE, despite living in the same little house with my mother and eating her cooking and letting her do my laundry, right? So I guess I actually have a one-in-*zero* chance. You think I'd be talking about joining up with the Quebecers separatists if I thought there was *any* chance at *all* I could catch M-SE?"

"Well, if that's the case," Marla said, a glint of defiance in her eyes, "how come you never go visit your mother in the hospital, huh? I thought maybe it was self-preservation, not wanting to catch what your mother has. But now I think maybe it's just 'cause you're an *asshole*."

She wanted to start something. Something hot that would maybe end up with them having insanely steamy make-up sex. But he didn't have the energy for it right now. "You don't know anything, Marla."

"Oh, I don't know *anything*, huh? Well, I know *this*." She poked him aggressively in his chest. "I know I've gone to visit your mother at least three times a *week* since she got admitted. She says I'm like a daughter to her, but all she wants is to see *you*. I've run out of excuses to tell her, Jean-Louis. I've told her you're way busy with school. Well, now you've flushed *that* excuse down the toilet. She's *dying*, you *fuck*. She needs to *see* you."

"They keep her all doped up. She probably wouldn't even know me." He realized how lame that sounded. "She'll be gone soon, anyway. There's no cure."

"And *that* gets you off the hook? She's your goddamn *mother*, Jean-Louis. Don't you have *any* feelings for her?"

*More than you'll ever know.* But he couldn't say that.

"Look, Jean-Louis, if you don't come with me tonight to visit your mother, you and I are *done*. *Finito*. I've got no reason to stick with you. You're a fucking *bum* who's dropped out of school, living in your dying mother's house like a leech. I mean, the sex is great and all, but guys like you are like buses—another one comes cruising along every fifteen minutes. You hear me?"

THE OLD YID'S BREATH smelled of garlic pickles. And he wouldn't stop yapping. "Whoever would've thought we'd see the day when refugees from *Canada* would be seeking political asylum in the *United States*? The world has turned upside-down . . . When I was your age, young man, those of us who were against the Vietnam War and the draft wanted to escape to Canada!"

Thanks to the waiting room's overcrowding and Marla's insistence that they occupy the last two available seats, Jean-Louis found himself a captive audience. The Jew in his skullcap ignored all of Jean-Louis's obvious signs of disdain and insisted on talking about the stories on the front page of the *New York Post*, most of them about the situation north of the border.

"What do you think about the Francophones' claims?" the man said. "Could there be any truth to that? That the Anglos hate them so much, they created the M-SE virus to perpetrate a genocide against the Quebecers?"

Jean-Louis knew silence wouldn't dissuade his repulsive neighbor. He decided to offer a minimal response, hoping this would discourage him, get him to turn his attention to someone else. "I don't know what to think," he said in a monotone.

"Well, here's what *I* think," the man said. "Of *course* the Francophones have every right and inclination to believe the worst. But the counterargument is that no Canadian Anglo has claimed *credit*. And the type of evil mamzer who would do this *always* claims credit. On the other hand, who *has* claimed credit? The neo-Nazis! The Christian Identity people! The Jew haters!

"So back to what I think? I think these poor Quebecers are collateral damage. I think they weren't meant to be the targets of M-SE at all. The *Jews* were the target. If French Canadians and Ashkenazi

Jews didn't share a genetic propensity for Tay-Sachs disease, the Quebecers would never have suffered this plague. There wouldn't be a war of secession going on. All accidental, I say. It was the *Jews* who were in the crosshairs."

At last, Jean-Louis could take it no longer. "Must 'the Jews' *always* be the center of attention? Can't anyone else be recognized as suffering, *only* the Jews?"

Jean-Louis realized he was speaking too loudly. The waiting room appeared to be filled with Jews, and several of the men directed censorious looks at him—but he didn't care. "Weren't millions of Gypsies and Polish Catholics killed in the concentration camps in World War II? But who talks about *them*? Who builds memorials and museums in *their* memory? No, it has to be the Jews, 'the saintly six million'! Gentiles aren't even *allowed* to question this, to try to correct the record.

"Listen to yourself! You're trying to make a Canadian national tragedy, the destruction of a proud, French-speaking people, all about *you*! How can you not be *disgusted* by yourself?"

A woman had begun weeping. Two men at opposite sides of the room stood, grim-faced, fists clenched.

Jean-Louis stood himself. He wasn't going to be intimidated. A fight would be cathartic. Then he felt a tugging on his right arm. Marla. "Jean-Louis, let's *go*," she whispered fiercely.

"I've got every right to be here," Jean-Louis said, "the same as any of *them* . . ."

"Yeah, sure you do, you dummy. But the whole room wants to *pound* you. Let's go find another waiting room. *Now*."

He let himself be dragged from the room, resisting just enough to show the threatening Jews that he had no fear of confronting them. They found a different waiting room at the opposite end of the floor, far from the m-se quarantine ward. This one was empty.

"Go get us cups of coffee, Jean-Louis," she said.

"I don't want a cup of coffee . . ."

"Well, *I* do. And maybe a walk down to the cafeteria will cool you off."

EVERYTHING ABOUT THE HOSPITAL cafeteria depressed him. The cracked Formica floor. The dirty tables, sticky with soda residue and littered with discarded napkins and wrappers. The aroma of over-boiled hot dogs, floating in grayish swill.

He heard a familiar voice intone in a stage whisper from one of the tables behind him, "Oh, my, *Gawd* . . . Over there, Adam, I cannot *believe* who it is. It's the guy I told you about, Mexican Marijuana Man . . ."

The Black fag. Small world. Jean-Louis paid for the cups of coffee. Marla called him a pit bull, because once he clamped an idea between his jaws, he refused to ever let it go. He supposed she had a point.

He approached their table. "You again," he said. "Sorry, I never learned your name. You vamoosed before I could finish. I was about to tell you about the Jews and the slave trade."

"Well, I am sure you are a *fount* of historical information," the Black man said, "but we were just finishing, and we have a dear friend in terrible extremis we need to visit."

"My first cousin," the man named Adam (*the Jew boyfriend?*) said. He looked bleary. "He just got diagnosed with M-SE. Basically a death sentence." His heavy-lidded eyes widened as he gave Jean-Louis a searching look. "Say, don't I know you from somewhere?"

"No," Jean-Louis said coldly.

Adam's face grew animated. "Yeah, yeah, I *do*. We went to high school together. You were in Mr. Greene's advanced placement chemistry class with me. You're, uh, John—"

"Jean-Louis . . ."

"Yeah, that's *right*—Jean-Louis! Holy shit! You were *ace* smart in chem class. Remember that?"

"Yeah," Jean-Louis said. He remembered being isolated, lonely.

"What a time to meet up again, huh? The world's going to *hell*, man. Crazy shit going on. This civil war up in *Canada*, of all places. This fucking new plague—it's AIDS for Jews and French Canadians. I mean, what chance have I, gay *and* Jewish, got? And if we all die off, who's gonna keep the Broadway theaters running?" He smiled awkwardly. "Oh, geez, I've got diarrhea of the mouth here, I haven't let you get a word in. You here to see a doctor, or are you visiting somebody?"

"My mother," Jean-Louis said. Then, without intending to, he blurted, "She's got M-SE too."

Adam blanched. "I'm *sorry*, man. Jesus Christ . . . that's fucking *awful*. And here I was, thinking I'd drawn the short stick 'cause I've got a *cousin* with the fucking plague. I mean, nobody should suffer what they are going through, but when it's your *mother* . . . I mean, your *mother* . . . shit . . ."

He pulled out his wallet. For one absurd moment, Jean-Louis feared Adam was going to try to console him with Jewish money. Instead, Adam removed a piece of note paper and began writing his phone number and email address. "Look, Jean-Louis, I figure we hardly know each other . . . I don't know what kind of a support group you've got, but if you find yourself wanting to talk, I mean, don't hesitate . . . You get in touch, okay?"

Jean-Louis found the very notion ridiculous. Him, sharing confidences with a gay Jew? Yet, somehow, the emotional generosity of Adam's offer affected him more than he cared to admit.

"I'm all right," he mumbled awkwardly. "I've got a girlfriend, sort of . . ."

"That's good," Adam said. "Girlfriend, boyfriend, everybody should have one. But just in case, hang onto my contact info, okay?" He shrugged. "Look, I won't bite. Not like Brandon, here." He gave his companion an affectionate punch to the shoulder. "I hear he gave you some shit outside the Sashay Club. Don't take it personally. He gives shit to *everyone*." He smiled. "I mean, everyone's got some goofy ideas. What's the harm in it? My great uncle thought he'd be struck dead if he ever put a slice of cheese on his hot dog. Y'know?"

Was he being condescended to? Jean-Louis wasn't sure what to think.

"Look, I don't wanna hold you up," Adam said, patting his shoulder. "I know you've gotta go see your mom. But stay in touch, all right? Tough times like these, people have gotta hang together, y'know?"

Adam and Brandon left the cafeteria. Jean-Louis pocketed the slip of paper Adam had given him, then picked up his two cups of coffee (one marked M+S for "milk and sugar"—Marla's) and walked toward the exit. He hadn't kept in touch with anyone from high school. They'd all been snobs, fakers, or assholes.

Could he have been wrong? Wrong about Adam? Wrong about . . . lots of things?

He felt dizzy. He found a bench by a window and sat down. He felt afraid he might fly apart, like a poorly made doll inside a spinning centrifuge. Existential terror. He had to focus, desperately focus on those things that made him *him*.

He mentally grabbed hold of a key memory. Sixth grade. Sara Weissberger. He'd idolized her. Spent endless moments sitting behind her in class, staring at the soft white flesh her dress revealed, breathing in the scent of her hair.

Then that day had come. That day in the school cafeteria when she'd realized she'd forgotten her lunch at home. Jean-Louis had been reading about King Arthur. He wanted very much to be like Galahad, a shining, pure knight, eager to do deeds of valor to win the heart of his lady. So he offered her his lunch in place of the one she'd left at home. A carton of milk. A pickle wrapped in tinfoil. A ham and cheese sandwich.

She unwrapped the sandwich. Asked him what it was. He told her. Her friends all gasped in unison, as though they were acting in a school play. And then she said them, the words he'd never forget, ever. "*Ham* and *cheese*? You're offering *me ham* and *cheese*? *Me*?" All her friends started laughing. And Sara started laughing, too, the cruelest laughter of all.

He remembered the ache. His dizziness receded. The centrifuge that had threatened to dismember him stopped spinning. He was himself again.

He dug in his pocket until he found the piece of paper Adam had given him. He crumpled it up into a tight ball and tossed it into a waste receptacle. He felt better. More himself.

A NURSE ANNOUNCED OVER a loudspeaker that Jean-Louis could go see his mother. Before he and Marla could enter the M-SE quarantine ward, an orderly handed them disposable gloves, masks, and paper coverings for their shoes.

His mother resembled one of those South American mummies in a natural history museum: shrunken, shriveled, too small to be an adult human. A bag of dried-up skin from which all the organs and bones had been removed. *It's not her*, he told himself. *It's a prop, a prop from a movie.*

She stirred. Afloat in a boggy marsh of opioids, she didn't open her eyes. But she moaned, and Jean-Louis could hear a muffled remnant of his mother's voice. This wasn't a prop from a horror movie. This was his mother, the only parent he'd ever known.

Her flaccid arm, a garish shade of purple, horribly thin, lay atop her sheet. Her hand, swollen and almost shapeless, quivered like the flipper of a beached, dehydrated sea lion. Afraid of what her hand would feel like but more afraid not to hold it a final time before she passed, Jean-Louis clasped her fingers. They felt like deboned sardines.

The stench of putrescence was almost unbearable.

*Someone had to do something*, he told himself, squeezing his eyes tightly shut. *Someone had to take action. Everyone complained about them, but no one ever* did *anything about them, not since the Germans. So they continued their march to world domination. They took over the media. They took over the banks. They set up social media companies to control our opinions. They used America's military to destroy their enemies, spilling our blood in the Middle East so they wouldn't need to do their own fighting.*

*Someone had to try to put an end to them.*

He squeezed her hand. He released it immediately, horrified by its repulsive squishiness.

*I made a mistake with the CRISPR virus. I used Tay-Sachs as a marker. I'd always heard about Blacks and sickle cell disease, Jews and Tay-Sachs. I didn't think it all out. I didn't research who else might be susceptible . . .*

"Jean-Louis, you look sick . . . ?"

"I'm *fine*, Marla. Just leave me alone . . ."

Who had thought marketing a home-brewed genetic-sequencing kit was a good idea? Who'd invented CRISPR? Jean-Louis might not know the inventor's name offhand. But he knew the most pertinent fact about him.

The inventor must have been a Jew. Because only a Jew would have been satanic enough to coax him into this self-made hell.

# FIVE

## Selecting the Tools to Build a Promethean Spyglass

### *A Brief Survey of Seventy Years' Worth of Forecasting Methods*

WE'VE ALREADY DISCUSSED HOW the future remains essentially unpredictable, how even the clearest of crystal balls will remain partially cloudy, at best. Fortunately, those who want to conduct a devil's toy box analysis can press into service several sets of predictive analysis techniques that have been developed since the end of World War II, all of which can help improve the clarity and accuracy of their crystal ball. Any of these techniques, used in isolation, will likely produce results that fly widely astray of the target, but used in conjunction, they can help bring the most likely and most consequential of possible futures into better focus.

**The Delphi Technique: Granddaddy of Predictive Analysis Tools**

The Delphi technique was created in the wake of World War II. During those five years of total war, the future had rushed inexorably upon humanity like a speeding panzer, taking the forms of radar, sonar, jet-propelled aircraft, carpet bombing, guided missiles, ballistic missiles, analog computers, and, towering above them all, the atomic bomb. It was not the first conflict to serve as an accelerator for new technologies. The Crimean War saw the introduction of iron-armored floating batteries, and the U.S. Civil War witnessed for the first time ship-to-ship clashes between armored warships, a submarine used to sink an enemy warship, and lighter-than-air observation platforms. The Russo-Japanese War introduced the widespread use of locomotive torpedoes, machine guns, and trench warfare, the latter of which resulted, ten years later, in the development and deployment of terrible new weapons—poison gas, mechanized tanks, and heavier-than-air aircraft—to break the stalemate of World War I.[1] Yet the atomic weapons of World War II were the first to cause thought leaders to fear for the future of the world. The atomic devastation of Hiroshima and Nagasaki led scientists and government leaders to anxiously question what the accelerating wave of technological advances would mean for warfare, society, and humanity itself.

This perceived need to predict potential future events and technological developments in a systematic way led to the development during the late 1940s of the Delphi technique, a systematized method for the elicitation of expert opinion. Olaf Helmer, one of the inventors of the Delphi technique, had this to say in 1967: "Fatalism . . . has become a fatality. The future is no longer viewed as unique, unforeseeable, and inevitable; there are, instead, a multitude of possible futures, with associated probabilities that can be estimated and, to some extent, manipulated."[2]

The earliest notable use of the Delphi technique for defense-related prognostication took place in 1953. In an experiment that remained classified until 1962, Norman Dalkey and Olaf Helmer used the technique to elicit the opinions of seven experts regarding the likely outcomes of nuclear war with the Soviet Union.[3] Helmer stated that he helped develop the Delphi technique because projections regarding the future can very rarely be based entirely upon mathematical models; rather, they are more appropriately based on the intuitive judgments of a number of experts spread across various disciplines. In his view, political, social, economic, and military leaders can either wait until such time as an adequate theory and models have been developed to project future events, or they can "obtain the relevant intuitive insights of experts and then use their judgments as systematically as possible."[4]

Dalkey, another of the technique's pioneers, listed the three essential elements of the Delphi technique as follows: (a) anonymity (none of the participants are aware of the others' identities, they do not engage in any face-to-face interactions, and all communications from the facilitators to the participants are in the form of written questionnaires); (b) formulated feedback (the individual participants are provided with statistics of the group responses); and (c) a finalized group statistical response resulting from a series of rounds of surveys.[5] Dalkey's partner, Helmer, noted that prior to the development and use of the Delphi technique, the most common method for eliciting expert opinions from a group of experts was a roundtable discussion. He helped develop Delphi to mitigate what he saw as the roundtable discussion's major shortcomings—the pressure among face-to-face interactors for a compromise between divergent or opposing positions and the undue influence of the participant with the most prestige or the most dominating personality. Helmer also called attention to the vulnerability of roundtable discussions to the "bandwagon effect," or the tendency of members of a group to alter their own stated opinions to better fit in with the majority's opinion.[6]

Abraham Kaplan, a philosopher employed by the RAND Corporation, gave the Delphi technique its name after its first use in an experimental setting. That initial use had nothing to do with prognosticating any of the great issues of the late 1940s. Rather, in a perfect illustration of how man's drive to satisfy his baser desires can often lead to advances of more general benefit, the initially nameless technique was tested to see whether it could improve the accuracy of horse-race betting.[7] For those devotees of the sport of kings who wish to know whether the Delphi method can indeed fatten one's wallet at the track, unfortunately, the results of this early experiment appear lost in the fogs of time. Olaf Helmer was the only participant who ever cited the experiment, in a 1963 RAND Corporation monograph titled *The Systemic Use of Expert Judgment in Operations Research*, and he neither confirmed nor denied that the winners of horse races could be predicted based on a statistically derived consensus of the handicappers' predictions.[8]

Other, more consequential uses of Delphi soon followed. During the early 1950s, the U.S. Air Force (USAF) sponsored one of the earliest uses of the Delphi technique. U.S. military experts role-played Soviet strategic planners and attempted to determine which U.S. industrial targets were most vital to sustaining the country's military capabilities and how many atomic bombs the Soviets would have to deploy to reduce U.S. outputs of munitions by various percentages.[9] This USAF Delphi study also served as an early strategic use of the technique of red teaming, or viewing one's own vulnerabilities through an adversary's eyes.

Different researchers have set forth varying methodologies for Delphi procedures. The steps for the classic Delphi, the format that Dalkey and Helmer originally developed, are as follows:

1. The first-round questionnaire offers open-ended questions intended to prompt the participants' brainstorming regarding the issue at hand.

2. The facilitator/researcher uses the participants' responses to this first questionnaire to prepare a more structured questionnaire for the next round. This second-round questionnaire asks the panel members to rank or rate the responses received from the open-ended first-round questionnaire, with rankings or ratings posted using a Likert scale.

3. The facilitator/researcher tabulates the results from the second-round questionnaire and calculates statistics for each questionnaire item. Such statistics typically include means, standard deviations, and frequency distributions for each item.

4. The third-round questionnaire, as well as questionnaires for any subsequent rounds, includes this statistical feedback for panelists to consider, sometimes in addition to comments that respondents have made regarding items. Panelists are offered the opportunity to use this informative feedback on the group's prior responses to change their responses in the current questionnaire if they so wish.

5. The facilitator/researcher either halts the Delphi procedure after a predetermined number of rounds of questionnaires or once a group consensus or a stability of responses has been achieved.[10]

The researcher Kenneth Brooks outlined an adjusted Delphi procedure, a variant often used in the field of educational administration research, with eight steps:

1. Identify a panel of experts, with the optimal number of participants being no more than twenty-five.

2. Determine the willingness of the prospective panelists to participate. Make certain that eliminating some whose enthusiasm for the project seems marginal does not remove all representation from a key demographic.

3. Gather input, allowing for some open-ended contributions and demographic data from each panelist.

4. Amalgamate the input from the panelists into a limited number of possible future states (the basis for a second questionnaire). Take special care that the researcher's biases or expectations do not play an overriding role in compiling this second, more structured questionnaire.

5. Send the second questionnaire to all the panelists. Solicit their reactions, which may consist of agreement/disagreement, rankings using a scale, or modifying the questionnaire's statements.

6. Analyze the feedback received from the second questionnaire and prepare a third questionnaire, which should contain summary statistics of the group's responses. Also, provide each panelist a reminder of his or her own response to each question or item.

7. Ask each panelist, in the context of the third questionnaire, to reconsider his or her earlier responses in light of the group's amalgamated responses. Ask a panelist, if he or she decides to stick to the divergent view, to provide a brief rationale to support this decision.

8. Repeat step 6 with a fourth questionnaire, and ask the panelists to repeat step 7. Repeat the process until a consensus is reached or little or no movement of opinions and responses occurs between rounds.[11]

### The Nominal Group Technique: A Response to Delphi's Deficiencies

Andrew H. Van de Ven and Andre L. Delbecq created the nominal group technique (NGT) in 1968. They noted that whereas researchers of small group dynamics and group decision-making processes had found group interactions *do not* promote the efficient and effective generation of ideas, identification of problems, or elicitation of facts (the initial phase of the problem-solving process), face-to-face discussion *does* promote improved evaluation, screening, and synthesizing of ideas that have already been generated (the latter portions of the problem-solving process).[12] So they designed their NGT to remove face-to-face interactions from the idea-generation stage of analysis but included those interactions in those stages of analysis where such interactions add value.

Delbecq and Van de Ven described the steps of an NGT procedure as follows:

1. The group's members, seven to ten in number and occupying the same room, silently brainstorm ideas and write them down.

2. A recorder writes all the group's ideas on a flip chart. In round-robin fashion, each participant offers one idea at a time. No discussion occurs in this phase. The round-robin process continues until all the members' ideas have been written on the chart. (This portion of the procedure gives the technique its name; the group is considered "nominal" because although the members are in one another's presence, communication between them is very limited.)

3. Members discuss each recorded idea one at a time, asking for clarifications when necessary and expressing their agreement or disagreement. The ideas' originators may opt to share supporting rationales.

4. Each member privately votes on the ideas, ranking or rating each. The facilitator mathematically derives the group's decision or consensus based on these private votes.[13]

### Techniques Derived from Futurism

*Futurism,* or the structured study of potential futures, developed as an academic discipline in the 1960s. Dr. Roy Amara, the president and a senior research fellow at the Institute for the Future in Menlo

Park, California, had this to say about the practitioners of this new field: "Our purpose is not to predict—much as we would dearly like to do so. Rather, our primary purpose is to generate images and to analyze and understand them so that we can act to increase the probability of producing futures that we prefer."[14] Notable works on futurism published during the 1960s included *Art of Conjecture* by Bertrand de Jouvenel (1964), *Der Wettlauf zum Jahre 2,000* by Fritz Baade (1960), *Inventing the Future* by Dennis Gabor (1964), and "The Future as a Way of Life" (1965) by Alvin Toffler, who later wrote the famed bestseller *Future Shock* (1970). Western governments formed advisory commissions during this period in hopes of harnessing forecasting techniques to help guide public policy formulation. These groups included the Futuribles association in France; the Commission on the Year 2000; the National Planning Association; the National Commission on Automation, Manpower, and Technological Progress; and Resources for the Future in the United States.[15]

### Technology Sequence Analysis

*Technology Sequence Analysis* (TSA) was first developed and utilized in the 1980s as a way to formulate probabilistic forecasts of the time it would take to develop a technological system.[16] TSA is a form of path analysis that breaks down a system into subsystems, which are further divided into individual components. Theodore J. Gordon provides an example of a harvesting robot, with simple Boolean logic laid out in picture form (see fig. 1).

The left side of the figure shows three alternate enabling technological sub-subsystems, any of which could enable the ripeness sensing subsystem. They are called OR nodes because only one—not all three of them—needs to be developed and available for the ripeness-sensing subsystem to work. The middle of the figure lists five critical subsystems: guidance, position sensing, ripeness sensing, cleaning, and packaging. All these subsystems are required for the overall system of the harvesting robot to work properly. Each of the five critical subsystems is termed an "AND node," since all of them must be present, and none of them can substitute for the others.

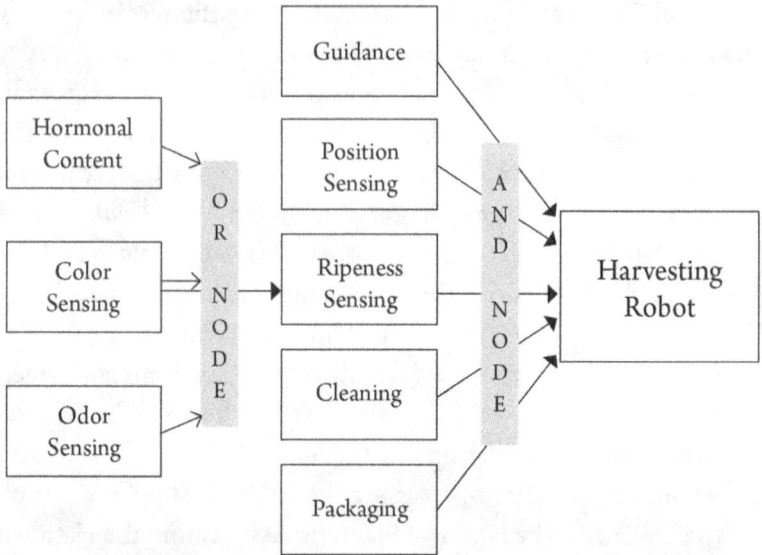

Fig. 1. Example of Technology Sequence Analysis (harvesting robot). From Theodore J. Gordon, "Technology Sequence Analysis," in *Futures Research Methodology*, Version 3.0, ed. Jerome C. Glenn and Theodore J. Gordon (Washington DC: The Millennium Project, 2009), CD-ROM article 16, 3.

Technical experts provide their estimates of the likelihood of nodes within the network being created by a certain date. An example might be, "Node XXY has a 65 percent likelihood of being developed within five years." Several hundred nodes leading up to the completed system on the right, such as the harvesting robot, might need to be included in a full TSA diagram. Gordon explained that a network could consist of six hundred to eight hundred nodes and seven hundred to a thousand associated "or" paths and "and" paths. Some charts may become so complicated that special software must be used to simulate the Monte Carlo simulations necessary to assign the ranges of probabilities opened up by all the alternate paths involving the different enabling technologies or components.[17] Gordon further explained:

The process begins with the technologies at the left side of the matrix. Using a random number generator, the time of occurrence of each of the downstream technologies is determined. Suppose, for example, that a given path from one node to another is judged to have a 25 percent probability of taking three years, a 50 percent of taking five years, and a 75 percent of taking ten years or less. These estimates form a probability versus time curve. A random number between 0 and 100 is chosen; this number is used to enter the curve and produce a single estimate of the required time. If the node being considered is at an "and" point in the network, the latest date of the contributing technologies determines when the development occurs. Similarly, the earliest date of the possible technologies determines when an "or" node is assumed to occur. When this process is completed for all paths, a single scenario will result. In this scenario, the anticipated sequence of events is the path through the network; in turn, this path leads to an estimate of the time of availability of the end system.[18]

If the entire path from the most basic components on the left to the finished system on the right consisted only of AND nodes, with no alternate OR nodes, Monte Carlo simulations would not be necessary, and the sequence of contingent probabilities could be calculated simply. This simplistic calculation can be used in the harvesting robot example since no OR nodes apply. For the sake of illustration, let's assume the estimated probabilities of the five critical subsystems (all AND nodes) being completed within five years are as follows: guidance, 80 percent likelihood; position sensing, 95 percent likelihood; ripeness sensing, 78 percent likelihood; cleaning, 93 percent likelihood; and packaging, 54 percent. In this simple example, the estimated probability of a harvesting robot being completed within five years is the product of these dependent probabilities, or about 30 percent. This is only true, however, if those critical subsystems are not themselves dependent upon enabling technologies for which several alternative solutions are available. This will very rarely be the case. Since most notional technological systems may be actualized through various alternate combinations of components or technical solutions for subsystems, Monte Carlo simulations are almost always a necessary part of Technology Sequence Analysis.

*Scenario Analysis*

Technology Sequence Analysis focuses on the likely time lines various potential future technologies may need to reach the market, a vital part of a devil's toy box analysis. Yet equally important are the human motivations that drive the uses and misuses of those emerging technologies—that is, the religious, political, ideological, and emotional factors that could influence human actors to harm or threaten to harm others through innovative tactics.

Nicole Rijkens-Klomp and Patrick van der Duin define *scenario analysis* as "the systematic analysis of a variety of uncertainties combined into distinctive stories about the future."[19] Herman Kahn and Anthony J. Wiener, two futurists associated with RAND who made prolific use of the scenario analysis technique in their writings, have this to say regarding the technique: "The scenario is suited to dealing with events taken together—integrating several aspects of a situation more or less simultaneously. Using a relatively extensive scenario, the analyst may be able to get a feeling for events and the branching points dependent upon critical choices. These branches can then be explored more or less systematically or the scenario itself can be used as a context for discussion or as a 'named' possibility that can be referred to for various purposes."[20] They go on to caution that "if a scenario is to seem plausible to analysts and/or policy-makers it must, of course, relate at the outset to some reasonable version of the present, and must correspond throughout to the way analysts and/or policy-makers are likely to believe decision-makers are likely to behave. Since plausibility is a great virtue in a scenario, one should, subject to other considerations, try to achieve it. But it is important not to limit oneself to the *most* plausible, conventional, or probable situations and behavior." Since history is replete with surprises, they continue, "we should expect to go on being surprised."[21] Along those lines, Kahn and Wiener list a key advantage of the scenario analysis technique; it helps to "illuminate the interaction of psychological, social, economic, cultural, political, and military factors, including the influence of individual political personalities upon what otherwise might be abstract considerations,

and . . . [scenario analyses] do so in a form that permits the compre-
hension of many such interacting elements at once."[22]

Scenario analysis can facilitate the asking of essential questions for
a devil's toy box analysis. Are there aspects of an emerging Promethean technology that make it especially appealing to the adherents
of an extremist ethnic, religious, or political group? Would using the
technology fit within an extremist group's ideology, worldview, and
goals, or would its use violate a taboo sacred to that group? What are
the levels of skill and technical expertise required to make effective,
malign use of the technology, and are such skill levels and expertise
found among members of the extremist groups under consideration?

Prominent American futurist Peter Schwartz, author of *Art of
the Long View: Planning for the Future in an Uncertain World*, long
considered a bible for scenario analysis, provided the following eight
steps for constructing scenarios:

Step 1: Identify the primary focal issue around which the scenario
will revolve. What challenges are faced by your organization or
company? What are the looming decisions that will need to be
made? (For a devil's toy box analysis, this would be selecting one
over-the-horizon technology of concern or a cluster of emerging
and existing technologies that might be combined in a new and
malign way.)

Step 2: Identify the environmental factors that will influence the
success or failure of your organization's or company's strategy. This
could include the availability of budgetary and material resources,
the capabilities of competitors, the regulatory environment, the
overall economic climate, and the political climate. (For a devil's
toy box analysis, the team would want to consider whether the
political climate might contribute to the rise of new extremist
groups or the rebirth of old ones and whether changes in the
economy and in the social acceptance of technologies might be
creating new societal vulnerabilities. An example might be the
Internet of Things making household appliances, climate controls,
and security features vulnerable to hacking.)

Step 3: Identify those specific driving forces that will have a significant impact on your organization or company. (For a devil's toy box analysis, the team would explore whether any formerly exclusive and expensive technologies of interest have recently become affordable for the typical consumer or soon will become so. The team could also research whether any new extremist groups are gaining traction domestically or internationally and what those groups' goals might mean for homeland security.)

Step 4: Rank key factors and driving forces on the criteria of the strength of their relationship to the success or failure of your organization's or company's strategy, and on the degree of uncertainty of those key factors and driving forces. The aim in this step is to identify a small group of factors and forces that are high both in significance to success or failure *and* in uncertainty.

Step 5: Select the logics of the scenarios by arraying the key factors and driving forces that are high in both significance and uncertainty along a spectrum (one axis), a matrix (two axes), or a volume (three axes). With three axes and assuming each separate scenario will be either high or low on each axis, you end up with eight possible scenarios: high-high-high, high-high-low, high-low-low, high-low-high, low-low-low, low-low-high, low-high-high, or low-high-low. The number of possible combinations would be extended if the key factors and driving forces are arrayed along more axes or low-moderate-high rather than just low-high. Do not assemble the scenarios mechanically, however. You want to keep the number of scenarios manageable, so decide which ones make the most sense in terms of internal consistency and plausibility.

Step 6: Flesh out the selected scenarios. Create plots that realistically bring the story forward from the present situation to the future situation portrayed in the scenario. Decide whether any key personalities or leaders might facilitate progress from the present situation to the future scenario.

Step 7: Determine the implications of the scenarios for your organization or company. Will your organization thrive or wither in the future world of the scenario? What are the implications of the scenario for the success or failure of your organization's strategy and goals?

Step 8: Select leading indicators that will show whether a scenario is on its way to becoming actualized. These leading indicators will typically consist of a movement in one of the key factors and driving forces identified in steps 3 and 4. Then monitor those leading indicators.[23]

Schwartz cautioned against identifying only three scenarios to work with, pointing out that participants in the analysis will tend to identify the one in the middle as the most likely scenario and then treat that scenario as a single-point forecast, defeating the whole purpose of scenario analysis. He recommended four scenarios as an optimal number for a single session of scenario analysis and further suggested that two scenarios should be of equally high probability and that the other two should be what he terms "wild card" scenarios, with a low likelihood but high impact.[24]

### The Wisdom of Crowds: Insights and Best Practices from Prediction Markets

In 1948 British economist Friedrich Hayek published his expansion on Adam Smith's eighteenth-century notion of the "invisible hand," the amalgamation of tendencies that guide unregulated markets in goods and services, resulting in the averaged welfare of all participants being increased. Hayek's efficient market theory posits that markets act to aggregate otherwise separate bits of knowledge concerning the environment within which a market operates, as well as the forces acting upon that market, and that they do so through the mechanism of prices. The market, by amalgamating vast amounts of scattered pieces of information, can be collectively far more intelligent than any of its individual participants.

The efficient market theory had received startling empirical support a little less than half a century earlier. In 1906 the British statistician Francis Galton used an already existing betting game to demonstrate the collective intelligence of a crowd of ordinary persons (nonexperts and nonspecialists). Approximately eight hundred persons participated in a betting game in which they were asked to guess the weight of an ox. Bettors placed their names and best guess of the beast's weight on a slip of paper, and the person who came closest to the animal's actual weight won a prize. Galton borrowed the eight hundred slips of paper and averaged all the guesses. This average varied from the ox's actual weight by less than 1 percent.[25] In 1968 Dr. John Craven of the U.S. Navy's Special Projects Division performed a similar experiment. He had been assigned to head up the search for the navy's missing nuclear submarine the USS *Scorpion*. Craven gathered a team of submarine officers, salvage specialists, and scientists; then he organized an internal prediction market in which they participated. Eventually, the *Scorpion* was discovered resting 220 yards from where Craven's team predicted it would be found.[26]

The team of Albert E. Mannes, Jack B. Soll, and Richard P. Larrick refined the "wisdom of the crowd" technique, calling it the select-crowd strategy. In a select-crowd forecasting procedure, the participants are ranked in terms of their forecasting ability based on an available indicator of such ability, such as their performance on recent forecasts. The group's amalgamated output, rather than being the average of all the participants' contributions, is instead the average of the inputs of the top five–ranked participants. Mannes, Soll, and Larrick compared the utility of three varieties of prediction markets: their select-crowd strategy, a whole-crowd strategy (the averaged or otherwise amalgamated opinions of all the members of a crowd, such as in a prediction poll), and a best-member strategy (participants on a forecasting team or panel select the opinion of the single member they collectively judge to be the best or most accurate to be the group's consensus opinion). The researchers point out that each of these strategies is most appropriate within a different type of environment and tends to produce the best or most accurate output when its respective environmental factors are present. In an environment in which the participants' forecasting abilities vary widely and the facilitators can access unambiguous indicators of those abilities, the best-member strategy tends to perform the best. Contrarily, in an environment distinguished by small differences in forecasting ability and frequent bracketing (i.e., participants' forecasting errors show an approximately equal likelihood of being either above or below the true value by approximately equal amounts), the whole-crowd strategy is preferable. The difficulty in selecting the appropriate procedure lies in determining what type of environment applies. If the type of environment is ambiguous, the select-crowd strategy is the most robust. This is based on the fact that in two types of environments (a low-bracketing/low-dispersion-in-expertise environment and a high-bracketing/high-dispersion-in-expertise environment), the select-crowd strategy is optimal, and in the other two types of environments (a low-bracketing/high-dispersion-in-expertise environment and a high-bracketing/low-dispersion-in-expertise environment), the select-crowd strategy ranks second best out of the three strategies.[27]

As part of their experiments, Mannes, Soll, and Larrick tried to determine the ideal number of the highest-ranked participants whose outputs should be averaged using the select-crowd strategy. They found that depending on the type of environment, select crowds varying in size between three and eight in number could be optimal. In situations where the type of environment is unknown, selecting five high-ranking judges serves as a "best compromise" optimal number.[28]

Other researchers have tried to determine the ideal number of forecasters to use in a whole-crowd strategy. Ville A. Satopää and his partners found that although aggregated accuracy of forecasts shows continual improvement as the number of forecasts aggregated increases, the majority of the improvement in accuracy occurs as the number of forecasters increases from ten to twenty. Only small increases in accuracy accrue from increasing the number of forecasters beyond twenty, and those moderate improvements taper off significantly after the number of forecasters reach forty.[29]

Regarding the select-crowd strategy, Mannes, Soll, and Larrick discovered that only short histories of prior forecasting performance— one to five prior forecasts, with the higher number being preferred for environments of high dispersion of levels of expertise—are required to productively rank the participants by ability. They found that under conditions of high dispersion of expertise, only minimal testing is required to differentiate between the participants; whereas under conditions of low dispersion of expertise, when all participants are approximately equal in their ability, no amount of testing would reveal significant differences.[30]

Mannes and his partners also determined that the participants' self-evaluations of confidence in their own levels of expertise could serve as a valid and reliable alternative judgment factor for the facilitators to use in selecting the five preferred participants from a crowd. They found that selecting five participants based on those participants' self-evaluations of confidence resulted in group average forecasting outputs about as accurate as those derived from a select crowd made up of participants chosen based on five of their past forecasts. The researchers pointed out that using self-evaluated confidence as an alternative selection cue is especially appropriate in situations where the forecasting task involves an unprecedented or unique event, such as the anticipated remaining tenure for a foreign dictator.[31] Clearly, this latter stipulation applies in the instance of a devil's toy box analysis, which, by its nature, attempts to forecast unprecedented events involving technological innovations. Researchers in the United Kingdom corroborated the results of Mannes's team. They found that the participants who rated themselves as being more expert proved to be less overconfident, better calibrated, and more likely to achieve higher accuracy scores than those participants who self-rated as less expert.[32]

The efficacy of even those prognosticators who are high performers on a battery of forecasting tests and who rate their own expertise and confidence highly can be significantly improved with even minimal training regarding how to recognize and overcome cognitive biases. Nicholas Rescher, the chairman of the University of Pittsburg's Center for Philosophy of Science, has noted the many cognitive biases that, if uncorrected for, tend to warp forecasts and result in false positives, false negatives, and omissions. The first of these biases is the tendency of prognosticators to exaggerate both the imminency and the scale of a predicted change or event. Forecasters tend to pull predicted events closer in time to the present and grant them greater magnitude. Another cognitive bias is *conservatism,* or the tendency to assume that present conditions are more durable and lasting than they are; that is, the forecaster believes the present's social, political, and economic features and patterns will persist into the future. Two related cognitive biases are what Rescher termed "wishful" and "fearful" thinking. Regarding the former, prognosticators tend to predict a future they prefer either because they feel they ought to express such an opinion or because they hope that making such a prediction of a preferred future will increase the likelihood of its becoming actualized. The flip side of wishful thinking is *fearful thinking,* or the tendency of prognosticators to have greater confidence in their expectation that what they most dread will come to pass.[33]

Rescher also highlighted how many persons tend to be radically off base in their judgments of probabilities. He provided the example of a coin tosser who predicts the next toss will result in heads because the last three flips have all resulted in tails (any flip has a 50 percent chance of coming up heads regardless of the results of earlier flips). Regarding probabilistic combinations, he pointed out that bettors (predictors) tend to overestimate the chances of long shots becoming actualized (an overestimation of the likelihood of conjunctive events) while underestimating the likelihood of small-probability/large-consequence events happening (an underestimation of disjunctive events). An example of the latter is the repeated willingness of town planners and homeowners to build homes and businesses in flood plains.[34] By having such common human cognitive biases explained to them, however, members of a forecasting team can take such biases into account and attempt to compensate for them.

Philip Tetlock, the coauthor of *Superforecasting: The Art and Science of Prediction,* assembled a team called the Good Judgment Project to compete in a forecasting tournament organized by the Intelligence Advanced Research Projects Agency. His team won the tournament by a wide margin. Tetlock's experience backs up Rescher's results regarding the usefulness of cognitive bias training for the efficacy of the prognosticators' performance. He was both surprised and gratified to discover how long lasting the beneficial effects of the initial, brief training sessions in overcoming cognitive biases could be. The topics covered also included reducing overconfidence in predictions and using Bayesian statistical methods to refine or change their forecasts over time as new information becomes available. Tetlock found that the benefits of the training stuck with the participants throughout an entire year's worth of forecasting activities.[35] Tetlock and his team also found that training in group dynamics—"how to disagree without being disagreeable"—improved the outcomes seen by forecasting teams.[36] Additionally, they learned that providing the participants with scenario training—that is, teaching them to envision a broad range of possible futures, how to use decision trees, and how to avoid biases in forecasting such as fabricating incoherent scenarios, overpredicting patterns of change, or assigning probabilities that exceed a sum of 100 percent to a range of mutually exclusive and comprehensive outcomes—was not as helpful as providing training in the use of Bayesian statistical methods, but scenario training resulted in higher levels of forecasting accuracy than that shown by the participants in a control group who received no training at all.[37]

### Red Teaming: Learning to See through an Adversary's Eyes

Col. Gregory Fontenot, U.S. Army (USA, Ret.), defined *red teaming* as "a structured and iterative process executed by trained, educated, and practiced team members with access to relevant subject matter expertise" that "provides the commander with an independent capability to continuously challenge OE [operational environment] concepts, plans, and operations from partner and adversary perspectives . . . emphasiz(ing) technical issue and vulnerability analysis, focusing on capabilities rather than the enemy's potential use of those capabilities . . . [and] provid(ing) a means to build intellectual constructs that replicate how the enemy thinks."[38] He traces the practice's origin to the kriegspiels (wargames) that the nineteenth-century German army instituted to train its officers.

Dr. Mark Mateski, in his "Red Teaming: A Short Introduction (1.0)," asserted that red teaming is a type of alternative analysis that assists leaders in making good decisions by avoiding rigidity and countering surprise. Red teaming does this through drawing on the benefits of a variety of alternative analysis techniques, including "key assumptions checks; devil's advocacy; Team A/Team B; red cell exercises; contingency 'what if' analysis; high-impact/low-probability analysis; [and] scenario development."[39] He divided red-teaming activities into two categories—passive and active—with each category serving two purposes. Passive red teaming helps decision makers better *understand* (how their adversaries think, how they view the defending organization, and what biases and assumptions the defending organization holds) and better *anticipate* (their adversaries' potential courses of action, which of the defender's vulnerabilities are most likely to be exploited, and potential surprises). Active red teaming serves the purposes of *testing* (probing and penetrating the defender's systems or security, identifying vulnerabilities and determining how far they can be exploited, and demonstrating their adversaries' likely moves and the defender's countermeasures interactively) and *training* (teaching defenders how potential adversaries think and how they might operate and preparing defenders to deploy effective countermeasures).[40]

Maj. David F. Longbine, USA, listed three key roles of red teaming: (1) challenging stale, outdated, or false thinking in an organization through filling the role of the devil's advocate; (2) strongly challenging what is accepted as conventional wisdom; and (3) providing a set of alternative analyses. Red teaming grants decision makers with alternative perspectives by describing the operational environment as it might be seen through the eyes of allies and partners, adversaries, or other actors within the environment. The goal of red teaming, in Longbine's view, is to avoid common perceptual errors such as *mirror imaging* (assuming that one's adversaries or allies share one's own motives, values, and cultural concepts) and *ethnocentrism* (the belief in the superiority of one's own culture). These biases can lead a decision maker to dangerously underestimate an adversary's skills, abilities, or determination.[41] Additionally, red teaming helps decision makers avoid falling into the pernicious trap of *groupthink*, the all-too-common phenomenon wherein a group of experts, with similar backgrounds and worldviews, reinforces one another's viewpoints and erroneously solidifies a sense that the right decisions are being made.[42]

Brian A. Jackson and his team, in *Breaching the Fortress Wall: Understanding Terrorist Efforts to Overcome Defensive Technologies*, emphasized the continual dynamic of measure-countermeasure and move-countermove that takes place between defending organizations within the homeland security enterprise and their opponents, either individual terrorists/criminals or terrorist organizations. The authors reviewed the tactics and strategies of four prominent terror groups or aggregations: Palestinian terror organizations, Jemaah Islamiyah and its allies, the Liberation Tigers of Tamil Eelam, and the Provisional Irish Republican Army. They identified four ways that these groups have attempted to defeat the defensive technologies or measures that homeland security organizations put into place: they altered their operational practices, which included incorporating camouflage, deception, or forgery into their tactics; switched their own chosen technologies (surveillance tools, communications systems, or weapons) to foil defensive technologies; avoided the defensive technology altogether by, for example, changing their target or zone of attack; and, finally, directly attacked the defensive technology. The authors assert that homeland security defensive systems should always be designed with the likely reactions of their opponents in mind. They recommend that designers of these systems utilize red-teaming techniques to test the resilience of their systems. The designers need to assess their potential adversaries' information requirements (i.e., what attackers would need to know to successfully defeat the system and how those attackers might acquire such information). Defenders also must consider how attackers may adjust to the defensive system; then they should change their own technologies and tactics in anticipation of this. Flexible systems are more valuable than inflexible ones, for the opponents' countermoves may swiftly render a defensive system's initial mode of operation obsolete. Also, the authors recommend that defensive system designers consider the relative costs both of the system they are designing and of the foreseeable efforts to defeat that system. They point out that a goal of some terror groups is to drain the defenders' ability and will to defend themselves by subjecting them to very high relative expenditures. In other words, a billion-dollar system that can be defeated by a ten-thousand-dollar countermeasure is not a wise expenditure.[43]

Red teaming introduces something new to our devil's toy box analytical tool kit. The techniques described earlier—the Delphi technique, the nominal group technique, the tools of futurism—focus on emerging and potential technologies from a scientist's, engineer's, or technologist's point of view. Red teaming, however, focuses on conflict, not on technological development. Its prime concern is the ever-shifting balance between attackers and defenders. When analysts look at new technologies through a red-teaming lens, they focus on the advantages or disadvantages that those new technologies may offer to attackers and defenders within a particular environment. In this view, new technologies may offer both benefits and threats to defenders. For example, the Internet of Things offers facility security managers new capabilities to remotely control their facilities' defensive features, yet it simultaneously increases those facilities' vulnerabilities by providing attackers with new pathways to remotely hack into the control systems.

Red teaming encourages defenders to take their potential antagonists' motivations, fears, strengths, and weaknesses into account. Why might one target prove more attractive than another to a certain type of attacker? What makes a type of weapon or mode of attack more appealing and to which sorts of attackers? Given the cultural, social, and psychological background of a particular category of attacker, how might a mode of defense be adjusted or improved to take advantage of that attacker's vulnerabilities, taboos, or fears?

To sum up, red teaming lies at the heart of a devil's toy box analytical effort. Fresh, innovative weapons do not use themselves. They do not attack office buildings, shopping malls, trains, aircraft, festive gatherings, religious processions, or entire cities of their own volition (the issue of future artificial intelligence systems going rogue aside). They are used by human beings, persons possessing human motivations, fears, hatreds, loyalties, honor codes, religious or ideological aspirations, and lusts, as well as hunger for destruction and its accompanying glory or infamy. Only a thorough red-teaming process can provide members of a devil's toy box analytical team with insights into the minds and hearts of potential adversaries.

The most useful red-teaming techniques developed by Western armed forces and law enforcement agencies are addressed in chapter 7, wherein all the tools described thus far are amalgamated into a process I call the Promethean Spyglass. Before that, we consider the question of who should wield this Promethean Spyglass—that is, what sorts of experts belong on a devil's toy box analytical team. One suggestion may surprise you!

# SIX

## The Core of a Devil's Toy Box Analytical Team?

*Science Fiction Writers*

GROUPINGS OF EXPERTS, SUCH AS Delphi panels, nominal groups, and conclaves of futurists, all need the right mix of participants to operate effectively—persons possessing specialized knowledge, not typically dispersed among the public, and/or individuals with life experience or personal knowledge that has specific bearing on the analytical task. Since we are focused on conducting an analysis of potential terror modalities, our grouping of experts should include senior officers from law enforcement agencies and special agents, senior analysts, and/or members of top management from homeland security agencies. However, a real danger exists that too large an "in-house" representation on a devil's toy box analytical team will lead to organizational groupthink, or the counterproductive steering of results in directions amenable to the sponsoring organization's existing initiatives and priorities. When one's only tool is a hammer, every problem conveniently looks like a nail.

What other sorts of experts would be most useful for a devil's toy box analysis? Certainly, we need to include scientific and technical experts whose fields are most relevant to the over-the-horizon Promethean technologies initially flagged by a forecasting system such as the Intelligence Advanced Research Projects Agency's FUSE Program. We would most likely want to involve geneticists to judge emerging gene-splicing technologies; explosives and firearms experts to judge emerging 3D printing technologies; robotics, machine intelligence, and radio spectrum communications experts to judge emerging automation technologies; and cybersecurity experts to judge the

vulnerabilities of new personal medical implant technologies connected to the Internet of Things.

Yet a focus on the future development of technologies is not
enough. A gun, by itself, does not murder. Nor will an automated
laser rifle, a micro drone carrying a payload of poison, or a software
worm written to turn off internet-connected pacemakers. For any
of these tools to contribute to acts of destruction and disruption,
a human actor would need to use them. Human actors choose all
the various attack options: mode, time, place, and target. Ideally,
our devil's toy box analytical team also would include experts on
the human motivations that lead to decisions to engage in acts of
terror. We would want to engage specialists who have studied the
desires, aspirations, fears, hatreds, taboos, loyalties, rivalries, social or
religious traditions, and cultural imperatives that shape the behaviors
and goals of terrorists.

An ideal addition to a devil's toy box analytical team would be
a person who combines the horizon-scanning habits of a futurist
or a technology forecaster with the conflict- and mayhem-inclined
mindset of a terrorist. Such an individual would be able to speak
not only to the feasibility of using Promethean technologies for
destructive purposes but also to the human, emotional factors that
prompt such use—the symbolic, religious, and psychological attractants inherent within certain technologies and why those attractants
appeal to persons with terroristic tendencies.

These notional ideal team members exist. They are called science
fiction writers.

### The Key Equation: Commercial Science Fiction = Future Technology + CONFLICT

Many persons with only a passing familiarity with the science fiction
field assume that the primary goal of writers of science fiction is to
successfully predict future developments in science and technology,
to be Delphic oracles. This impression is furthered by the accurate
prognostications of two of the science fiction field's earliest and most
prominent writers—Jules Verne and H. G. Wells. The former predicted

electricity-powered submarines (*Twenty Thousand Leagues under the Sea*), manned flight to the moon (*From the Earth to the Moon*), and round-the-world travel by air (*Around the World in Eighty Days*). The latter foresaw the development of armored tanks ("The Land Ironclads"), the genetic engineering of animals (*The Island of Doctor Moreau*), and the advent of nuclear weaponry (*The World Set Free*).

Yet as John Clute and Peter Nicholls, the editors of the authoritative *The Encyclopedia of Science Fiction*, point out, the record of science fiction writers as soothsayers is decidedly mixed. Since the start of science fiction as a distinct commercial genre with the publication of the first issue of *Amazing Stories* in 1926, the most consequential scientific prediction by a major science fiction writer has been Arthur C. Clarke's 1945 article about communications satellites; the most amusing has been Robert Heinlein's accurate prognostication of the invention of the waterbed. Clute and Nicholls indicate that many science fiction writers have never set out to predict what *will* happen. Instead, they predict, then dramatically envision, what *could* potentially happen either to warn their readers about possible dire developments in the future or, less frequently, to provide a beacon to an attractive possible future.[1]

If science fiction writers have not demonstrated a widely shared talent for accurately predicting future technological developments, what do they have to offer a devil's toy box analysis? Their most valuable contribution would be their science fiction mindset, inculcated in them by a career spent chasing opportunities to sell stories and novels to a certain readership—a mindset that combines conflict seeking (within the realm of storytelling) with continual horizon scanning in search of innovative technological extrapolations upon which to base their fictions.

Conflict lies at the heart of any story or novel. Absent conflict (which can be between persons, between a protagonist and society, or opposing impulses of a protagonist), a story or novel is no more than a character sketch, a philosophical or sociological essay, or an excursion into speculative psychology. Although a relative handful of science fiction stories and novels have been accepted into the literary canon as works of literary art, and science fiction has made inroads in recent decades into the academy as an object of study, science fiction is primarily a commercial genre of fiction. It is subject to the same marketplace pressures and influences as other popular fiction genres, such as romances, mysteries, suspense thrillers, and westerns. If acquiring editors do not judge a story or novel as having the potential to earn a profit, they will not buy the piece, no matter how much they may personally like it. (Exceptions to this marketplace rule exist for media that are not primarily profit driven, such as academic publications, subsidized publishing, self-publishing, or agenda-focused publishing.)

The mode of creative extrapolation of scientific and social possibilities inculcated in writers of commercial science fiction is ideally suited for a devil's toy box analysis. Their preferred storytelling mode, centering around believable conflict between persons (or in the case of aliens, beings) with intelligible and compelling motivations, grants science fiction writers insight into (returning to our initial parable) the devil's mindset—his desires, preferred goals, and choice of many gestating toys. In fact, including science fiction writers on a devil's toy box analytical team is the next best thing to recruiting former terrorists who have brainstormed new weaponry and new modes of attack.

The science fiction field has traditionally been an iterative one, like jazz or modernist art. Newer writers build on the concepts and tropes developed by earlier writers. In the science fiction genre (as opposed to the related commercial genres of fantasy and horror, which rely more heavily on repeated, well-worn tropes and effects), a fresh approach to the material is highly sought. Writers who can provide innovative, novel approaches are highly thought of by their colleagues, are often the recipients of prestigious awards, and are lauded by discriminating readers. Some (not all) acquiring editors in the science fiction field seek freshness and novelty and will immediately reject what they perceive as the same old story (unless that same old story is written by a highly marketable author with a huge built-in readership). Thus, science fiction writers—or at least those who write what is called *hard science fiction* (or hard SF, defined as "imaginative literature that uses either established or carefully extrapolated science as its backbone")—compete with one another to offer fresh takes regarding rigorous extrapolations of evolving science and technology.[2] This science and technology is often cutting-edge or highly notional.

Throughout much of its existence as a genre of popular fiction, science fiction has been marketed as reading material for teenage boys and young men of approximately college age. With good reason, a saying common in the field cynically states that "the Golden Age of Science Fiction is 14."[3] (Varying versions of the epigram peg the golden age as twelve years old.) With this primary audience in mind, science fiction writers who hope to have a remunerative career have traditionally loaded up their stories and novels with plenty of conflict, generally of the sort that intrigues teenage boys and young men. This audience gravitates to stories of future military conflicts, invasions by alien beings, and underground rebel movements using new technologies or social doctrines. Stories about exploring and conquering new frontiers, primarily outer space, have always been popular with boys. Young males also appreciate stories centered around acquiring vast new personal capabilities, such as machine-enhanced intelligence or physical strength and dexterity, superpowers gained through genetic engineering, or esoteric abilities such as telepathy or telekinesis.

Publishing billets are a limited good. In recent times, they are a shrinking good. The competitive pressures of commercial science fiction publishing push writers of more technology-oriented hard SF to present hot takes on plausible extrapolations of current or foreseen developments in science and technology *and* to present those extrapolations in the form of exciting conflicts that induce readers (most especially acquiring editors) to swiftly turn the pages. Any successful writer of hard SF has learned to continually scan available sources for new information on scientific and technical developments with story potential. He or she then furiously extrap-olates the potential implications (both good and bad, but the latter typically makes for more exciting plots) of said developments before a competitor writes the same or similar extrapolation, sells it to one of the limited numbers of acquiring editors, and renders the tardier author's work unmarketable. These highly proficient commercial writers extrapolate these scientific or technical developments in the most thrilling, reader-engaging way possible while maximizing the levels of conflict in their stories.

To maintain even a modest income from their writing, these authors must continually ask themselves the following:

What are the *newest* developments in science and technology?

What developments are anticipated in the foreseeable future?

What are theorists of science speculating about as possibilities?

What might happen because of these developments in science and technology?

What is likely to happen? What might plausibly happen?

What trends currently exist in science and technology and in societal adjustments to science and technology? What would happen if those trends were extrapolated into the future and greatly exaggerated?

What are the possible social impacts of these trends and developments? Political implications? Cultural implications? Religious implications? Psychological impacts? Impacts on behaviors? Impacts on health and longevity? Impacts on the physical environment?

What are the *scariest* things that might result?

What are the most interesting, exciting *conflicts* that might arise because of these potential, extrapolated trends and developments in science and technology?

These exact sorts of questions are key to any devil's toy box analysis. But just as valuable for this purpose is the tendency of science fiction writers to write fiction from the vantage point of rebels, insurgents, subversives, and terrorists. In seeking to please an audience of young men who oftentimes view themselves as an oppressed, overlooked, unappreciated "secret elite," science fiction authors have often cast insurgents and rebels as their heroes (thus flattering their reading audiences and providing them with the power fantasies they crave). Popular writers Robert Heinlein, A. E. van Vogt, Fritz Leiber, and L. Ron Hubbard wrote about future insurgencies against various types of political or religious tyrannies. Emblematic works of this type during the golden age of science fiction (1938–46, corresponding with the most innovative period of editor John W. Campbell Jr.'s helming of *Astounding Science-Fiction*) include Heinlein's *Sixth Column* and *Revolt in 2100*; van Vogt's *Slan*, *The Weapons Shops of Isher*, and *The Weapon Makers*; Leiber's *Gather, Darkness!*, and Hubbard's *Final Blackout*.

This special focus on the actions and interior lives of rebels and subversives was not limited to the golden age. The subgenre of science fiction called cyberpunk, popularly launched by William Gibson's innovative novel *Neuromancer* (1984), became the dominant subgenre in the field during the 1980s and the 1990s. It remains popular and influential to the present day both in written and filmed forms. Cyberpunk fiction focuses, as the portmanteau suggests, on both *cyber* (the impact on individuals and their societies of computer networks, highly advanced information technologies, machine intelligence, and the fusion of computers and machines with human biology) and *punk* (resistance to authority, convention, control, and the Establishment). In cyberpunk stories, novels, and films, hackers are the heroes who struggle against oppressive, authoritarian constructs, either governmental or corporate (or a malign fusion of both). Their clashes, often highly romanticized, take place in both the physical realm and the realms of virtual reality and cyberspace. How difficult is it to transpose James Dingley's overeducated and underemployed into the role of cyberpunk antiheroes or to imagine them seeing themselves that way? Not very.

The cyberpunk movement in science fiction was praised in some quarters as having restored a missing element of swagger, avant-gardism, romanticism, fashion sensibility, and sexiness to science fiction. According to some critics, these qualities had been missing in action since the work of the New Wave cohort of writers in the 1960s that formed an influential part of that decade's counterculture. Writers associated with the cyberpunk movement include Gibson, Bruce Sterling (the movement's primary writer of manifestos), Greg Bear, Elizabeth Hand, and Jack Womack. Key early cyberpunk films include *Blade Runner* (1982, based on Philip K. Dick's 1968 novel *Do Androids Dream of Electric Sheep?*) and David Cronenberg's *Videodrome* (1983).[4]

The cyberpunk work that has arguably enjoyed the greatest mass popularity and cultural impact is *The Matrix* (1999) film trilogy, which prominently features the cyberpunk tropes of humanity enslaved by technology (in this case, literally as intelligent machines have subjected humanity to virtual reality suspended animation in which individuals unknowingly serve as biological batteries to power their machine oppressors); a charismatic group of heroes, possessed of otherwise hidden knowledge (derived from the Red Pill, which allows them to perceive that what they thought to be reality is merely virtual reality) and who serve as the vanguard of a revolution; a long-prophesized, technocratic messiah (Neo); dynamic conflicts within cyberspace; and vertiginously shifting, seemingly psychedelic environments. Recent films and television productions—including a sequel to *Blade Runner, Blade Runner 2049* (2017), which was nominated for five Academy Awards, and a 2018 Netflix series based upon Richard K. Morgan's popular 2002 cyberpunk mystery-thriller *Altered Carbon*—illustrate the continuing relevance and popular appeal of the subgenre.[5]

Eric Frank Russell's novel *Wasp*, first published in 1957, provides an extraordinary example of how beneficial the science fiction mindset would be for a devil's toy box analysis. This astoundingly prescient work—not predictive of future technologies but rather of insurgency doctrine, strategy, and tactics—serves as a fictionalized how-to manual for an insurgency or terror campaign with limited resources and personnel. Russell's accomplishment is especially noteworthy because he wrote *Wasp* prior to the great explosion of insurgencies in the latter half of the twentieth century: the Viet Cong's campaigns against the government of South Vietnam and its American allies in the 1960s, the Palestinian terror offensive against Israel beginning in the late 1960s, the various leftist and Maoist terror campaigns in the United States and Europe in the late 1960s and 1970s, the Liberation Tigers of Tamil Eelam's insurgency in Sri Lanka as of the mid-1970s, the leftist insurgencies and terror campaigns in Latin America in the 1980s, and the current wave of Islamist terror, arguably begun with the 1979 Iranian Revolution and the subsequent rise of both Hezbollah and an array of Sunni terror organizations. When Russell wrote his novel, the Algerian War between the Algerian National Liberation Front and France, the century's first anti-colonial war, had only begun three years earlier.

Russell likely drew upon accounts of the French resistance during World War II and the anti-Nazi partisans in Eastern Europe in working out his fictional terror campaign. But he used his science fiction–trained imagination to extrapolate new tactics that would allow a single individual with no actual followers to appear to be the secret leader of an insurgency of hundreds or thousands of operatives. Best-selling British author Terry Pratchett, in a back-cover blurb for a reprinting of Russell's book in 2000, writes, "I'd have given anything to have written *Wasp*. I can't imagine a funnier terrorists' handbook."[6]

The central conceit of the novel is this: just as a tiny, half-ounce wasp that flies through the window of a car loaded with passengers and stings the driver can cause the destruction of a two-ton automobile and the deaths of five human beings, a single secret operative, using tactics that appear to enormously magnify his actual strength, can goad the government and military forces of an entire world into ruinous overreactions, tying down a force of thousands of police and soldiers. The book's protagonist is James Mowry, an earthman who was born and raised in Masham, the capital city of Diracta on the home world of the Sirian Combine. Mowry is recruited by the special operations division of the Terran defense forces, which have been engaged in a long interstellar war with the Sirian Combine. The Terrans want Mowry as their operative because of his Sirian language skills, his knowledge of Sirian culture, and, following plastic surgery procedures to make him appear Sirian, his presumed ability to infiltrate a Sirian planet. Although the Terrans are in some ways technically superior in their war-making capabilities to the Sirians, the Sirians outnumber the Terrans by twelve to one. The Terran defense forces hope to overcome this stalemate through a campaign of sabotage, subversion, propaganda, and recruitment of local criminals, culminating in what a present-day reader would recognize as carefully targeted acts of terror.

A stealthy spacecraft inserts Mowry in a backwoods area of Jaimec, the ninety-fourth planet of the Sirian Combine, along with a large cache of supplies and equipment that Mowry hides in a secluded cave. He uses the cave as his base of operations as he travels between various cities on Jaimec, sowing confusion, misdirection, targeted murders, and terror. The initial tactic Mowry deploys is very simple and extremely effective in spreading a sense of unease and apprehension among both Jaimec's population and its law enforcement cadres: he uses a machine in his cave hideout to print up hundreds of stickers with slogans purportedly from an indigenous insurgent group opposed to the Sirian war with Terra. Designed to be applied to glass surfaces, the sticker's chemicals etch the printed slogan into the glass, making it impossible to remove the slogan without replacing the entire pane. Mowry surreptitiously affixes the stickers to phone booths, restaurant windows, storefronts, and the windows of public facilities. The resulting effects are twofold: not only does he induce fear that a widespread underground organization opposed to the war exists but he also spreads suspicion among law enforcement that the building and businesses owners who are unable to remove the slogans from their properties, at least not quickly or easily, are supporters or even members of this organization. Mowry's use of this sticker campaign can be viewed as a precursor of how today's Islamist terrorists use the internet, in part, to make their support, reach, and capabilities appear greater, perhaps, than they truly are. On the internet, no one knows you're a dog . . . or a lone wolf.

Mowry focuses his initial terror campaign on high-ranking officers of the Kaitempi, the Sirian secret police who are his chief foes. After he manages to insinuate himself with a mid-ranking Kaitempi, kills him, and steals his credentials along with a list of fellow Kaitempi officers, Mowry hires a trio of local criminals and murderers to assassinate a more prominent Kaitempi officer. Simultaneously, he mails hundreds of notes threatening assassination to other top-ranking Kaitempi and signs them only with the name of his imaginary insurgent organization, Dirac Angestun Gesept (the Sirian Freedom Party). Then he mails copies of the letters to members of the Sirian media and government so that his terror message will be disseminated even more widely. Mowry intuits that this mail-facilitated information-terror campaign will cause the Kaitempi to circle the wagons and assign a goodly portion of their manpower to protecting their own leaders rather than searching for Mowry and his imaginary followers. He provokes his foes into declaring martial law in Jaimec's largest cities and drawing military forces away from the primary campaign against the Terrans.

The climax of Mowry's "wasp" campaign of terror involves Jaimec's merchant fleet, a key piece of Sirian infrastructure on the primarily ocean-covered planet. Mowry deploys a small fleet of inexpensive, oil drum–sized, automated seacraft that travel just beneath the ocean's surface and randomly extend periscope-like devices above the waves, thus (to surface observers) appearing to be enemy submarines. He then infiltrates Jaimec's largest commercial harbor and attaches a mine to the side of a merchant ship, timing its explosion to occur when the vessel is on the open sea so it will appear as if the ship has been attacked by a submarine. He accurately anticipates this will result in vast military forces being deployed to hunt enemy submarines, which are merely Mowry's cheap, harmless drones.

Although I am not aware of any evidence that the leaders of the Palestine Liberation Organization (PLO) ever read *Wasp*, the PLO of the late 1960s and early 1970s carried out a *Wasp*-like campaign with such near similarities to Mowry's tactics on Jaimec that Eric Frank Russell seemingly could have written its operations manual. Just as Mowry monopolized the attention of Jaimec's governmental and security leadership by threatening a key transportation system, so did the PLO gain the world's headlines by threatening the viability of commercial aviation with its campaign of hijacking passenger airliners.

Just as Mowry made his imaginary organization seem far, far larger and more consequential than it truly was through a handful of carefully chosen and targeted assassinations, so did the Palestinians succeed in forcing their cause to the center of the international community's agenda by assassinating eleven Israeli athletes and coaches at the 1972 Summer Olympics. Only two years later, PLO chairman Yasser Arafat was invited to address the United Nations General Assembly, achieving a legitimacy few world leaders would have anticipated he and his cause would ever gain.

The PLO, however, was (and remains) an actual organization with a leadership structure and cadres of armed operatives. What Russell foresaw with *Wasp* was a more advanced terror apparatus, a *virtual* terror organization consisting of a single operative with limited physical assets who is able to vastly expand his perceived potency and deadliness through various communications networks. Making use of his science fiction mindset, Russell envisioned terror organizations and individual terrorists whose primary weapons are the psychology of fear and the power of suggestion rather than actual capabilities to physically destroy and kill.

The fictional Mowry is a Terran patriot, working for the military victory of his home society. Real-life Mowrys, likely to arise from the ranks of the overeducated and underemployed, will more resemble Jonah Sebold (from "The Happiest Place on Earth"), Fabiana Silvio (from "Initiation Rites"), or Jean-Louis (from "More Than You Bargained For") in their motivations: an angry rejection of their home society, a bitter resentment toward those they see as being undeservedly more successful, a craving for infamy and recognition, or simply a slap against a pervasive boredom and sense of uselessness. They will take advantage of the powers Promethean technologies hand them and, if they are clever, will pursue tactics strikingly similar to those of Eric Frank Russell's protagonist.

### SIGMA, the Science Fiction Think Tank

By 1992 Dr. Arlan Andrews, a member of the American Society of Mechanical Engineers and part-time science fiction writer who was serving as a White House fellow and staffer in the White House Science Office, had had enough. First, he witnessed Dr. Joe Bordogna, the National Science Foundation's deputy director for engineering, being made the butt of jokes from his foundation colleagues for suggesting that a decade hence, nanotechnologies and micromachines would become prominent on the scientific horizon. Then he had to sit silently as his boss, Dr. Alan Bromley, President George H. W. Bush's science adviser, suffered humiliating laughter from a roomful of scientists and bureaucrats for mentioning that virtual reality could potentially become an important aspect of future computer systems. Andrews would soon put his thoughts from those two infuriating meetings to paper: "I have heard more appropriate and realistic forecasts of technology and the future at any given science fiction convention than in all the forecasting meetings I have attended here in Washington, D.C."[7]

Those thoughts formed part of the founding manifesto for SIGMA, the science fiction think tank Andrews founded in 1992 to provide insights from the science fiction community to U.S. defense, intelligence, and homeland security institutions. Andrews hoped that SIGMA could counter what he saw as a crippling lack of imagination in the federal science establishment. "The Future is too important to be left to the futurists," Arlan wrote in SIGMA's founding document. "We science fiction writers have spent our literary careers exploring the future, we owe it to the rest of humanity to come back and report on what's out there."[8]

Andrews initially limited SIGMA's membership to science fiction writers with doctorate degrees in science or engineering, or medical degrees, to avoid giggles from the federal partners with whom they hoped to work as pro bono consultants. His initial recruits included fellow science fiction authors Dr. J. Douglas Beason, who also served as an air force lieutenant colonel assigned to the president's Office of Science and Technology Policy; Dr. Charles Sheffield; Dr. Yoji Kondo (who wrote under the pen name Eric Kotani); Dr. David Brin; Dr. Gregory Benford; Dr. Stanley Schmidt (then editor of *Analog Science Fiction & Fact*); Dr. Robert Forward; Dr. Geoffrey A. Landis; and Greg Bear. Although in its early years, SIGMA's efforts to engage with the government were rebuffed, individual members were permitted to brainstorm educational technology ideas for DARPA, deliver a lecture to a standing-room-only audience at Sandia National Laboratories, and serve as paid consultants. Andrews himself contributed an endorsement of nanotechnology to the April 1993 edition of *The President's Report to Congress on Science and Technology* (a response, perhaps, to the humiliation he had seen heaped upon his colleague Dr. Bordogna).

The organization's first formal interaction with the federal government occurred in 1999, when the group offered a discussion seminar titled "Future National Threats" to the Sandia National Laboratories' Advanced Concepts Group. SIGMA did not hold its second formal interaction with federal employees until May 2007, when six of its members were invited to participate in the Department of Homeland Security's Science & Technology East Coast Stakeholders' Conference. SIGMA member Dr. Jerry Pournelle chilled the audience by leading them in a discussion of what sorts of mitigations the government should have ready after an attack on the United States that left the country's twenty largest cities devastated and all communications systems inoperable. Other SIGMA participants offered DHS S&T officials ideas regarding post-disaster resilient communications and how DHS might best deploy the cell phone–installed biochemical agent detectors that S&T teams were developing.[9]

SIGMA's participation in this event led to a flattering interview of SIGMA members by a reporter from *USA Today*. This positive publicity led other federal agencies to invite SIGMA members to advise them regarding potential future developments in fields as diverse as demography, sociology, computer science, politics, communications, and culture. Clients for SIGMA's no-cost consultations, lectures, and panel or roundtable discussions have included the U.S. Army's Tech 2025 Conference (also called the Mad Scientist conference), the North Atlantic Treaty Organization's NATO 2030 conference, the 2012 Global Competitiveness Forum, and other conferences sponsored by DHS S&T and the Joint Services Small Arms Program.[10]

As of November 2020, SIGMA comprised fifty-one members. (*Disclosure*: I have been a member since 2017.) Members are no longer required to have a doctoral degree in science or engineering or a medical degree, although a professional background in the sciences or engineering is highly valued in the group. Current members include some of science fiction's most popular living authors. Among them are Dr. Catherine Asaro, John Barnes, Dr. Gregory Benford, Alan Dean Foster, Nancy Kress, Dr. Geoffrey A. Landis, Elizabeth Moon, Dr. Larry Niven, Dr. Stanley Schmidt, Bruce Sterling, Steve Sterling, Michael Swanwick, and Walter Jon Williams. Recently deceased authors Dr. Ben Bova and Kathleen Goonan also served.[11] According to the SIGMA Forum website:

> With sufficient notice, SIGMA can provide a panel of distinguished science fiction authors with real-world expertise ranging over physics, astrophysics, nuclear science, advanced weaponry, engineering, nanotechnology, biomedicine, human factors and a common element of practical futurism. Other members can be recruited as needed; a large pool of potential SIGMANs exists within the professional science fiction community. SIGMA members have each committed to consult with Federal authorities for taskings on vital national issues for several days, for travel and lodging expenses only. For extended effort or research, compensation may be based on individual contracts, as appropriate.[12]

Thus, homeland security has already experienced a proof of concept for the involvement of science fiction writers in brainstorming and advisory efforts. The work of SIGMA collectively and that of its members independently should ameliorate any skepticism on the part of homeland security professionals to incorporating science fiction writers, with their vital science fiction mindset, into a devil's toy box analytical venture.

And those writers' participation is vital. Only science fiction writers have rigorously trained themselves both to imagine what may await on the horizon and what looms far beyond the visible horizon and to extrapolate not only the primary impacts of technological changes but also their secondary and tertiary impacts. In 2019 the Mad Scientist team of the U.S. Army's *Small Wars Journal* invited me and other members of SIGMA to participate in its science fiction writing contest. The theme of the contest was the various forms a U.S. conflict with a near-peer competitor might take in 2030.

Rather than writing about robot tanks, stealth drones, cyborg soldiers, and the like, I decided to focus my scenario on a new and very frightening vulnerability our society may choose to subject itself to in the not-very-distant future in the interests of securing the best possible educations and futures for our children. Plausible? Read for yourself.

### Scenario 5: The Supreme Art of War

"Secretary MacKennan, this is what satellite imagery showed as of oh-three-thirty this morning. The Imperial Macedonians are massing their forces on their border with Greater Albania." Acting chairman of the Joint Chiefs of Staff Gen. Lauren Goldwaithe, USAF, aimed her laser pointer at a holographic image that had suddenly appeared in at the front of the conference room.

Secretary of Defense William MacKennan's stomach churned due to both the vertigo induced from the sick-making hologram and the situation's deadly significance. "There's no chance this is just an exercise, a drill?" he asked.

"No, sir. The Macedonian military has always been very up front about announcing their exercises. They made no announcement in this instance. These significant movements of kinetic assets have followed on the heels of repeated cyber degradations of Greater Albanian communications and public utilities, as well as suspected reputational assaults on key Albanian political and business leaders."

*"Suspected reputational assaults,"* MacKennan thought. *Such a bloodless, analytical way to refer to what amounts to social annihilation. That's their specialty, isn't it? The Imperial Macedonian art of war-short-of-war . . .* And hadn't it begun here, too, in America? In Michigan?

He forced himself to look at the satellite imagery the joint chiefs had acquired from Space Command. They displayed the Macedonian formations in two formats—holographic three-dimensional and, at his request, old-fashioned flat screen. They knew he hated the holos. Walking among the seemingly floating Macedonian weaponry, their particle-beam generators mounted on tracked transports and automated armored fighting vehicles, swirled his innards. *But the joint chiefs would feel deprived without their latest toys to play with,* MacKennan told himself. And so the holos filled the conference room like obnoxious poltergeists, his stomach be damned.

He forced himself to focus exclusively on the reassuringly old-school flat-screen display. "What about their space assets?" he asked. "Any provocative movements?"

"They've positioned their Global Devastator satellite in geostationary orbit directly above the Albanian capital."

"I see . . ." His nausea intensified.

"State's phones have been ringing off their hooks with pleas from the Albanians. They want to know what our response will be. They've been citing our treaty obligations chapter and verse, sir."

MacKennan wiped a sheen of sweat from his upper lip. "I'm sure they have . . ."

"Give us the green light, sir, and we can make Global Devastator a nonfactor. We can boost it out of orbit. We can blind it, either kinetically or electronically—"

"That would be an act of war, wouldn't it?"

"Of course it would, sir. I'm merely offering options—"

"That's your job, General. Mine is to ensure the will of the political branches is carried out by you uniformed types. I'll bring your contingency plans to the president's attention."

"When do you anticipate the president will make his decision, sir?"

"Soon," MacKennan said. "But don't expect a decision within the next twenty-four hours. The administration is rather . . . distracted right now. This business in Michigan. I'm sure you're aware of it."

"The Macedonians are behind it, sir," General Goldwaithe said. "They're stirring up political instability to keep us off balance—"

"Do you have *proof* of that, General?" MacKennan said, exasperated almost beyond measure. "Not informed speculation but hard, fast *proof?* Strong enough for us to take to the media and the American people?"

The general fell silent for several seconds. "Uh, . . . no, sir. We don't."

"Well, you'd better damned well call me as soon as you do."

"MR. PRESIDENT, THE MACEDONIAN SITUATION—"

"Not now, MacKennan. Michigan has us twisted up like a fucking pretzel. If we don't manage to unwind some, we'll strangle." President Naddler shoved a rolled-up yoga mat into MacKennan's arms. "Off with the suit jacket, MacKennan. Five minutes of deep stretches for everybody. No exceptions."

MacKennan had gone through this same rigmarole before during multiple meetings with this president. Still, he wouldn't forgive himself if he didn't make his best effort to impress the nation's chief executive with the gravity of the present situation. "Sir, we could be mere hours away from a national security crisis—"

"Sure, *sure! Everything's* a crisis! You want to know a fucking *crisis*, MacKennan?" He stepped close, too close for MacKennan's comfort, and drummed a finger on the defense secretary's chest. "*Michigan.* Michigan is a fucking crisis. You want to know why? Should the governor of Michigan, the lieutenant governor of Michigan, the attorney general of Michigan—hell, at this point we might as well include the fucking *chief dog catcher and head ice cream licker* of Michigan—should those fine, upstanding gentlepersons get referendummed out on their asses, the Populists take over the state. The Populists and their senile, retarded great-uncles, the Balanced Budget Republicans. If those pukes take over Michigan, they'll steamroll the voters, those ignorant cow-fuckers, into referendumming *me*. You may not like riding Air Force One, MacKennan, you with your delicate stomach. *Me?* I fucking *love* riding Air Force One. I want to be riding that sweet bitch for another six and a half years. But if Michigan goes Populist, Gaia forbid, the dominoes will start falling in the Midwest. I could be riding a fucking *electric scooter* six months from now, not Air Force One, puttering between street corners in downtown Santa Barbara, rattling pencils in a tin cup, trying to raise money for my fucking presidential library."

MacKennan slowly sucked in a breath. A lifetime in politics had taught him Zen-like control of his visible emotions. "Mr. President, unless the Imperial Macedonians pull their forces back from the border, the Albanians are going to formally—and very publicly—call upon the United States to fulfill our treaty obligations. That will mean either we go to war with the Macedonian Empire, or we perform a climbdown so humiliating our international reputation will likely never recover. The time to get the Macedonians to back down is *now*, sir. Before this all begins spiraling out of control—"

"Have the Albanians formerly requested treaty assistance yet?"

"No, sir. I believe they want to give us a chance to work behind the scenes before they pull out the diplomatic big guns . . ."

"Well, there you go, MacKennan. We've still got time. And there's *always* time for a good stretch. Jesus, the fucked-up chi in this room! I mean, look at her—my secretary of state's in a *terrible* state. Worsened by your news, I might add. My secretary of transportation looks like she's just been run over by one of those Macedonian robo-tanks. My secretary of health and human services, poor bastard, looks like he's got ulcerative bowel syndrome. So *five minutes of stretching* before we sit down at the conference table! No exceptions, *anyone!*"

THE CABINET MEETING ENDED inconclusively insofar as the Albanian crisis was concerned. MacKennan hadn't expected any different outcome. President Naddler wouldn't do the right thing until events forced his hand. *If even then . . .*

As soon as MacKennan strode into his office, Cynthia Cormorant, his chief of staff, handed him an urgent message. It was from Gerald Throkston, the governor of Michigan.

*Christ, I hope Jerry's holding up.* Throkston was MacKennan's former protégé. A politician he'd pulled up the steep ladder of Michigan politics, rung by rung. A man who looked to him as a father figure, who'd proven to be a more loyal "son" than Franklin, MacKennan's biological offspring, ever had.

MacKennan sealed his office door, then he returned the call. Throkston's face appeared on the screen perched at the edge of

MacKennan's desk. He looked exhausted. Worse than tired, he looked *old*. No longer the matinee idol of Michigan politics, "Merry" Jerry Throkston now appeared as though he'd slept a couple of lost decades on a urine-stained mattress in a slum alleyway, clutching an unending succession of bottles of two-dollar wine.

It hurt MacKennan to see his protégé reduced to this. Hurt him in his soul. "Jerry, my boy, it's Bill. What can I do for you?"

The Michigan governor's lower lip, marred by scabs resulting from compulsive lip chewing, trembled. "He's going to cut me loose, isn't he?" Throkston said. "President Naddler . . . he's going to denounce me, insist the legislature impeach and replace me before I can be referendummed, right? I'm going to be thrown to the ravening wolves, aren't I? *Aren't I?*"

"Jerry, this isn't the place to talk about this—"

"Bill, I have to *know* . . ."

"All right. All right, Jerry. I was thinking about the propriety of it, talking dirt about my boss, the head of my party, here in my office. But proprieties be damned. You're in a hell of a fix."

"When will the guillotine fall?"

"The president . . . he hasn't decided on his course of action yet. He's still considering all options. There's a lot going on at once, Jerry. A whole lot of moving parts. There's this developing Macedonian crisis. The Albanians, our allies—"

"Naddler'll cut them loose, too, won't he?"

"That's a *precipitous* thing to say, Jerry. Didn't I always tell you not to fall prey to snap judgments?"

"You know another thing you always told me? *Character is destiny.* What kind of *character* do we have sitting in the Oval Office, huh? A man who made his money and fame starring in feelies for lovelorn women. Back in the old days, we would've called Naddler a *porn star*. But today, somehow, the man half the country voted for isn't a *porn star*. No, he's a *techno-romance entrepreneur*. The thought of that man, that low-down *sleaze*, standing up in front of America and denouncing *me*—me and Hugh Goldblatt and Samantha Pace—Bill, it makes me want to *puke* . . ."

"I know. I know, Jerry. It's awful. But he's got to think about the fate of the party, of the whole country. If the Populists and Balanced Budget Republicans take over—"

"*Fuck* all that! Fuck *politics*, Bill! There's more at stake here than whose goddamn team comes out on top! The president's got to push back on the Macedonians, Bill. Push back *hard*. Otherwise, this goddamn crap will never stop. The Macedonians and their hackers will destroy whoever they want, anyone whose destruction will help destabilize our country. *Anyone*, Bill. *You*. The *president*. Please tell me the three-letter agencies are on this! The FBI, the CIA, the NSA?"

"They're all working it, working it hard. I can't share details, of course. But the Macedonians, they employ some of the finest hackers on the planet, and they sure as hell know how to cover their tracks."

"You don't . . . you don't know what it's *like*, Bill." Throkston's voice cracked. His face seemed to cave in on itself. "What it's *like* . . . to have your own kids look at you as though you're a *monster*. It's *crazy* . . . I mean, I've never said a racist word my entire *life* . . . In high school, in college, in the legislature, I always tried to be a good ally to people of color . . . But now, *now* I'm some kind of super racist, a Michigan version of George Wallace setting dogs loose on civil rights marchers. I've got crowds picketing the governor's mansion, night and day, chanting for me to be wrapped with chains and tossed into Lake Michigan.

"Janette and I, we can't go anywhere, not even the goddamn *grocery store*, without being hounded by reporters. The worst of it, Bill? My *own daughters* won't share a meal with me, won't even *look me in the eye*. They're the ones who denounced me. Oh, *God*, it's like the old Soviet Union, children ratting out parents, but now it's all super high-tech . . ."

MacKennan said, "I know, Jerry, I know. It's all implanted memories. It's those goddamn knowledge shunts, the so-called boosters. We let doctors inject programmable nanobots into our kids' brains, our grandkids' brains, wanting to give them a step up in life, open them to a world of immediately upgradable knowledge and skills. But what we've really opened them up to is Macedonian hacking . . ."

"You *warned* me, Bill. A decade ago, when my girls were little, you *pleaded* with me not to let them get fitted with boosters . . ."

"And I made the same pleas to my own children regarding their kids. And they still went ahead and fitted them out with boosters anyway. You can't blame yourself, Jerry. Parents . . . parents will do whatever they can to ensure their kids have a leg up in life. They'll expend sweat and treasure and blood trying to give their kids every advantage. It's what we *do* as parents."

"Good intentions." Throkston managed a pained smile. "The road to hell is paved with 'em. I'm getting to know that road pretty well, Bill. All the rest stops, all the damn scenic overlooks . . ."

"I know, Jerry . . ." He was running out of things to say.

Throkston made a visible effort to compose himself. "I'll let you go. I'm sure you've got a lot on your plate, without having to listen to me . . ."

"No, no, it's all right, Jerry. You call me any time." He couldn't help but feel relieved this train wreck of a call was over. "Anytime you feel the need. You're going through hell."

"I just hope you never have to experience this, Bill. I hope you never learn what it's like to have your loved ones shun you . . ."

"You hang in there, Jerry."

"Oh, I'll be hanging . . ." Throkston cut the connection.

DID I DO THE *wrong thing? Bringing Jerry up in politics the way I did? Did I doom him to this personal demolition the day I first stoked his ambitions?*

MacKennan stared out the security glass rear windows of his chauffeured Suburban. The trees of Alexandria had recently been stripped of their autumn plumage by an early season ice storm. His familiar surroundings seemed changed, somehow darkened, as though a malevolent enchantment had taken hold of the town while he'd been at work in Washington.

He was glad he wasn't driving alone. Strictly speaking, Don Nogami, his chauffeur, wasn't necessary—the electric Suburban could drive itself—but the uniformed man up front served the twins needs of tradition and security. By the standards of the day, Nogami was a perfectly solid young man—a former U.S. Army Ranger, spawned from a long line of patriots going all the way back to the Nisei regiment of World War II—yet even he couldn't resist flashy trends. The Suburban's front compartment bathed in a glow that didn't issue from the vehicle's touch screens. Instead, it seeped from the cuffs and collar of Nogami's uniform jacket.

"Don?"

"Yes, sir?"

"How long have you had your nano tattoos? If you don't mind my asking."

"Not at all, sir. I got them right after high school graduation. An army recruiter told me Colt's Manufacturing was looking to sponsor young men in the armed forces."

"You mean the gun manufacturer?"

"That's right."

"And the army—back then, they didn't have a problem inducting recruits covered in bioluminescent tattoos? What about the visibility issue on the battlefield?"

"Well, y'know, sir, most soldiers nowadays don't set foot on any battlefields. They send mechs to do the fighting for them. And if you're a member of special forces, like I was, you use camo paint to cover up your tats. It's not a problem. Just about everybody in my platoon had them. I remember this one guy who got himself sponsored by Disney. Most of the time, he was covered in really macho art, martial stuff. But three times daily, at noon, seventeen hundred hours, and twenty-one hundred hours, the Disney bots took him over, and for twenty minutes he lit up with the Little Mermaid and Dumbo. Funniest damn thing."

*Lack of standards. Disgraceful. Lord knows, I've wrestled with that issue plenty during my eighteen months as secretary of defense. And gotten precious little support from the joint chiefs. "We can't afford to alienate the recruits." "If we try to fight the civilian culture, we lose, and we'll never make our numbers." "Maintaining morale is more important than maintaining traditions." It's all of a piece, this lack of firmness, this giving in to the whims of the mob. All those amendments to the Constitution over the past decade . . . direct democracy, national referenda, instant recall elections. No more electoral college. Forget extended debate, giving important issues time to congeal, passions time to simmer and cool. Everything turns on a dime now. One minute you're a messiah, the next you're a goat . . .*

*No, I can't blame myself for ruining Jerry Throkston's life. We lived in a different world, we both did, when he first walked into my office as a college intern. Crazy as the world seemed back then, in retrospect, it was a far saner place. I couldn't have known what was to come.*

"Don, are you up for a little stroll? The missus and I are supposed to meet our grandchildren at a pizza parlor on King Street in forty-five minutes. I think a nice walk might help my constitution. Would you mind accompanying Nan and me? It's only about half a mile's walk."

"No problem, sir. I'll just wait in the car until you and your wife are ready. I've got some paperwork to fill out."

"You're sure you wouldn't rather do it in the house?"

"That's all right. Thanks, though. My secure comms link works best from the vehicle."

They parked on a quiet street of colonial revival houses. MacKennan walked up to the front door, unlocked it, and entered his parlor. "Nan? Are you getting ready? We're supposed to meet Bradley and Christina for pizza."

No answer.

"Nan?"

*Well, maybe she walked over to the neighborhood store for something. A carton of milk, perhaps.*

He could use a glass of milk. Something to counteract the acid seething in his stomach. He found no milk in the refrigerator. He settled for a pair of Tums tablets. Best he should skip the spicy toppings tonight.

It wasn't just the Macedonian situation or the bad aftertaste of that fiasco of a cabinet meeting or his pained conversation with Jerry Throkston. Rather, it was *all* those things, plus the edgy anticipation of his having to sit at the same table as his son, Franklin, tonight. Having to pretend to be sociable and pleasant for his grandkids' sake.

Franklin hadn't gotten himself inked with nano tattoos as his form of rebellion. No, that wouldn't have been nearly outrageous enough. Instead, he'd joined the Young Populists League in college. Oh, had that led to salacious backstage whispering in Lansing and Washington! A source of continuous embarrassment for MacKennan, then the junior Democratic-Communitarian senator representing Michigan and former head of the state assembly. MacKennan had hoped Populism would be a distasteful stage that Franklin would pass through once rebellion against patriarchal authority had lost its luster, once he'd realized his father, far from being an omnipotent ogre, was just an ordinary man with good intentions who'd always striven to do the best he could. Yet Franklin had only doubled down on his rebellion. After graduation, he'd gone to work for the People's Heritage Foundation as a policy researcher, then climbed through the ranks of Populist political magazines to become a leading pundit.

MacKennan and Nan had tried mightily not to allow political disputes to color their relationship with their son and his young family, but Franklin hadn't obliged them. The headstrong fool had used MacKennan's two grandchildren as a weapon in the family's civil war. Until very recently, MacKennan and Nan hadn't seen their twin grandchildren, Bradley and Christina, in nearly three years. Precious years lost to needless enmity. Nan had worked assiduously behind the scenes with Franklin's wife, Natalia, to regain access to the children. Her efforts met with success, finally. But the children's tenth, eleventh, and twelfth years, years that could have been filled with boat trips on the Potomac and afternoons flying kites on the National Mall, were forever lost to MacKennan.

*Useless to dwell on what's been denied you, what you can never regain,* he told himself as he climbed the stairs to his bedroom. *Concentrate on what you have now, what you have to look forward to.*

He headed for his closet to put away his suit and change into casual clothes. Passing the shut bathroom door, he heard soft weeping from inside.

"Nan?"

He opened the door. He found his wife slumped on the bath mat, her shoulders convulsing with sobs.

"*Nan?* What's happened? What's wrong, honey?"

He knelt down next to her and tried embracing her. She squirmed away from him.

The word crawled out of her throat. "*Horrible . . .*"

"What is it? What's horrible?"

"What . . . what they told me you *did* to them . . ."

MacKennan felt an iciness on the back of his neck. His throat went dry. "Who told you this, Nan? What did they say?"

"The *children . . .*"

"You mean Bradley and Christina?"

"They said . . . they told me you *violated* them . . . *repeatedly . . .* when they were hardly more than *babies . . .*"

His mind flashed red. *Franklin orchestrated this.*

That abominable suspicion lasted only an instant before logic's harsh light dispelled it. *No, even if he could stoop that low, he couldn't force them to lie so despicably to their grandmother. They aren't robots that he can program to do his bidding . . .*

Then he knew. The boosters. The same implants that had enabled Bradley to master advanced calculus and Christina to effortlessly recall the notes of the entire classical piano repertoire . . .

His grandchildren had been hacked by the Macedonians or by their confederates. They'd implanted false memories in their brains. He was being targeted the same way Jerry Throkston and other leaders in Michigan had been targeted.

He took hold of his wife's shoulders and forced her to face him. "Nan, this isn't *real*. It's the work of foreign enemies. How can you *believe* I'd do such a thing? An enemy country wants to start a war with one of our allies, and they don't want us to intervene. So they're destroying the reputations and lives of our leaders, one by one, remotely. They've infiltrated our grandchildren's minds through those goddamn boosters Franklin had them implanted with. They've corrupted their memories—"

She pulled herself away again. "That's just what Franklin *insisted* you'd say . . ."

"I'm going over there."

Her tear-reddened eyes grew wide. "Bill, *don't*. He doesn't want you anywhere near the children. He'll call the *police*—"

"He can call the FBI and the military and the goddamn Harlem Globetrotters, if he wants. I'm going."

HE RANG HIS SON'S doorbell repeatedly. No response. Franklin was home; his car sat in the driveway. MacKennan could feel the tiny cameras of the house's security system eyeing him. He pounded the door with his fist, yelling into the intercom. "Franklin! I *insist* that you speak with me! I'm not leaving this porch until you let me in!"

Finally, the door opened. Franklin quickly stepped out onto the porch, locking the door behind him. "I won't have you causing a scene," he said coldly. "You've got ten seconds to get back in your car before I call 911."

"Franklin, I've got to talk with the children—"

"No way. They're *terrified*. They don't want to ever see you again."

"Franklin, what they're thinking and feeling, it's not *real*. It's the Macedonians, their hackers. Maybe Macedonian sympathizers here in our country. Look, the Macedonians are on the verge of invading Albania. They don't want the United States to intervene, so they're warning us off by destroying the reputations of key leaders. Hackers have infiltrated the children's minds through the boosters—"

"Always with the boosters, huh? You didn't think I was smart enough to make that decision for my children. So these are *fake* memories, are they? Let me tell you, it's not just Bradley's and Christina's claims, Dad. Half a dozen of their friends back them up. They've come forward, told their school counselors that either Bradley or Christina talked about your abuse. Told them about it *years ago*, while it was going on."

"They've been hacked, too, don't you see?"

"Oh, yeah—*all* of them, right? Hell, the Macedonians hacked the *whole school*, didn't they? Just to get at *you*? Jesus Christ, I always knew you had an inflated ego—"

"It's not *ego*, Franklin—I'm the goddamn *secretary of defense*. Of *course* they'd go to these lengths. Why else would the children be making these accusations *now*, when the Imperial Macedonian Army is massing on the Albanian border?"

"Repressed memories. You've been on the news a lot lately, Dad, with that iron-toned voice of yours. Maybe it's the same tone you used when . . . when you ordered them to submit to you, out at the lake house. The kids have seen you on their devices. They knew they'd be having dinner with you tonight. It triggered repressed memories."

"'Repressed memories' are a load of pop psychology *horseshit*, and you know it!"

Franklin's face took on a haunted look. "No, they're not."

"How would you know? You've never even studied psychology!"

"I know from *personal experience*, Dad. The kids, they aren't the only ones who've had unbearable memories surface. You've been a sex criminal and a pedophile for a *long time*. Do you remember needle-nose pliers? What you *did* with them? I've had an aversion to them for years. Until a day ago, I never knew why. You're *scum*. The worst scum in the world. And once my column appears tomorrow, the whole world will know you the way I do. Now get the fuck off my porch."

MacKennan realized then what his son had never told him. The insight squeezed all hope from his chest. "My God . . . you got *yourself* boosted, too . . ."

"YOU'VE BECOME A LIABILITY, Bill. You've got to see that. It's clear as a fucking bell."

"Mr. President, I am the victim of a precisely targeted character assassination. You and every man and woman in this room know that."

"Yeah, well, maybe so. But I've still gotta ask for your resignation. You aren't going to drag the rest of this administration down with you, Bill. It's not right that one drowning man flips over the lifeboat and causes everybody else to drown." President Naddler scanned the faces of his department heads, arrayed around the long conference table. "Aren't I right?"

MacKennan did his best to ignore the mumbled affirmations. "I'm *not* handing in my resignation. If you want me gone, you'll have to fire me. And I doubt you want to do that in the midst of an international crisis. I insist that we address the Macedonian situation, right now. The Albanian ambassador called me personally. He says the secretary of state hasn't been returning his urgent calls."

Secretary of State Zegatsky cleared his throat, then straightened his tie. "That's not *precisely* true . . ."

"The Albanians have officially requested military and diplomatic support due to them under authority of treaty. All power to the Albanian capital and their five largest cities was cut off this morning, forty-five minutes before the Macedonians crossed the border. This aggression cannot be ignored. How are we going to respond, Mr. President?"

All eyes turned to the president. He squeezed his left hand with his right, cracking his knuckles. "The Albanians are on their own."

"Mr. President, our treaty obligations—"

"I've had my people look very closely at that," Secretary Zegatsky interjected. "There are loopholes. Off-ramps. Our obligations are nullified in cases where the Albanians incited foreign aggression through aggressive acts of their own."

"Just this last week, there were bomb attacks in the Macedonian capital, a bunch of them," President Naddler said. "The Macedonians claim it was the Albanians or Albanian sympathizers."

"Mr. President," MacKennan said indignantly, "that's just Macedonian propaganda! *Misinformation!* They're *experts* at that! Have our own intelligence services verified the Macedonians' claims?"

"It's not in our interest to go to war against Macedonia or even to threaten to go to war," President Naddler said. "Look, Bill, the Albanians aren't innocent. They made their bed, and now they can lie in it. Secretary Zegatsky says we've got a diplomatic off-ramp, and I agree. Putting American lives at risk for Greater Albania isn't something I'm willing to sanction. I'm sure the American public will back me on this."

"*Which* American lives are at risk? The lives of our soldiers, sailors, and aviators? Or the comfortable lives of those of us *here in this room*?" MacKennan stared at the faces of his peers around the table—sheepish, embarrassed expressions, every one of them. "I'll tell you what I think. I think you're all *terrified*. Terrified that what's been done to me and to Jerry Throkston and the others in Michigan will happen to you next. You're willing to sell out America's international standing so you won't risk having your children and grandchildren and the fashionistas in Georgetown shun you like you're some abomination. If we cut the Albanians loose, America's credibility on the international stage is shot for a generation. In your hearts, each of you must recognize that."

He plunged ahead, heedless of the personal consequences. "Mr. President, the rest of you, I'm going to give you all a chance do the right thing. I'll give this administration until zero eight hundred hours tomorrow to declare through diplomatic and public channels that we're backing the Albanians and fulfilling our treaty obligations. Otherwise, I'm taking my story to the media. I'm explaining to every major outlet how personal moral *cowardice* is warping American foreign policy in a time of international crisis. I'm going to share our intelligence estimates that indicate the Macedonians have been manipulating our political processes and inflaming political passions through targeted memory hacking—"

"Revealing intelligence sources and methods is a federal crime," Attorney General Monique Legrande said. "Don't do it, Bill. I'll be forced to bring you up on charges. Serious charges that could put you away for life."

"My life is already over," MacKennan said, rising decisively from his seat. "All I have left are my honor and my country."

MACKENNAN SAW NO REASON to go home. No wife or other family awaited him. He had a couch here at his satellite office suite in the Eisenhower Executive Office Building. He could catch a few hours of sleep on it between sessions of monitoring international news feeds.

He glanced out his sixth-story window. Rows of street lamps along Pennsylvania Avenue revealed a cordon of protesters. *How many of them were actually Macedonian agents of influence?* He wondered whether other protesters surrounded his home. At least Nan wouldn't be subjected to that. She'd left him a message that she and Franklin's family had fled the area. And that he shouldn't try to locate them.

Even if every street lamp on Pennsylvania Avenue lost power, the protesters' messages would still shine through the darkness. Most wore transparent outerwear, so that even on a night as chilly as tonight, their nano-tattooed messages would glow forth.

*Pedophilia has no place in the Democratic-Communitarian Party.*

*William MacKennan—Secretary of* OFFENSE.

NO WAR/NO BABY FUCKERS.

He could read the slogans from up here. Camera crews surrounded the protesters. Cameras from all over the world.

He stepped out to use the bathroom down the hall. The old building's long hallways stood empty, dimly lit by after-hours ceiling fixtures. *As dim and deserted as my life has become.*

He stood over a sink and splashed handful after handful of cold water on his face. Zero eight hundred hours was just six hours away. He truly doubted Naddler would find his spine. So MacKennan would be forced to betray his country in a small way—to redeem it, he hoped, in a far more profound way.

He stared at himself in the bathroom mirror. He'd aged at least a decade and a half in the last few days. And the Macedonians and their agents hadn't needed to physically touch him.

He'd read Sun Tzu as part of his preparation for becoming the secretary of defense. Now the Chinese philosopher's immortal aphorisms glowed like beacons in his mind.

*One need not destroy one's enemy. One need only destroy his willingness to engage.*

*The supreme art of war is to subdue the enemy without fighting.*

In the mirror, he saw a stall door behind him swing open. He hadn't noticed any shoes resting on the floor of the stalls when he'd entered.

Don Nogami silently exited the stall. He held an automatic pistol, its barrel lengthened by a silencer.

"I assume you've been ordered to make this look like suicide," MacKennan said, not turning around.

His former driver wasn't wearing a shirt, only an unzipped black windbreaker that exposed his chest and its transitory tattoo. The last thing MacKennan ever did was to decipher the backward message in the mirror.

...YRROS M'I

# SEVEN

## The Promethean Spyglass

*Doing a Devil's Toy Box Analysis Right*

WE'VE REACHED THE BOOK'S CAPSTONE! In this chapter, I
describe my recommended method for carrying out a devil's toy
box analysis. I call it the Promethean Spyglass, and it is based on
seventy years' worth of best practices from the fields of expert analysis,
futurism, and forecasting (described in chapter 5). But first, I need to
set forth the assumptions on which I base my chosen methodology,
as someone beginning from a different set of assumptions than mine
would produce a different set of blueprints. So here we go!

*Assumption 1*: Intelligence of the enemies' intentions can never
be complete. Defensive measures can never be made infallible. The
homeland's defenders will not be able to prevent every attack. Despite
the defenders' best efforts, their antagonists will still be able to achieve
surprise sometimes. In an environment of limited resources and
capabilities, the best the homeland security enterprise can hope to
achieve is to deter those attacks with the most onerous consequences
or to mitigate the effects of those attacks if they cannot be deterred
or countered.

*Assumption 2*: The purpose of a devil's toy box analysis is not to
predict which over-the-horizon malign technologies will be used
to harm the United States or when. That's the job of intelligence
agencies. Rather, the role of the Promethean Spyglass is to help
homeland security leaders decide which doorways to destruction
most urgently need to be closed. Not all such doorways can be
slammed shut simultaneously. Choices need to be made.

In other forecasting arenas, "success" is defined as forecasters seeing
a high percentage of what they predicted actually come to pass. For

a devil's toy box analysis, however, seeing forecasted developments become actualized represents *failure*.

*Assumption 3*: Most, but not all, groups and individuals who seek to harm the United States are rational actors. On the one hand, they are more dangerous than irrational actors because they are more capable of teamwork, extensive planning, and maintaining operational security and secrecy. On the other hand, *rational actors are capable of being deterred.* The threat of incarceration or death may not deter the most committed; however, a high likelihood of failure to achieve their goal will tend to either redirect them toward a different strike modality or make them wait until a more fortuitous time to attack.

Irrational actors are far less deterrable, if they are deterrable at all. However, since they exhibit less self-control and higher impulsivity, they are far more likely than rational actors to trip themselves up by boasting of their intentions to friends, relatives, or anonymous crowds on the internet. Being less likely than rational actors to extensively plan, they are also less likely to seek and use innovative, future-shock attack modes and will usually pursue imitative attacks using conventional weapons.

*Assumption 4*: The members of a devil's toy box analytical team and the universe of malign actors will have a dynamic, interactive relationship; that is, the actions of one group will influence the decisions and actions of the other. Efforts made by a devil's toy box analytical team to promulgate defensive measures against a particular Promethean threat modality will result in a reactive shift by potential attackers away from that attack mode and to a different modality that is less well defended. Forecasts made by a devil's toy box analytical team will tend to have a self-denying prophecy effect.

For such deterrence to work, antagonists must be aware of the defenders' efforts, of course. To quote Peter Sellers's confounded Dr. Strangelove (in the classic dark comedy *Dr. Strangelove, or: How I Learned to Stop Worrying and Love the Bomb*) when the Soviet ambassador informs him that by mistakenly dropping an atomic bomb on Russian territory, an American bomber crew will automatically trigger a hitherto secret doomsday device: "Of course, the whole point of a Doomsday Machine is lost if you *keep* it a *secret!*"[1]

Members of a devil's toy box analysis team will want potential antagonists to at least *believe* that effective countermeasures are being developed to negate dangerous Promethean technologies. General, nontechnical information about the government's R&D efforts should be widely disseminated. To do otherwise would be to ignore Dr. Strangelove's wise counsel.

### Overview of the Promethean Spyglass Procedure

If the constraints assumed in the explanatory example outlined in this chapter are adhered to—thirty core team members assemble; conduct an environmental scan that surfaces thirty emerging, over-the-horizon Promethean technologies with malign potential; and initially brainstorm 180 scenario stubs and winnow them to a "deadly dozen" scenarios—the Promethean Spyglass procedure takes approximately six months. For participants, a face-to-face portion of three to four weeks is sandwiched between two distance portions, with the first taking eight weeks and the second taking fourteen weeks. Participants and facilitators, working together, are engaged for seventeen to eighteen weeks, and the facilitators work on their own for an additional eight weeks. During the two distance portions, participants work on a part-time basis from their homes or normal work locations, with their daily inputs likely taking between forty-five minutes and an hour.

I assume that the Promethean Spyglass procedure is used to support an annual R&D project selection cycle. Given the time required for the procedure, the sponsoring organization would likely choose to perform the Promethean Spyglass every two years, initiating the R&D projects for half of the participants' selected deadly dozen scenarios in the first year and the R&D projects for the remaining half in the second year.

## Table 2. Phases, steps, and duration of a Promethean Spyglass analytical procedure

| Phase | Step | Planned duration | Distance or face-to-face portion? | Sequential or concurrent? |
|---|---|---|---|---|
| Phase 1: Environmental scanning | 1 | Two weeks | First distance | Sequential |
| Phase 2: Assemble the team | 1—Recruit team members | Four weeks | First distance | Sequential |
| | 2—Administer a forecasting pretest | One day | First distance | Sequential |
| Phase 3: Brainstorm scenarios | 1—Push out the results of environmental scanning | One day | First distance | Concurrent with step 2 |
| | 2—Distribute questions to promote brainstorming | Two weeks | First distance | Concurrent with steps 1 and 3 |
| | 3—Train the science fiction writer members of the team in small group processes and optimally facilitating small group interactions | Half day (four hours) | Face-to-face | Concurrent with step 2 |
| | 4—Bring the participants together for the face-to-face portion of the analysis and emphasize personal accountability and the importance of the mission | Half day | Face-to-face | Sequential |

| | | | | |
|---|---|---|---|---|
| | 5—Apply convergent thinking to the scenario stubs | Half day | Face-to-face | Sequential |
| Phase 4: Red team the scenario stubs | 1—Introduce the concept of red teaming to the full group and provide training on avoiding cognitive biases | Half day | Face-to-face | Sequential |
| | 2—Randomly divide the full team into groups of four | Ten minutes (repeated at the beginning of each workday spent in phase 4) | Face-to-face | Sequential (facilitators assist eight teams concurrently) |
| | 3—Randomly assign a scenario stub to each group to red team; designate each group a red-teaming method to use | Twenty minutes (repeated at the beginning of each workday spent in phase 4) | Face-to-face | Sequential (facilitators assist eight teams concurrently) |
| | 4—Red team each scenario stub, then present results to the entire team and allow for questions | Three to four days | Face-to-face | Sequential |
| Phase 5: Rank the scenario stubs | 1—Facilitators provide participants with a list of scenario stubs | Five minutes | Face-to-face | Sequential |

| | | | |
|---|---|---|---|
| 2—Participants rate each scenario stub regarding the severity of its potential consequences | 2.5 to 3.75 days (twenty to thirty hours; forty minutes per scenario stub; each half team responsible for thirty to forty-five stubs) | Face-to-face | Sequential |
| 3—Participants receive refresher training in the laws of probability and how to calculate probabilities | Three hours | Face-to-face | Sequential |
| 4—Participants rate each scenario stub regarding the likelihood of its becoming actualized | Four to six days (rating each stub takes 1.75 hours; each half team can rate four stubs per workday; each half team responsible for thirty to forty-five stubs) | Face-to-face | Sequential |
| 5—Facilitators calculate the estimated risk levels for each scenario stub | Thirty minutes | Face-to-face | Sequential |
| 6—Facilitators finalize determination of the deadly dozen scenarios | Two hours | Face-to-face | Sequential |

| | | | | |
|---|---|---|---|---|
| Phase 6: Flesh out the deadly dozen scenarios | 1—Divide the full team into scenario expansion sub-teams | Ten minutes | Face-to-face | Sequential |
| | 2—Select the three key axes of driving environmental forces most significant to facilitating malign uses of the scenario's Promethean technology | Two hours (process takes one hour per scenario; six teams perform this step for two scenarios apiece) | Face-to-face | Sequential (however, six teams are working concurrently, evaluating two scenarios apiece) |
| | 3—Apply "through the terrorist's eyes" exercise to the scenario | Two hours (process takes one hour per scenario; six teams perform this step for two scenarios apiece) | Face-to-face | Sequential (however, six teams are working concurrently, evaluating two scenarios apiece) |
| | 4—Brainstorm precursors | Two hours (process takes one hour per scenario; six teams perform this step for two scenarios apiece) | Face-to-face | Sequential (however, six teams are working concurrently, evaluating two scenarios apiece) |
| | 5—Apply strengths, weaknesses, opportunities, and threats (SWOT) analysis to the scenario | Two hours (process takes one hour per scenario; six teams perform this step for two scenarios apiece) | Face-to-face | Sequential (however, six teams are working concurrently, evaluating two scenarios apiece) |

| 6—Apply measure-countermeasure, move-countermove exercise to the scenario | Two hours (process takes one hour per scenario; six teams perform this step for two scenarios apiece) | Face-to-face | Sequential (however, six teams are working concurrently, evaluating two scenarios apiece) |
| --- | --- | --- | --- |
| 7—Sub-teams present their scenarios to the full group for feedback and critique | Twelve hours, or 1.5 days (process takes one hour per scenario) | Face-to-face | Sequential |
| 8—Sub-teams reconvene to decide whether to adjust their scenarios in response to the full group's feedback | Two to three hours (between an hour and ninety minutes per scenario, with each sub-team assessing two scenarios) | Face-to-face | Sequential (however, six teams are working concurrently, evaluating two scenarios apiece) |
| 9—Lead scenario writers prepare fifteen-to-twenty-page scenario narratives with one-page executive summaries | One week | Second distance | Sequential (however, six sub-team leads are working concurrently, writing up two scenarios apiece) |

| Phase 7: Rank the deadly dozen scenarios | 1—Apply Technology Sequence Analysis to estimate the likelihoods of the Promethean technologies reaching market within a five-to-ten-year window | Eight to ten weeks | Second distance | Concurrent with phase 6, step 9; and with phase 7, steps 2 and 3 |
|---|---|---|---|---|
| | 2—Participants estimate the severity of the potential consequences for each of the deadly dozen scenarios | Twelve days (about 2.5 weeks) | Second distance | Sequential (but concurrent with phase 7, step 1) |
| | 3—Participants determine consensus values for each of the six probability factors that influence the likelihoods of the come-to-market Promethean technologies being used for malign purposes | Forty-two days (about 8.5 weeks) | Second distance | Sequential (but concurrent with phase 7, step 1) |
| | 4—Facilitators calculate estimated risk levels for each of the deadly dozen scenarios and rank them in descending order of risk | One hour | Second distance | Sequential |

| 5—Facilitators prepare a Promethean Spyglass analytical report including scenario narratives, in ranked order of descending estimated risk, of the deadly dozen scenarios | Two weeks | Second distance | Sequential |

## Phase 1: Environmental Scanning

Recent advancements in machine learning and big data analysis have made the process of environmental scanning for emerging, over-the-horizon technologies far more efficient and comprehensive than before. I've already mentioned the Intelligence Advanced Research Project Agency's FUSE Program. At least one commercial firm has developed a comparable product—Quid, a software platform developed specifically to facilitate technology scouting by government agencies.

> Quid is a platform that searches, analyzes and visualizes the world's collective intelligence to help answer strategic questions. Quid is a web-based platform that leverages proprietary algorithms to read millions of text-based documents for fast insight by visualizing relationships in the underlying language. . . . The platform can analyze public and private company data, news and blog articles, patent data, academic research as well as myriad custom text-based datasets. . . . Government stakeholders utilize Quid to identify near (6–12 months), medium range (1–5 years), and extended (5–10 years) technology scouting trends.[2]

Promethean Spyglass facilitators would be wise not to rely entirely on FUSE, Quid, or a comparable platform for establishing the universe of emerging Promethean technologies. Although the ability of these tools to mine news and blog articles, company data, worldwide patents, and academic papers at scale eclipse any human team's ability to examine and sift through such gargantuan amounts of material, human specialists in various technical fields may be aware of embryonic developments that have not yet surfaced in patent applications, academic papers, or companies' R&D reports.

The commercial firm Recorded Future facilitates data mining from dark web sources to scout for emerging behaviors of criminal, terror, and extremist groups. The company's website states, "Recorded Future arms threat analysts, security operators, and incident responders to rapidly connect the dots and reveal unknown threats. Our patented technology automatically collects and analyzes threat intelligence from technical, open, and dark web sources to provide invaluable context for faster human analysis."[3] The firm employs its own team of intelligence analysts who continuously locate new onion sites on the dark web. These analysts develop data dictionaries that allow clients to develop their own customized searches.[4] Promethean Spyglass facilitators would do well to work with Recorded Future's analysts (or their counterparts at a competing firm) to determine whether terror groups, extremist groups, criminal organizations, or lone wolves are already fixating on and brainstorming future uses of emerging technologies.

### Phase 2: Assemble the Team

*Step 1—Recruit Team Members*: Based on the results of their environmental scanning efforts, Promethean Spyglass facilitators should seek to recruit technical experts and researchers who have collectively worked within all the fields covering the identified emerging Promethean technologies. Based on best practices from Delphi procedures, nominal group technique procedures, and wisdom of the crowd techniques, I recommend assembling a team of twenty-five to forty participants. The same environmental scanning procedures that surfaced over-the-horizon technologies should also provide lists of researchers and technologists who have applied for applicable patents, as well as academics who have published papers in relevant fields of interest.

To ensure institutional support from their sponsoring organization, the facilitators should recruit representatives from upper management, or homeland security institutional insiders. Their inclusion will greatly facilitate the later "selling" of the analytical effort and its resulting recommended R&D projects to the powers that be. Terror group analysts should also be included, as the environmental scanning phase may have indicated certain types of groups are growing in prominence and are expressing interest in pursuing technically innovative modes of attack.

Very importantly, Promethean Spyglass facilitators need to acquire the science fiction mindset by recruiting writers of hard SF. SIGMA, the science fiction think tank, can recommend participants from its own membership or the broader science fiction writing community. Science fiction writer members of the team will serve as the lead scenario writers. Each scenario writing sub-team will consist of a scenario lead (a science fiction writer), between one and three technical experts (depending on how many emerging technologies are considered in the scenario), and at least one nontechnical expert, either a terror group expert or an institutional homeland security insider.

Since the Promethean Spyglass procedure will encompass both a face-to-face portion that will make use of the modified nominal group technique and two remote portions that will implement Delphi procedures, a reasonable rule of thumb would be to aim for a team size of twenty-five to forty members.

*Step 2—Administer a Forecasting Pretest*: Once the members of the team have been recruited, but prior to their physically being brought together, members should take a forecasting skills pretest. The results from this pretest will be used to weigh individual responses during the latter remote portions of the analysis (the assignation of estimated consequence and probability scores to the deadly dozen scenarios, which will be based on the consensus Delphi panels). Some researchers suggest that a prior history of just five forecasts is needed to establish a performance history to use as a differentiator.[5] Other researchers state that a forecasting pretest of twenty to twenty-five forecasts is necessary to establish a performance differentiator.[6] I

**Table 3. Makeup of a Promethean Spyglass analytical team**

| | |
|---|---|
| Overall team size: twenty-five to forty members (may be expanded during the remote Delphi portion) | |
| Technical experts | 50–60 percent (this portion may be expanded during the remote Delphi portion if the initial team did not adequately cover all the areas of technical subject matter expertise indicated by the environmental scanning phase) |
| Science fiction writers | 20–25 percent |
| Mix of terror group analysts and homeland security insiders | 20–25 percent |

recommend that facilitators split the difference and assign a pretest of twelve to fifteen forecasts.

All forecasting tests should concern events that will be actualized prior to the latter remote portions of the Promethean Spyglass, when the facilitators will be required to assign weights to the individual members' assignation of estimated consequence and probability scores to the deadly dozen scenarios. To do this, facilitators will need to calculate Brier scores indicating comparative levels of accuracy in forecasting for each team member (see an explanation of how to calculate a Brier score in phase 7, step 2). The pretest may consist of questions regarding any event that will become actualized within the required time and that can be predictively responded to with a "yes" or a "no." Participants will be asked to indicate how confident they are in their answers by stating what percent chance there is that their answers are correct.

Here are some examples. For each question, the respondents would respond yes or no and offer a statement: "There is an X percent chance this answer will prove correct."

"Will Candidate X achieve the nomination of Party Y for the upcoming Iowa gubernatorial election?"

"Will the closing Dow Jones Industrial Average equal or exceed twenty-five thousand points on date xx-xx-xxxx?"

"Will General Motors sell more than four thousand Chevrolet Suburbans during the month of xx-xxxx?"

"Will the opening weekend theatrical gross ticket sales of soon-to-be-released film *Revenge of the Fast and Furious Jedi* exceed $80 million?"

Prior to administering the pretest, facilitators should share written, audio, or video links to brief training sessions for team members on these topics: reducing overconfidence in their predictions, self-calibrating their predictions, avoiding common cognitive biases, and using Bayesian statistical methods (starting with a hypothesis of probability and updating it as new data becomes available, allowing for the continuous refinement of forecasts).[7] They should follow up with instructional materials on the laws of probability, including compound and contingent probabilities.[8]

### Phase 3: Brainstorm Scenarios

Phase 3 is split between the initial remote portion of the analysis and the middle, face-to-face portion. This allows team members to benefit from the best features of both the nominal group technique and the Delphi technique. Researchers of small group dynamics and group decision-making processes have found that individual work is better suited to certain phases of the brainstorming process, and group interaction is better suited to other phases. Individual work is preferable during the initial phases of the problem-solving process—idea generation, identification of problems, and elicitation of facts—whereas face-to-face discussion is better in the latter portions, which are spent promoting the improved evaluation, screening, and synthesizing of ideas already generated.[9]

*Step 1—Push Out the Results of Environmental Scanning*: Facilitators should share the reports generated by the environmental scanning activities with team members (summarization may prove necessary). Some participants may have specialized knowledge to add and should be encouraged to share their knowledge of embryonic developments that have not yet surfaced in public or semipublic sources.

*Step 2—Distribute Questions to Promote Brainstorming*: At this stage, the objective is not to solicit fully developed scenarios from participants regarding the dangers of emerging technologies. At this stage, divergent thinking needs to be encouraged. Facilitators should instruct team members to provide "stub" scenarios, or brief, one-paragraph descriptions of potential outcomes that would result from the dispersion, adoption, and potentially malign use of the technologies. They should encourage participants to brainstorm at least four stub scenarios that could play out of each of the identified technologies (or combinations of them). Half of the stub scenarios should be ones that are judged to be of high-likelihood and high-probability, and half should be ones that are considered wild card, black swan, low-likelihood, and high-impact scenarios.[10]

The numbers can quickly grow daunting, so facilitators should avoid overwhelming the analytical effort with too many scenario stubs. If the team consists of thirty members, the environmental scanning process identifies ten strands of technological development with malign Promethean potential, and each participant is encouraged to provide at least four scenario stubs for each technology, then this would result in a minimum of 1,200 scenario stubs! To avoid creating overwhelming numbers of scenarios, facilitators should distribute the identified emerging technologies among the participants so that each team member has at least one from which to create a minimum of four scenario stubs. Facilitators should strive, as best as possible, to match the identified emerging technologies with the technical experts in those fields. Emerging technologies may be randomly distributed to the remaining team members.

Since this stage of the analysis emphasizes divergent thinking, the facilitators do not want to inadvertently foreclose the development of divergent scenarios by limiting participation. All participants should be supplied with the full list of emerging technologies with Promethean implications. They should be instructed that although they are primarily responsible for generating scenario stubs only for the technology assigned to them, they are free to volunteer scenario stubs for other technologies on the list as well if they choose. This will allow flexibility without swelling the number of scenario stubs beyond reason. If the team consists of thirty members, the number of identified emerging technologies is also thirty, and each participant generates four scenarios for one assigned technology, plus half the team members (fifteen) opt to generate four scenarios for one additional technology on the list, the team will be responsible for sorting and evaluating a total of 180 scenario stubs. While still a large number, it is much more manageable than 1,200!

Facilitators should provide questions to participants to assist with their brainstorming. These questions are not for participants to answer and submit; rather, they are meant to prompt creative thinking and the use of their imaginations. The participants should be advised to put critical thinking aside for the moment, although they will be called upon to use that skill in later phases.

The Evil Genius questions listed in chapter 4 provide a good starting place to jump-start creative thinking (see table 1). Team members should be encouraged to think through the questions from the vantage points of the three categories of malefactors identified in the Defense Threat Reduction Agency's *Thwarting an Evil Genius* study—jihadists, nihilists, and thrill seekers—as well as the categories of left-wing terrorists, right-wing terrorists, and adherents of apocalyptic cults.

Additionally, the facilitators should distribute the following variant of the "science fiction mindset" questions from chapter 6:

What trends currently exist in science and technology and in societal adjustments to science and technology? What would happen if those trends were extrapolated into the future and greatly exaggerated?

What are the possible social, political, cultural, religious, and psychological impacts of these trends and developments? What possible impacts could these trends and developments have on behaviors, on health and longevity, and on the physical environment?

What are the *scariest* things that might result?

What are the most interesting, exciting *conflicts* that might arise because of these potential, extrapolated trends and developments in science and technology?

What *precursor developments* are required for the technologies to be used in malign ways to produce conflict? (In plotting terms, what is the backstory of the conflict, or the steps that will lead to the malign use of the technology?)

What *new vulnerabilities* might these emerging technologies create in society, in infrastructure, and in individuals' lives? In what ways do these emerging technologies make society *more fragile*, less resilient? What *new threats* could result from those vulnerabilities?

Team members should avoid self-censoring in this phase. At this stage, there are no bad, stupid, crazy, or wrong ideas. Participants should allow their imaginations to run freely and follow them wherever they may lead. All scenario stubs will be submitted anonymously. The facilitators will not identify the scenarios' originators when they distribute the list of stubs, and the originators will not be required to identify themselves during the face-to-face portion of the analysis unless they choose to do so to offer clarifications. Thus, no participants should fear being stigmatized for submitting wild or far-out scenario stubs.

The facilitators will gather all the scenario stubs and remotely disseminate the full set of stubs to the entire group. Participants are allowed to submit additional scenario stubs if their reading of the consolidated list results in further brainstorming, and the facilitators will then distribute the new additions. Team members will continue to have the opportunity to submit additional scenario stubs until the first day of the in-residence meeting of the full group.[11]

*Step 3—Train the Science Fiction Writer Members of the Team in Small Group Processes and Optimally Facilitating Small Group Interactions*: The science fiction writer members of the team will serve as the facilitators of the fleshing out of the deadly dozen scenarios and then as the lead writers for the twelve fleshed-out scenarios. Although they will have all had copious experience with the latter task, most will not have had experience leading small groups. The facilitators of the overall effort should have the science fiction writer members of the team arrive at the face-to-face meeting location a day earlier than the other members and provide them with a three-to-four-hour training on small group processes and behaviors. This training should include not only ways to get the best, most productive interactions out of the participants but also methods of discouraging counterproductive group behaviors, such as nonproductive argumentation, repetitious restatements of the same inputs by participants, withdrawal by the less-confident or nonassertive members from offering input, and domination of the group by one or two of the loudest or most aggressive members. The main goal is to teach the science fiction writers how to allow for disagreement without it becoming disagreeable.

*Step 4—Bring the Participants Together for the Face-to-Face Portion of the Analysis*: Now the face-to-face portion of the Promethean Spyglass begins. The facilitators should emphasize from the start the importance of this analysis for the nation's future safety and that of the participants' own families, neighbors, and friends. They should fully explain how the process will work, including descriptions of the ground rules for the Delphi and nominal group technique procedures, and how their analysis will guide homeland security R&D priorities. They should share the parable of the devil's toy box to spur discussion of the unique challenges inherent in this type of forecasting and threat analysis (see the prologue). Also, the facilitators should provide a brief overview of the usefulness of the science fiction mindset to offset any skepticism regarding the inclusion of science fiction writers on the team.

*Step 5—Apply Convergent Thinking to the Scenario Stubs*: The University of Foreign Military and Cultural Studies' *Red Team Handbook* recommends that the final stage of a brainstorming effort should apply convergent thinking to the brainstormed ideas. In a fashion visible to all, the team does this by removing duplicate ideas and grouping the most similar ideas.[12] The facilitators should edit each scenario stub to its basic elements, such that each can be printed on a large (about six by four inches) sticky note.

Let's assume thirty team members have generated the 180 scenario stubs. Having the entire team initially sort the full list of scenario stubs would be cumbersome and time consuming. The nominal group technique procedure, thankfully, gives us a way to sidestep this headache:

1. The project manager divides the full team into five sub-teams of six members apiece. That person randomly divides the 180 scenario stubs into five sets, with each set having thirty-six scenario stubs for a different sub-team to sort, and assigns a facilitator to each of the sub-teams.

2. The project manager provides each sub-team with its own work and discussion space and outfits each with two portable easel boards that are big enough to accommodate all thirty-six scenario stubs' sticky notes without overlapping.

3. The facilitator randomly assigns turns to the members of the sub-team. The person assigned the first turn silently goes to the easel board holding all thirty-six sticky notes, groups identical or strongly similar stubs, and groups any stubs that can be logically combined into a larger scenario, moving any or all the sticky notes to the second, initially empty easel board. Or the participant may opt to not move any of the sticky notes.

4. Each of the other participants, one at time, is given the opportunity to question why the currently active team member chose to move a sticky note. The questioning participants may pose only one query at a time. The active team member is not obligated to provide his or her reasoning if he or she does not wish to do so. The rounds of questions continue until no non-active participants have any more questions.[13]

5. Instructions 3 and 4 are followed for each member of the sub-team. Team members may take more than one turn, and turns continue until no member of the sub-team wishes to move any

of the sticky notes. This point is then considered the sub-team's consensus. If the sub-team deadlocks regarding the placement of any of the sticky notes (if after all members have had two chances, sticky notes are just going back and forth between previous placements), the facilitator will put those sticky notes aside and will make this lack of consensus known to the full team when it reconvenes.

6. Each sub-team brings its easel board holding the sticky notes for its respective thirty-six sorted scenario stubs back into the shared discussion/work space (in the current example, the five easel boards would be placed side by side in a single room and be viewable by the entire team). The shared space should include a display board that is large enough both to hold all 180 of the scenario stubs' sticky notes without overlapping and to allow for the separation of grouped items. The members of each of the sub-teams select a single representative to serve as their sorter during this consolidation round. Just as in instruction 3, the facilitators randomly assign turns to each sorter. The first sorter silently moves all 180 sticky notes from the small easels to the large display board. The sorter retains the groupings already established by the sub-teams. He or she may consolidate some preexisting groupings with others that have duplication, strongly similar elements, or shared features that would allow them to be logically combined into a larger scenario. However, the active sorter is not forbidden from moving individual sticky notes from one previously assigned grouping to a different grouping if the sorter can explain the reason for making this change. The active sorter should also consider to which of the existing groups the contentious sticky notes, or those not assigned to any groups in the earlier stages, should be assigned. The active sorter may choose to leave the contentious sticky notes as outliers, off on their own, but they still need to be moved to the large display board.

7. Just as with instruction 4, each of the members of the full team, one at time, is given the opportunity to question why the active

sorter chose to move a group of sticky notes or any individual sticky note. The questioners may ask only one question at a time. The active sorter is not obligated to provide his or her reasoning if he or she does not wish to do so. Rounds of questions continue until there are no more questions.

8. Instructions 6 and 7 are followed for each of the sub-teams' representatives. These representatives are not limited to only one turn at the display board. Turns will continue until no representative wishes to move any of the sticky notes any further. This state of play represents the full team's consensus. If the representatives deadlock regarding the placement of any of the sticky notes (if after all representatives have had two chances, the sticky notes or groups of sticky notes just go back and forth between previous placements), the facilitators will print out duplicates of the sticky notes in contention. They will then place these duplicate sticky notes within each one of the groupings for which the various sub-team representatives have been unable to come to agreement.

9. The facilitators take photographs of the final groupings of the sticky notes on the display board. While the other team members are on break, the facilitators work with the science fiction writer members of the team to remove duplicate ideas from the grouped scenario stubs and arrange the non-duplicative elements into logical progressions. Ideally, this process will narrow down the original number of scenario stubs (180 in this example) to a more manageable number, perhaps between a third to half the original number (in this case, somewhere between 60 and 90 scenario stubs).

### Phase 4: Red Team the Scenario Stubs

Red teaming the consolidated scenario stubs takes place entirely during the face-to-face portion of the process. This phase allows the participants to practice applying critical thinking, so they can more effectively flesh out the selected deadly dozen scenario stubs in the following portion of the Promethean Spyglass.

*Step 1—Introduce the Concept of Red Teaming to the Full Group and Provide Training on Avoiding Cognitive Biases*: Using introductory material from the University of Foreign Military and Cultural Studies' *Red Team Handbook* and/or the *Red Teaming Guide* from the Development, Concepts and Doctrines Center of the UK Ministry of Defence, present the full team with the basic concepts of red teaming. Grant special focus to the goals of learning to see situations from multiple vantage points—those of the defender, the attacker/antagonist, and the key allies—and understanding and avoiding common cognitive biases that affect decision making. Discuss the different goals, motivations, taboos and boundaries, and typical educational and socioeconomic backgrounds of the various types of jihadists, nihilists, thrill seekers, right-wing terrorists, left-wing terrorists, and members of apocalyptic cults; and focus on those characteristics that make members of the categories distinctive.[14] Teach participants to avoid the pitfalls of mirror imaging and ethnocentrism (see chapter 5).[15] Train participants to consider the cognitive distortion caused by the *availability heuristic*, or the tendency for people to assign higher levels of risk and consequence to the types of malign events with which they have the greatest familiarity or those recently highlighted in the news media.[16] Other examples of cognitive biases that participants should be familiarized with include the anchoring effect, the status quo bias, the confirmation bias, the sunk-cost bias, the framing trap, the halo effect, the narrative fallacy, and the self-fulfilling prophecy bias (*The Applied Critical Thinking Handbook* from the University of Foreign Military and Cultural Studies provides good, brief explanations of all these).[17] Nicholas Rescher also provides a useful overview of the cognitive biases most applicable to forecasting efforts in his book *Predicting the Future: An Introduction to the Theory of Forecasting*.[18]

*Step 2—Divide the Full Team into Groups of Four*: At the start of each day in this phase, the facilitators will randomly assign participants to groups of four. Each group will be responsible for red teaming randomly assigned scenario stubs. If the size of the full team is not divisible by four, facilitators should round out the short team themselves. Existing groups break up at the end of a working day, and new groups are formed at the beginning of the next working day. Facilitators should try, as best as is practicable, to ensure that each team member serves on groups with people they have not previously worked with during this phase, thus helping to familiarize each team member with as many other participants as possible.

*Step 3—Randomly Assign a Scenario Stub to Each Group to Red Team and Designate Each Group a Red-Teaming Method to Use*: At the beginning of each workday, facilitators assign each of the working groups one of seven red-teaming techniques to use in critically examining their scenario stubs. Each group's facilitator will spend fifteen minutes explaining the assigned red-teaming technique and answer any questions. If there are more groups than there are red-teaming techniques, more than one group will be assigned the same red-teaming technique, and the red-teaming technique that gets double coverage will change from day to day. The red-teaming techniques are outlined in the following paragraphs.

TEAM A/TEAM B: The group separates into two debating sub-teams of two members apiece. One sub-team will argue that the scenario stub will become actualized, and the other will argue that the scenario stub will never actualize. Each sub-team will assemble evidence for its own hypothesis and present it in an oral debate format. The two sub-teams spend the first five minutes brainstorming evidence for their hypothesis; then each group has five minutes to deliver a first-round oral presentation to the other. In the next five minutes, the sub-teams come up with rebuttals of the other sub-team's evidence. A second round of oral presentations follows, with five minutes allotted for each sub-team. The sub-teams are then allowed three minutes to assemble their closing arguments and two minutes each to present them. The last eight minutes of the red-teaming procedure are for an open discussion period during which group members may offer their opinions regarding the strengths of the arguments presented. They are also encouraged to make notes for an upcoming presentation on the debate for the entire team.[19]

STRENGTHS, WEAKNESSES, OPPORTUNITIES, AND THREATS ANALYSIS: The group separates into two sub-teams of two members apiece. Each sub-team, based on the scenario stub, creates a four-quadrant diagram outlining the strengths, weaknesses, opportunities, and threats, and brainstorms entries for each quadrant. One sub-team does so from the viewpoint of the attackers, and the other sub-team does so from the viewpoint of the defenders. After spending thirty minutes preparing their respective SWOT analyses, the sub-teams take the last fifteen minutes of the session to compare their notes with one another and prepare a brief presentation for the entire team.[20]

DEVIL'S ADVOCACY: The group spends the first ten minutes of the session deciding on the shared conventional wisdom regarding the scenario stub, the most widely held and strongly held consensus view. The members take the next thirty minutes to construct the strongest possible case for a competing explanation that contradicts the consensus view, striving to disprove it by uncovering evidence that was either faulty or ignored in the original analysis and seeking to prove the assertion opposite to the consensus view. The group spends the last five minutes of the session preparing a brief presentation for the entire team.[21]

MEASURE-COUNTERMEASURE, MOVE-COUNTERMOVE: This exercise is meant to explore the secondary and tertiary impacts of acts of terror. The group explores this in rounds, with each round taking ten minutes. At the beginning of the first round, the group "plays" the attackers and decides how the scenario stub's Promethean technology will be used in an attack. Then the group brainstorms what might be the prompt/primary, secondary, and tertiary effects of this attack. Members should consider the impacts on the economy, vital infrastructure, politics, social psychology, and individual liberties. At the beginning of the second round, the group takes the defenders' roles. The participants decide what would be the most likely countermove or countermeasure that homeland security and law enforcement would deploy in response to the attack. Then the group brainstorms the possible prompt/primary, secondary, and tertiary effects of putting this defense in place, focusing on its impacts in the same areas mentioned in the first round. At the beginning of the third round, the group shifts back to the attackers' roles. This time, the members brainstorm how the attackers would most likely respond to the defenders' initial countermove(s); they should include the same considerations assessed during the first round. In the fourth and final round, the group once again assumes the defenders' role. The group spends the final five minutes of the session preparing a brief presentation for the entire team.[22]

ALTERNATIVE FUTURES ANALYSIS: At the beginning of this exercise, the participants spend eight minutes deciding which two sets of influencing forces they wish to apply to the scenario stub. For example, the two sets chosen might be economic health (recessionary economic climate versus vigorous economic growth) and environmental stability (a period of violent weather events and drought versus a period of climate stability). The two sets of influencing forces are placed on two axes, forming a matrix that allows for an analysis of four potential alternative futures. In this example, the group would consider the scenario stub being played out within the following four future environments: (a) recessionary economic climate and severe weather events, (b) recessionary economic climate and environmental climate stability, (c) vigorous economic growth and severe weather events, and (d) vigorous economic growth and environmental climate stability. If the group selected the two axes to be domestic political stability (severe domestic political conflict and violence versus stable, cooperative domestic political environment) and international political stability (numerous international conflicts and high instability versus relative peace and international stability), the four future environments would be (a) severe domestic political conflict and violence with numerous international conflicts and high instability, (b) severe domestic political conflict and violence with relative peace and international stability, (c) stable, cooperative domestic political environment with numerous international conflicts and high instability, and (d) stable, cooperative domestic political environment with relative peace and international stability. The group spends eight minutes per future environment brainstorming how that particular environment might affect the terroristic use of the scenario stub's Promethean technology. Would the likelihood of its use be increased or decreased by the particular environment? Would the likelihood of its *malign* use be increased or decreased? Would the resulting severity of consequences be increased or decreased? Would the defenders' tasks be made more difficult by environmental factors? The group spends the final five minutes of the session preparing a brief presentation for the entire team.[23]

ANALYSIS OF COMPETING HYPOTHESES: The group spends the first five to ten minutes of this exercise identifying three or four plausible or compelling hypotheses related to the scenario stub. Examples could include "Malign use of the Promethean technology will result in severe curtailment of civil liberties in the United States," or "Repeated terroristic use of the Promethean technology will result in a U.S. economic recession due to an increased reluctance by consumers to engage in economic activities online." The hypotheses may conflict with one another. The group spends seven to ten minutes discussing each hypothesis. With each, two members brainstorm supporting evidence, or factors that would need to be present for the hypothesis to come true, and two members brainstorm disproving evidence, or factors whose presence would make it very likely for the hypothesis to be false. If time allows, members analyze how sensitive their hypotheses are regarding supporting or negating factors. For instance, if an evidence factor is removed, does the hypothesis then become unreasonable? The group spends the final five minutes preparing a brief presentation for the entire team.[24]

THROUGH THE TERRORIST'S EYES: The group spends the first fifteen minutes "trying on the shoes" of various types of terrorists, including jihadists, nihilists, or thrill seekers, and right-wing terrorists, left-wing terrorists, or members of apocalyptic cults. The members should discuss which groups or types of terrorists would be most likely to seek to use the scenario stub's Promethean technology and which would be less likely; then they should explain why. The group chooses one category of terrorists whose viewpoint they will adopt for the remainder of the exercise. The participants then spend twenty-five minutes filling in the Sandia National Laboratories' Generic Threat Matrix, keeping in mind the type of terrorist or terror organization selected for analysis. The group will assign ratings of high, medium, or low to matrix categories that include (a) *intensity* (the level of dedication to the cause that the antagonist brings to an attack), (b) *stealth* (the ability of the antagonist to keep his or her activities hidden), (c) *time* (the period required to plan, organize, supply, and carry out an attack), (d) *technical personnel* (the number of subject matter experts required to carry out an attack successfully), (e) *cyber knowledge* (the antagonist's level of expertise in computer systems, computer networks, and computer security), (f) *kinetic knowledge* (the antagonist's level of expertise regarding the defender's physical barriers and the methods with which to defeat them), and (g) *access* (the adversary's level of accessibility to the target). The group spends the final five minutes preparing a brief presentation for the entire team.[25]

*Step 4—Red Team Each Scenario Stub, Then Present Results to Entire Team and Allow for Questions*: Each group has now red teamed one randomly assigned scenario stub, a process that has taken forty-five minutes. All groups reconvene for a plenary session. Each group takes five minutes to present a summary of its findings to the entire team and follows with up to ten minutes of taking questions. The facilitators should compile notes of the groups' findings regarding each scenario stub as well as the answers to any questions posed. Prior to the participants' ranking the scenario stubs, the facilitators will distribute these notes together with a list of all the scenario stubs.

With eight sub-teams, carrying out this step takes about 165 minutes (45 minutes for the red-teaming exercises themselves, 40 minutes for eight presentations, and 80 minutes for eight question and answer [Q&A] sessions). With breaks and a 45-minute lunch, three such sessions could be accomplished in an extended workday. If the initial set of scenario stubs numbers sixty to ninety, red teaming the whole set would take three to four workdays.

Facilitators may consider sharing the five fully fleshed-out scenarios that are included in this book with the full team for the members to read on their own. Once the entire group has red teamed the full set of scenario stubs, they can apply their newly sharpened critical thinking skills to any or all of the five scenarios during a plenary session. Discussion questions might include the following:

> What are the social, economic, and psychological factors that influenced the attackers in the various scenarios to select the modes of attack they chose?
>
> What could homeland security or law enforcement agents do to try to deter those modes of attack?
>
> If deterrence fails, how could these attacks be defended against?
>
> What factors might make the scenarios' attacks more likely to succeed? Less likely to succeed?
>
> If such attacks can't be deterred or defended against, what sorts of societal changes or precautions could plausibly mitigate the primary, secondary, and tertiary consequences of such attacks?

### Phase 5: Rank the Scenario Stubs

This phase also takes place entirely during the face-to-face portion. During phase 5, the participants collectively rank the scenario stubs in ordinal fashion based on the scenarios' severity of consequences and likelihood of being actualized. Their output is a deadly dozen of scenario stubs, or the twelve scenarios that the participants have judged to be the very worst.

Research has shown that individual judges are typically capable of productively ordering no more than nine items or ideas at one time.[26] I therefore don't recommend that each participant individually rank all the scenario stubs. Instead, the participants should use the consensus Delphi technique to arrive at collective judgments of the potential consequences and likelihoods of the scenario stubs being actualized. Many online tools have been developed to facilitate Delphi procedures, including the Delphi Learning Package for Moodle; the Mesydel package developed at the University of Liège; Delphi Blue, an open source, Java/JSP version of the Delphi technique originally developed by DARPA; and Calibrum, a commercial product that allows users to select different variations of the Delphi technique. Additionally, online polling software such as SurveyMonkey or Slido can be adapted to ease the administration of consensus Delphi procedures.

The very large number of consensus Delphi procedures that need to be conducted during this phase reflect both the high quantity of scenario stubs that need to be rated and the fact that participants will rate each scenario stub nine times: once on the severity of the consequence, once on the likelihood of the emerging Promethean technology being developed and marketed within a five-to-ten-year window, six times on six different limiting or retarding factors that influence the likelihood of the come-to-market Promethean technology being used to promulgate the catastrophic outcome(s) envisioned, and once on the overall probability of the scenario becoming actualized. To shorten the length of this face-to-face portion, the facilitators should randomly divide the full team into two groups at the beginning of each workday. Each scenario stub will be rated by half of the members of the full team; consequently, each participant will be tasked with rating half the scenario stubs.

*Step 1—Facilitators Provide Participants with a List of Scenario Stubs*: All participants receive a complete list of the scenario stubs. A summary of both the results of the red-teaming exercise and the answers or clarifications that resulted from the Q&A sessions is included with each stub's description.

*Step 2—Participants Rate Each Scenario Stub Regarding the Severity of Its Potential Consequences*: Rather than using a numeric scale (one to ten or one to a hundred, for example) for rating the severity of potential consequences, the participants should be instructed to consider their severity in dollar terms. This will help them distance themselves from emotional reactions when contemplating the relative weights of various malign consequences. Although the assignment of a dollar value to a human life may strike some participants as cold-blooded or even offensive, it helps minimize the bias in this analysis. Different insurance companies and governmental institutions have already calculated various estimates of the dollar value of the life of an American; consistent use of any of them is acceptable. The U.S. Department of Transportation utilizes a value of a statistical life of $4.4 million for its cost-benefit analyses of proposed new traffic safety regulations.[27] For ease of calculations, this value may be rounded down to an even $4 million.

Participants should also consider the dollar values of the secondary and tertiary consequences. Some of these secondary and tertiary consequences may involve the loss of human life, injuries, or illnesses, but most will take the form of economic impacts, such as losses to the local, regional, or national economy. Since participants may feel overwhelmed by this task, the facilitators should remind them that no one is expected to perform as a professional econometrician; they should make use of back-of-the-envelope estimates. During the first round of the consensus Delphi to collectively decide the severity of potential consequences, participants are allotted twenty minutes to calculate an economic estimate of the primary, secondary, and tertiary impacts they see arising from the scenario stub. They should provide brief statements explaining why they settled on their dollar figure. All responses will remain anonymous; participants enter their dollar value estimates and their brief rationales through software that allows for anonymous online polling and/or Delphi procedures. Participants should be reminded to be consistent with their assumptions from scenario to scenario. So long as their assumptions remain consistent from evaluation to evaluation, any errors they may make in estimating costs will be uniformly applied across their range of ratings and will thus not affect their ordinal rankings. Facilitators should also instruct participants to build for themselves a personal "assumptions dictionary" as they go. It will allow raters to reuse assumptions they have made earlier, allowing for both consistency and for increased speed and convenience in ranking.

For the second round of the consensus Delphi, each participant should be electronically provided with the following data: (a) their own previously submitted dollar value estimate; (b) the full team's median dollar value estimate; (c) the summary statistics, including standard deviation, mean, mode, and minimum and maximum values; and (d) a list of the rationales anonymously submitted by the full team. Participants should be allotted fifteen minutes to reassess their initial dollar value estimate, if they choose to, in light of these materials. They may opt to either stick with their initial estimate or adjust their estimate. Again, all responses to the second round of the consensus Delphi are submitted anonymously. During this round, participants aren't required to submit rationales.

The facilitators then calculate the median dollar value of the full team's estimates from the second round, and it becomes the consensus value for this scenario stub. The facilitators then share the consensus value with the participants. This process is repeated for each of the remaining scenario stubs in turn.

*Step 3—Participants Receive Refresher Training in the Laws of Probability and How to Calculate Probabilities*: At this point, the facilitators provide a more in-depth version of the training they previously offered in an online format during phase 2. This training session, running between two and three hours, should include material on the laws of probability, including compound and contingent probabilities.[28] Also, per Philip Tetlock and Dan Gardner's guidelines in their book *Superforecasting*, the training should also include how to use Bayesian statistical methods to refine or change probability estimates in response to new information. Douglas W. Hubbard provides a helpful set of calibration tests and answers that may be included as part of this session as well.[29] Facilitators should allow adequate time throughout for questions and clarifications.

*Step 4—Participants Rate Each Scenario Stub Regarding the Likelihood of Its Becoming Actualized*: At the beginning of this step, facilitators should instruct participants that when they estimate the probability of a scenario stub becoming actualized, they should consider not only the likelihood of the key enabling technologies reaching market within the next five to ten years, or the *independent base probability*, but also the magnitude of the following six probability limiting or retarding factors that may influence the likelihood of a developed Promethean technology being used for malign purposes.

These limiting or retarding factors in using the Promethean technology include:

the affordability of its anticipated acquisition cost or of its enabling components in five to ten years' time;

its appeal to the various types of terrorists and terror groups (jihadists, nihilists, thrill seekers, right-wing terrorists, left-wing terrorists, and acolytes of apocalyptic cults) compared with alternative modes of attack;

the logistical complexity, or the number of personnel and the amount of time required to plan, organize, supply, and carry out an attack;

the level of cyber knowledge or other scientific and technical expertise required in such fields as computer systems, computer networks, and computer security, or in chemistry, biology, physics, or engineering;

the level of kinetic knowledge required, or the level of expertise to assess the defender's physical barriers and to develop the methods with which to defeat them; and

the level of access to a target that an attacker requires to successfully carry out an attack.

The team will collectively rate on a low-to-high scale each of these probability limiting factors in turn, working one scenario stub at a time.

The probability figure calculated for the independent base probability also represents the highest possible probability of the Promethean technology not only coming to market but also being used to promulgate the catastrophe envisioned in the scenario. In other words, if the team calculates that the likelihood of Promethean technology X coming to market within a five-to-ten-year window is 45 percent, the ceiling, or the absolute maximum, probability of technology X being used for the malign purpose envisioned in the scenario in question is 45 percent. The highest value (which represents the lowest retarding effect) that can be assigned by the team to any or all the probability limiting factors is 1.00, or 100 percent. If all six probability limiting factors are assigned scores of 1.00, or 100 percent, the likelihood of technology X being used for the malign purpose envisioned in the scenario would be 45 percent, or the same probability estimated for technology X coming to market within a five-to-ten-year window.

As their name implies, the probability limiting factors act to decrease the probability of the malign use of an actualized Promethean technology. The stronger the limiting factors are judged to be, the more they will tend to drive the probability of a malign use downward. The lower the probability limiting factors (expressed as percentages) are estimated to be, the stronger they are in their impact. Each of the probability limiting factors is judged on a scale ranging between zero and one, inclusive of one, with a score just above zero representing the highest limiting or retarding impact of that factor and with a score of one representing a complete absence of limiting or retarding impact. (I have chosen not to allow a score of zero for a probability limiting factor because this would imply an infinite retarding power for that factor, rendering the malign use of an actualized Promethean technology an impossibility. I assume that once a technology is invented, there is always at least *some* likelihood, no matter how small, that it will be used for destructive purposes.)

Scores are then converted into percentages. By not assigning participants a three-point, five-point, or ten-point scale to use, but rather allowing them to choose any decimal (percentage) figure between zero and one, inclusive of one, I avoid several problems that Douglas W. Hubbard has identified with using scales for evaluating risks, such as range compression, the presumption of regular intervals, and the tendency of a large proportion of respondents to select either three or four when offered a five-point scale.[30]

Regarding the *likelihood of the key enabling technologies reaching market* within the next five to ten years, participants will assign a probability score of any number between 0 percent (no possibility of the enabling technologies being developed and brought to market within the next five to ten years) and 100 percent (full certainty that it will occur). Facilitators should provide participants with following adjectival scale to help guide their selection of a probability score:

impossible = probability of 0 percent

extremely unlikely = probability between 0 percent and 19 percent

unlikely = probability between 20 percent and 44 percent

about equally unlikely as likely = probability between 45 percent and 54 percent

likely = probability between 55 percent and 79 percent

extremely likely = probability between 80 percent and 100 percent

certain = probability of 100 percent

Participants will follow the same consensus Delphi procedure as described in step 2 but with a few differences. Participants are given *fifteen minutes* to make their first-round estimate and to submit supporting rationales; then they have *ten minutes* during the second round to review their fellow team members' rationales, the *mean* of the full team's responses (rather than the median value), and the additional summary statistics to consider whether to stick with their original estimate or to adjust it. The facilitators calculate the *mean value* of the full team's estimates from the second round. This mean value is the consensus value for the *likelihood of the key enabling technologies reaching market* for this scenario stub. The facilitators share the consensus value with the participants.

For the first scenario stub, in rating each of the six limiting factors, the participants use the same consensus Delphi procedure outlined earlier. The only changes are that participants are given *five minutes* to make their first-round estimate and to submit supporting rationales. Then they have *five minutes* during the second round to review their fellow team members' rationales, the *mean* of the full team's responses, and the additional summary statistics, and to consider whether to stick with their original estimate or to adjust it. Rating scales for the six probability limiting factors follow the next instruction, and the qualitative descriptions should be used merely as guides in their selection of values.

I encourage facilitators to provide these instructions to participants regarding the scoring of limiting factors: "You will judge the strength of each limiting factor individually for each scenario, in isolation from consideration of any other factors. In judging each factor, presume it is the *sole* retarding factor impacting the likelihood of a developed technology being used for the malign purpose described in a scenario. If you feel this factor makes it virtually impossible that the developed technology will be used for the malign purpose envisioned, score the factor close to zero. If you feel this factor exerts very little or no retarding influence on the likelihood of the use of the developed technology for the malign purpose envisioned, score it close to one (hardly any retarding influence) or one (no retarding influence at all). If you feel the influence of the limiting or retarding factor falls somewhere between these two extremes, please use the provided descriptions to guide your rating."

*Affordability* of the anticipated acquisition cost of the Promethean technology or its enabling components five to ten years in the future:

> 0–0.19 = highly unaffordable, save for well-funded organizations ($200,000 or more)

0.2–0.49 = mostly unaffordable, save for well-funded organizations (between $50,000 and $200,000)

0.5–0.79 = affordable for organizations, mostly unaffordable for individuals (between $10,000 and $50,000)

0.8–0.94 = somewhat affordable for individuals (between $1,000 and $10,000)

0.95–1.0 = highly affordable for individuals (less than $1,000)

(If the scenario involves an individual using the technology, the participant should score the affordability retardant more strongly—that is, numerically lower—than if the scenario involves an organization using the technology. If a team member estimates that the acquisition cost falls near one of the extremes of a suggested dollar range, that team member should select a fractional value close to the top or bottom of the suggested range. This stipulation applies to all the remaining limiting factors as well.)

*Appeal* of the Promethean technology to the various types of terrorists and terror groups as compared with alternative modes of attack:

> 0–0.19 = extremely unappealing (use of the technology conflicts with the attacker's religious precepts, morality, or ideology *and/or* attacker judges that use of the technology promises a much lower likelihood of success than use of alternate attack modes *and/or* use of the technology will very likely bring condemnation from the attacker's allies and potential supporters *and/or* use of the technology will very likely incite a powerfully disproportionate punitive response from a nation-state or coalition of nation-states; that is, the technology is judged to be too hot to handle and/or more trouble than it is worth)

0.2–0.79 = unappealing (the attacker judges use of the technology promises at least some marginal decrease in the likelihood of success than use of alternate attack modes *and/or* use of the technology is more likely than not to bring condemnation from the attacker's allies and potential supporters *and/or* use of the technology is more likely than not to incite new punitive measures of increased severity from targeted nation-state[s] and powerful enemies, representing a risk that the attacker's use of the technology will retard the attacker's goals more than the use advances those goals)

0.8–0.89 = neither especially unappealing or especially appealing (attacker judges that use of the technology suffers no significant disadvantages or offers no significant advantages when compared with alternate modes of attack; choice to use technology over alternate modes of attack most likely due to availability or convenience rather than any real preference)

0.9–0.94 = appealing (attacker judges use of the technology promises at least some marginal increase in likelihood of success than use of alternate attack modes *and/or* use of the technology is more likely than not to bring approbation from the attacker's allies and potential supporters *and/or* attacker judges use of the technology will reduce the morale and will to resist of target nation-state[s] and powerful enemies and advance the attacker's goals)

0.95–1.0 = extremely appealing (use of the technology is an excellent fit with the attacker's religious precepts, driving narrative, or ideology *and/or* attacker judges use of the technology promises much higher likelihood of success than use of alternate attack modes *and/or* use of the technology will very likely bring great approbation from the attacker's allies and potential supporters *and/or* attacker judges use of the technology will very likely significantly cow and intimidate target nation-state[s] and powerful enemies and greatly advance the attacker's goals)

*Logistical complexity,* or the number of personnel and the time required to plan, organize, supply, and carry out an attack using the Promethean technology:

> 0–0.19 = very high complexity (three years or more, fifty personnel or more)

0.2–0.39 = high complexity (one to three years, twenty to fifty personnel)

0.4–0.69 = medium complexity (two months to one year, ten to twenty personnel)

0.7–0.94 = low complexity (two weeks to two months, three to ten personnel)

.095–1.0 = very low complexity (days to two weeks, one to two personnel)

Level of *cyber* knowledge or other scientific/technical expertise required:

> 0–0.19 = very high (postgraduate-level skills and expertise needed, and/or five years or more of professional experience in the field)

0.2–0.49 = high (baccalaureate-level skills and expertise needed, and/or three years or more of professional experience in the field)

0.5–0.69 = moderate (associate's-level or certificate program–level skills and expertise needed, and/or one year or more of professional experience in the field)

0.7–0.94 = low (skills and expertise can be easily acquired and absorbed through books or internet research, and/or three months or more of professional experience in the field)

0.95–01.0 = very low (no special skills or expertise are required, nor is any work experience in the field; Promethean technology is consumer-grade and comes with instructions that the average user can follow, with assistance, if needed)

Level of *kinetic* knowledge required:

> 0–0.19 = very high (to carry out a successful strike, attackers must penetrate or bypass highly sophisticated defensive systems *with* multiple layers of defense, including both automated or passive defenses *and* manned defenses)

0.2–0.39 = high (to carry out a successful strike, attackers must penetrate or bypass a sophisticated defensive system *or* multiple layers of defense, including automated or passive defenses and/or manned defenses)

0.4–0.79 = moderate (to carry out a strike, attackers must penetrate or bypass ordinary, unsophisticated barriers such as might be found at a special event or a school, and might include fences, walls, locked entrances, bollards or traffic barriers, or areas with restricted access, *and* avoid detection by law enforcement or security guards assigned to protect the site)

0.8–0.94 = low (to carry out a successful strike, attackers must penetrate or bypass ordinary, unsophisticated barriers such as a fence, a wall, and/or locked entrances, and avoid detection by patrolling law enforcement not specifically assigned to the site of the attack)

0.95–1.0 = very low (to carry out a successful strike, attackers must access a space normally open to the public with no restrictions and not normally patrolled by law enforcement or security guards)

Level of *access* an attacker requires:

> 0–0.29 = very high (to carry out a successful strike, attackers need to become vetted employees or contractors of an institution that uses vigorous background checks in its hiring process and requires at least a public trust clearance level or its equivalent, *and* significant surveillance is necessary)

0.3–0.79 = high (to carry out a successful strike, attackers need to be vetted visitors, getting permission to access a facility from security staff *and* having to pass through a metal detector and have one's belongings be searched or electronically scanned, *or* significant surveillance is necessary)

0.8–0.89 = moderate (to carry out a successful strike, attackers need to enter a facility with no restrictions on entrance, without raising suspicions from employees, security guards, or other visitors, *and* moderate surveillance is necessary)

0.9–0.94 = low (to carry out a successful strike, attackers do not need to enter a facility or site but only require physical proximity, such as from a street or sidewalk; moderate surveillance may be necessary)

0.95–1.0 = very low (attackers can carry out a strike remotely, from a secure base of operations, and do not require any access or proximity to the site of the attack)

After team members have performed consensus Delphi procedures regarding the independent base probability and regarding all six probability limiting factors for a scenario stub, they will then estimate the probability of that scenario becoming actualized. Facilitators allot participants twenty minutes for this procedure. I provide examples of various ways the six retarding factors could be weighted and how these weightings affect the likelihood of a developed technology being put to malign use. Facilitators should share these examples with the participants. Additionally, they should provide participants with the group's amalgamated mean for the independent base probability and for each of the six probability limiting factors, the participants' own second-round scores for the independent base probability and each of the six probability limiting factors, and the summary statistics for each of the seven calculated figures.

Terror attacks are highly individualistic events. Each event is strongly affected by the psychology of the terror group's leaders and followers or that of the individual terrorist, by local environmental factors, and by chance. For this reason, I don't recommend that facilitators provide participants with a mathematical formula that assigns weights to the various retarding factors and mechanically outputs an overall probability figure. Any such model the facilitators might come up with could only be validated by examining many diverse terror attacks and working backward, trying to estimate as best as possible what the levels of the various retarding factors were prior to attacks being carried out. However, models constructed and validated in this fashion would only be valid for a combination of terror group/category of terrorist, attack mode, type of target, and environment of target. A model judged to have very high validity, or measure of fit, for one such combination might have next to no validity for other combinations. Therefore, a staggering number of varying models would need to be constructed and validated to cover all possible combinations. This, however, defeats the purpose of modeling, which is to simplify predictions by providing standardization.

My reservations about the facilitators providing participants with a recommended or assigned model must not be misconstrued to imply that participants should be forbidden from creating and using their *own* models. Participants act as judges, and formulating their own models, with the six retarding factors weighted individualistically (or not assigned any weights at all), is itself a judgment activity.

The simplest method for making use of the six retarding factors would be for a participant to weight them all equally and calculate a simple mean of their scores. An example of this simple model follows.

**Scenario Stub XYZ**

likelihood of reaching market (independent base probability) = 74 percent

affordability = 0.92

appeal = 0.96

logistical complexity = 0.82

cyber knowledge/scientific-technical expertise = 0.66

kinetic knowledge = 0.94

access = 1.0

In this example, the probability score of the Promethean technology not only coming to market but also being used for malign purposes would be $0.74 \times [(0.92 + 0.96 + 0.82 + 0.66 + 0.94 + 1.00) / 6.0] = 0.65$, or 65 percent. In this instance, none of the retarding factors had a very strong effect, with the highest-strength limiting factor being cyber knowledge/scientific-technical expertise.

Should participants decide to create a weighted formula using the six retarding factors, they should first arrange them in order of descending importance. For the example above, the selected order might be (1) appeal ("if the attackers are not emotionally motivated to use the technology rather than alternative modes of attack, none of the remaining factors matter"), (2) cyber knowledge/scientific-technical expertise, (3) logistical complexity, (4) affordability, (5) kinetic knowledge, and (6) access. Then participants should select one of the factors to use as a *base value* against which to weight the others. Is there a factor that should be weighted twice as heavily as another? If so, assign the latter factor a weight of one and assign the former a weight of two, and work from there, gauging the weights of the remaining factors relative to the weights assigned to those two factors. Here's an example:

### Scenario Stub XYZ (weighted example)

likelihood of reaching market (independent base probability, no weighting) = 74 percent

appeal: raw score = 0.96; weight = 4.0

cyber knowledge/scientific-technical expertise: raw score = 0.66; weight = 2.0

logistical complexity: raw score = 0.82; weight = 2.0

affordability: raw score = 0.92; weight = 1.0

kinetic knowledge: raw score = 0.94; weight = 0.5

access: raw score = 100 percent; weight = 0.5

In this example, my two base values are appeal and affordability; the former is judged to be four times as important as the latter. Both cyber knowledge/scientific-technical expertise and logistical complexity are judged to be half as important as appeal and twice as important as affordability. Both kinetic knowledge and access are judged to be half as important as affordability. The following formula shows how to calculate the weighted mean of this example, with the denominator (in this example, 10) being the sum of all six weights: 0.74 × {[(0.96 x 4.0) + (0.66 × 2.0) + (0.82 × 2.0) + (0.92 × 1.0) + (0.94 × 0.5) + (1.00 × 0.5)] / 10.0} = 0.64, or 64 percent.

Now let's have a look at the same example but with different estimates for some of the retarding/limiting factors. Let's say that both logistical complexity and affordability are significantly retarding factors rather than having hardly any limiting effects at all. Logistical complexity, formerly scored at 0.82, is now scored at 0.12; and affordability, formerly scored at 0.92, is now scored at 0.21.

### Scenario Stub XYZ (alternate weighted example)

likelihood of reaching market (independent base probability, no weighting) = 74 percent

appeal: raw score = 0.96; weight = 4.0

cyber knowledge/scientific-technical expertise: raw score = 0.66; weight = 2.0

logistical complexity: raw score = 0.12; weight = 2.0

affordability: raw score = 0.21; weight = 1.0

kinetic knowledge: raw score = 0.94; weight = 0.5

access: raw score = 100 percent; weight = 0.5

$0.74 \times \{[(0.96 \times 4.0) + (0.66 \times 2.0) + (0.12 \times 2.0) + (0.021 \times 1.0) + (0.94 \times 0.5) + (1.00 \times 0.5)] / 10.0\} = 0.49$, or 49 percent.

With the retarding power of two of the probability limiting factors significantly increased, even for two variables that are not weighted the most heavily, the probability of the malign use of the Promethean technology declines by more than a third of its earlier value, from 74 percent to 49 percent.

Participants should be encouraged to play with their weightings in a spreadsheet so that they can see how altering the weights affects the overall probability of malign use. This will help participants decide whether the formula they have created passes the "smell test" of plausibility. Alternatively, participants may opt to consider the group's aggregated means of the six retarding factors separately and individually, without any weighting at all, to guide their intuitive judgment of the probability of the scenario described in the stub becoming actualized. Whatever method is used, participants should perform a gut check regarding whether the probability result they end up with seems reasonable based on the information they have absorbed. If their gut tells them the result is *not* reasonable, they should reexamine the assumptions they have made.

The final, consensus probability score of a scenario stub becoming actualized is the mean of the group's overall probability scores. Once the facilitators calculate this probability value, they share the consensus value with the group. Then the group moves on to performing the same set of consensus Delphi procedures for rating the probability for the next scenario stub and so on until participants have ascertained consensus probability ratings for all the scenario stubs.

*Step 5—Facilitators Calculate the Estimated Risk Levels for Each Scenario Stub*: Estimated risk levels are all expressed in dollar terms to allow for easy ranking and comparisons. For our purpose, the formula for risk is risk = consensus estimated dollar value of scenario's consequences × consensus estimated probability of the scenario becoming actualized.

Facilitators then provide participants with a list of all the scenario stubs ranked in descending order of risk, with the risk formula figures provided for each. Only the twelve scenario stubs at the top of the risk estimation list will be further worked on and fleshed out into full scenarios for a final ranking process.

*Step 6—Facilitators Finalize Determination of the Deadly Dozen Scenarios*: At this point in the process, some participants, upon reviewing the ranked list of all the scenario stubs, may feel the cutoff at twelve discards vital elements of the threat scenarios. Any participants who feel that especially likely and deadly scenarios are being improperly culled should indicate their concerns through anonymous electronic means. If this should happen, the full group will then follow a nominal group technique process to arrive at a consensus resolution of a revised list.

The preferred option for incorporating scenario stubs or elements of scenario stubs that are ranked below the deadly dozen is to combine the excluded elements with one of the top twelve scenario stubs, should such amalgamations be logical and complementary. If this does not prove to be possible, the group, using NGT processes, may opt to expand the list of scenario stubs and further flesh it out from a deadly dozen to a "threatening thirteen," a "frightening fourteen," or a "ferocious fifteen."

Here is how this would work. In the context of an NGT procedure, any participant may anonymously electronically submit his or her ideas for the amalgamation of a lower-ranking scenario stub with one of the top twelve or for adding a lower-ranking scenario stub to the list of survivors. Submitting participants should also provide a brief rationale supporting their suggested change. If called for, facilitators should allot ten minutes for this part of the procedure. Then the round-robin question and answer session begins. Facilitators should instruct participants to keep their round-robin inputs brief and to the point. Only one suggestion should be considered at a time. Speaking one at a time, participants may ask one question or make one observation regarding the suggestion or offer a reason to support or disagree with the suggestion. The suggestion's contributor, anonymous until now, may opt to respond or decline to answer.

After a full round of Q&A, the facilitators should ask whether another round is needed; then the facilitators ask for anonymous yes or no electronic votes. Round-robin Q&A and follow-on voting take place first for amalgamation suggestions. If the group votes yes on an amalgamation suggestion and that amalgamation integrates a lower-ranking scenario stub into one of the top twelve, no round-robin Q&A or follow-on voting is done for a suggestion that this same lower-ranking scenario stub be added as a separate scenario. Round-robin Q&A sessions and follow-on voting are carried out last for suggestions to add additional scenario stubs to the list of survivors.

### Phase 6: Flesh Out the Deadly Dozen Scenarios

Phase 6 is the last phase that takes place during the face-to-face portion of the Promethean Spyglass. Our bedraggled participants are begging to go home! But I have saved perhaps the most fun part of the face-to-face portion for last. Participants get to apply the scenario development and red-teaming skills they have learned thus far in a creative, interactive fashion. Earlier, the far more numerous scenario stubs were each subjected to only a portion of our basket of red-teaming techniques. These selected deadly dozen scenarios now each get fleshed out using the full set.

*Step 1—Divide the Full Team into Scenario Expansion Sub-Teams*: Facilitators should aim to assemble half as many sub-teams as there are surviving scenario stubs so that each sub-team will be responsible for fleshing out two scenarios. Each sub-team should have a science fiction writer as the lead scenario writer and scenario expansion facilitator. Facilitators should try to match team subject matter experts (the scientific, technical, academic, or homeland security practitioners) with appropriate scenarios (match biologists with scenarios involving gene manipulation, for example).

*Step 2—Select the Three Key Axes of Driving Environmental Forces Most Significant to Facilitating Malign Uses of the Scenario's Promethean Technology*: Sub-team leads (all science fiction writers) need to emphasize to their teammates that the primary goal of phase 6 is to promulgate the *worst-case scenario* from each stub addressed. In fleshing out each scenario, participants, when choosing between alternative, branching plot lines ("what happens next?"), should aim to pave the path that leads to the most catastrophic outcomes. Make it as bad as possible! Remember, the goal of a devil's toy box analysis is not to judge which of the many, many gestating toys are most likely to jump out of the box first but rather to decide which of those gestating toys are the most terrible in their potential impacts and thus the most important to seal inside. Participants, in devising worst-case scenarios, should strive for plausibility; however, a devil's toy box analysis does not call for devising *probable* futures.

Peter Schwartz, in his book *The Art of the Long View*, describes selecting key axes of driving environmental forces as one of the essential steps in developing scenarios of various plausible futures. Scenario analysis, in the traditional view, is not a tool for making predictions but rather for gaming a variety of plausible futures and exploring how different decisions made in various sectors might shift the unfolding pathways of those futures. In this phase of the Promethean Spyglass, however, participants select key axes of driving environmental forces with a different purpose in mind: they try to judge, within a volume (three axes), which combination of points along the three intersecting axes results in the worst-case scenario for using the Promethean technology under consideration; then this *most malign* combination of points along the three axes can be used as the scenario's enabling background. This most malign combination should be plausible and internally consistent, but it need not be probable.

You may wish to review the alternative futures analysis red-teaming technique, which was described in phase 4, step 3 (Randomly Assign a Scenario Stub). In that example, participants selected two sets of critical or uncertain influencing forces and placed them on sets of axes, forming a matrix containing four quadrants of combinations of forces having various strengths or intensities. This time around, rather than considering two axes of influencing forces, participants will consider three axes of influencing forces. So instead of four quadrants, participants must contend with eight possible combinations. If the choice along each axis is restricted to low and high, for instance, the possible combinations include high-high-high, high-high-low, high-low-low, high-low-high, low-low-low, low-low-high, low-high-high, or low-high-low.

First, the sub-team lead facilitates the brainstorming of different influencing forces that could possibly be assigned to the three axes. Since the time frame being considered is the next five to ten years, participants may want to focus on already-emerging trends that might possibly continue into that near-term future (or participants may collectively decide to go in a different direction and insert a black swan into the scenario's time line). Then the sub-team decides which three influencing forces are most relevant to the use or nonuse of the Promethean technology at the heart of the scenario: Health of the economy? Level of political unrest? Activity level of Terror Group X? Conflict in the Middle East? In Asia? Rate of societal diffusion and adoption of the Internet of Things? The sub-team lead, working with the assistance of a facilitator, creates a volume of eight possible combinations of the three influencing forces at either low strength/intensity or high strength/intensity. Then the sub-team members vote on which of the eight possible combinations is most conducive to the catastrophic malign use of the Promethean technology under consideration. This backdrop of influencing forces is used to help guide the development of the full scenario.

Since the sub-teams are small face-to-face groups, I encourage using nominal group technique procedures during this phase. Voting on the most malign combination may be undertaken in this fashion:

Participants take five minutes to anonymously select their top three choices, with the first choice receiving three points, the second choice two points, and the third choice one point. Facilitators sum the points of each alternative combination, with the combination receiving the most points being the sub-team's consensus choice. The entirety of this step 2, including the round-robin discussion session, should take no more than an hour per scenario.

*Step 3—Apply Through the Terrorist's Eyes Exercise to the Scenario*: In this red-teaming exercise, participants aim to select the terror group or category of terrorist (jihadists, nihilists, thrill seekers, right-wing terrorists, left-wing terrorists, and acolytes of apocalyptic cults) that they judge to have the greatest affinity for the Promethean technology under consideration. They also choose the group or category of terrorist that is most likely to make the worst, most catastrophic use of the Promethean technology. Participants should build on the results of the previous exercise, alternative futures analysis, and make use of the previously developed backdrop. This will be the case for all subsequent exercises carried out during this phase, with each exercise adding a new layer to the scenario. Sub-team leads should ensure that the full "library" that participants develop for this scenario, or all the products produced by the team, is available for members to consult in either electronic or hard-copy form (preferably both to accommodate differing working styles). I again recommend that the sub-team leads use the same NGT procedures that they used in the prior step. In voting for the featured terrorists, participants should take three minutes to anonymously select their top two choices, with the first choice receiving two points and the second choice one point. Facilitators then sum the points received by each, and the option receiving the most points becomes the sub-team's consensus choice for the scenario's protagonist. Step 3 should take no more than an hour per scenario.

*Step 4—Brainstorm Precursors*: What events or developments lead up to the malign use of the Promethean technology? What needs to happen for the worst-case scenario to actualize? What are world leaders doing in the months and years leading up to the worst-case use of the technology? What are technology and business leaders doing? Based on the materials created so far by the sub-team, do any wars occur during the five-to-ten-year period leading up to the worst-case use of the Promethean technology? Do any revolutions occur? Any insurgencies or terror campaigns? Have there been any major environmental disasters that have significantly impacted the world of the scenario? Are people's standards of living rising or falling? What social changes take place in the five to ten years leading up to the catastrophic use of the technology?

The sub-team leads should decide which brainstormed precursors enjoy consensus support following the round-robin idea submission round and the round-robin discussion round, and which brainstormed precursors have less than unanimous support and require voting. Voting should follow the same process used in the prior steps. Step 4 should be completed within an hour per scenario.

*Step 5—Apply Strengths, Weaknesses, Opportunities, and Threats Analysis to the Scenario*: The full sub-team performs the SWOT analysis together—first for the attackers, then for the defenders—using nominal group technique processes to reach a consensus. The sub-team leads should decide which brainstormed additions to the various quadrants enjoy consensus support following the round-robin idea submission round and the round-robin discussion round; they may then be added as elements to the scenario. Those suggestions that have less than unanimous support will require a voting procedure. Step 5 should be completed within an hour per scenario.

*Step 6—Apply Measure-Countermeasure, Move-Countermove Exercise to the Scenario*: In this step, participants should decide whether defenders benefit from any form of useful intelligence prior to the Promethean technology attack or whether they are taken completely by surprise. They should thoroughly brainstorm the prompt/primary, secondary, and tertiary consequences of *both* the catastrophic attack *and* the countermeasures the defenders put into place either in anticipation of the attack or in response to the attack.

The sub-team leads should decide which brainstormed consequences enjoy consensus support following the round-robin idea submission round and the round-robin discussion round, and these consequences should be added as elements to the scenario. Those suggestions that have less than unanimous support will require a vote using NGT procedures. Step 6 should take no more than an hour per scenario.

*Step 7—Sub-Teams Present Their Scenarios to the Full Group for Feedback and Critique*: The full group reconvenes after each sub-team has completed steps 2 through 6 for one of their assigned scenarios. The facilitators randomly assign the order for sub-teams to present their scenarios and respond to questions or comments. The sub-team leads take eight to ten minutes to summarize the results of their team's fleshing-out exercises for the assembled group. Following NGT procedures, the full group (minus the members of the sub-team) engages in two or three rounds of round-robin questioning and commenting, with each speaker offering a single question or comment per round. Facilitators should remind participants to keep their questions and comments succinct and to the point. Sub-team leads or members may respond, but they should also keep their responses brief and to the point, avoiding extended digressions. Each scenario receives an hour's attention from the full group. The sub-team leads should take notes regarding comments made about their respective scenarios and the question-and-answer exchanges.

*Step 8—Sub-Teams Reconvene to Decide Whether to Adjust Their Scenarios in Response to the Full Group's Feedback*: This step is the last one to take place during the face-to-face portion of the Promethean Spyglass. The sub-team leads reconvene their teams and use NGT procedures to perform a round-robin discussion of the feedback received from the full group. The sub-team then decides whether it wishes to make any changes to its scenario based on this feedback or any new ideas generated by it. Leads should aim to have this step take between sixty and ninety minutes per scenario. The sub-team members finalize their scenarios before departing the face-to-face portion of the analysis, knowing they will be sending their science fiction writer team leads home to polish the scenarios and write them up in a compelling, dramatic fashion. Before departing, the sub-teams repeat steps 2–8 for their second assigned scenarios.

The in-person portion of the Promethean Spyglass is both lengthy and emotionally and intellectually taxing. Some participants may be far from their homes and families; many will likely need to contend with issues arising from their normal jobs and lives. On the positive side, participants spend several weeks getting to know a cohort of very interesting people, many of whom come from professional backgrounds quite different from their own. They benefit from developing new critical thinking skills and the opportunity to think more deeply about issues important to their country and communities. Facilitators should take every opportunity to foster the growth of team spirit. Team members should be encouraged to share meals and enjoy shared leisure activities: nature hikes, excursions to historical or cultural sites, shopping trips, even karaoke. If participants are interested and the authors are willing, perhaps some of the science fiction writer team members could offer live readings of their work as after-dinner entertainment.

*Step 9—Lead Scenario Writers Prepare Fifteen-to-Twenty-Page Scenario Narratives with One-Page Executive Summaries*: This step represents the beginning of the second distance portion of the Promethean Spyglass. The science fiction writers who have served as sub-team leads take up to a week to write scenario narratives of approximately fifteen to twenty pages in length, complete with a one-page executive summary. The writers should strive to make their narratives vivid, relatable, and emotionally compelling while keeping within the constraints their team members have collectively established. They also should select memorable names for each scenario. Writers should keep in mind that these narratives will serve varying purposes. The narratives will provide the basis for the remaining phases and steps of the Promethean Spyglass analysis, of course. Homeland security and law enforcement agency administrators will also likely use them with congressional appropriations committees when requesting funding for counter–future-shock R&D projects. Should funding be attained, the narratives will likely be included with acquisition solicitation packages to inform potential offerers (federal research labs, academic labs or consortiums, commercial R&D firms, tech entrepreneurs, etc.) of project requirements. In this way, the narratives will also serve as recruiting tools, potentially attracting some of the country's best minds to work on countering some of the country's most dangerous threats.

### Phase 7: Rank the Deadly Dozen Scenarios

All steps of phase 7 take place within the second distance portion of the Promethean Spyglass. The purpose of this phase is to rank the deadly dozen scenarios in terms of awfulness (risk = the likelihood of the actualization of the malign use × the dollar value of the worst possible consequences). The reason for ranking individual scenarios within the already-prioritized deadly dozen group is that in any given funding cycle, the available funding may not be adequate to initiate R&D programs to counter all twelve scenarios. The deadly dozen themselves must be prioritized so that the worst risks get addressed first.

*Step 1—Apply Technology Sequence Analysis to Estimate the Likelihoods of the Promethean Technologies Reaching Market within a Five-to-Ten-Year Window*: See chapter 5 for a description of how to carry out a Technology Sequence Analysis. This step can be carried out concurrently with step 9 of phase 6 since the polished scenario narratives aren't needed for the team's technical experts and their confederates to carry out TSAS on the deadly dozen Promethean technologies.

Facilitators should have already arranged either to temporarily expand the team with an additional cadre of technical experts sufficient to carry out Technology Sequence Analysis on all of the deadly dozen technologies or to have a contract prepared with an outside consulting firm that specializes in such analyses. The technical experts who are already team members will not be able to accomplish this step on their own or at least not in a timely enough fashion. For any complex technology or system of systems, Technology Sequence Analysis is a lengthy, involved process that encompasses hundreds of estimates of the likelihoods of individual components being available within a five-to-ten-year period. The process may be expedited if more than one of the deadly dozen scenarios share the same Promethean technology or if two or more Promethean technologies share components or if some of the components or subsystems necessary for a Promethean technology have already been developed.

The Promethean Spyglass facilitators will use the TSA results for each of the deadly dozen scenario technologies as the independent base probabilities, or the likelihood of the Promethean technologies reaching market within the next five to ten years. Although the other team members will not be asked to estimate these base probabilities in this phase, they will still be required to assign scores to the six retarding factors as well as estimate dollar values for plausible, worst-case scenario consequences (primary, secondary, and tertiary). Fortunately, the results of the Technology Sequence Analysis will not be needed until step 4 of this phase.

*Step 2—Participants Estimate the Severity of Potential Consequences for Each of the Deadly Dozen Scenarios*: This step begins with participants receiving copies of the polished scenario narratives. Consensus Delphi procedures should be used for this step. Since participants will not be sharing a physical space and possibly not a time zone, facilitators will need to establish windows of time in which participants may electronically submit their first-round estimate and later electronically retrieve the group's median estimate, other summary statistics of the group's inputs, rationales from other (anonymous) group members, and a reminder of their own estimate. Participants will then submit their second-round estimate, either sticking with their original estimate or adjusting it and, either way, providing a justification for their decision. All the stipulations that apply to phase 5's step 2 also apply to this step except I recommend giving participants in this phase a half day's window for their first-round submission and another for their second-round submission. In the interests of keeping assumptions consistent across scenarios, participants should be given electronic access to the assumptions dictionaries they compiled earlier in the process.

A new feature in this step is that facilitators ask participants to rank their own level of confidence and self-perceived expertise regarding each individual estimate or ranking submitted. Facilitators should instruct participants to use the following ranking scale (participants may either choose to select an integer value or a decimal value between zero and five):

1 = very low confidence, no sense of expertise regarding this question

2 = low confidence, minimal sense of expertise regarding this question

3 = moderate confidence, level of expertise regarding this question is probably average

4 = high confidence, higher-than-average expertise regarding this question

5 = very high confidence, very strong sense of expertise regarding this question

At this point, facilitators calculate the Brier scores for the participants' forecasting skills pretests, which team members took in phase 2, step 2. (Forecasting questions on the pretest were chosen so that their answers would be known by this time, allowing levels of accuracy to be compared.) Brier scores are calculated in the following fashion: Events that occur are coded as one, and events that do not occur are coded as zero. The Brier score is the sum of the squared errors between what actually occurs and the probability forecast.[31]

As an example, a participant might have predicted a 70 percent chance that the Academy Award for Best Actor would be won by Sterling Silver (and, accordingly, the chance an actor other than Sterling Silver would win the award was predicted as 30 percent). However, in a shocking upset that made academy members collectively gasp, Thomas Tomas walked away with the golden trophy. The participant's Brier score for this question would be calculated as $(0.7 - 0)^2 + (0.3 - 1)^2 = 0.98$. The best possible Brier score is zero, representing a perfect forecasting ability, and the worst possible score is 2.0, representing a complete failure at forecasting. Had the participant predicted the reverse set of probabilities—that is, a 30 percent chance of Sterling Silver winning the Oscar and a 70 percent chance that a different actor would win—the Brier score would have been calculated as $(0.3 - 0)^2 + (0.7 - 1)^2 = 0.18$. Being much closer to zero, this latter answer would represent a large improvement in the Brier score.

Facilitators will calculate a power score for each participant for each estimate given. The power score is calculated using this formula: power score = self-assessed confidence/expertise rating − (mean Brier score from all pretest questions × 2.5).

The power score may be a negative number. The lowest possible power score is negative five, and the highest possible score is five. If a participant scores the lowest on self-assessed confidence/expertise (zero) but the highest on adjusted mean Brier score (zero), his or her power score would be zero. If a participant scores the highest on self-assessed confidence/expertise (five) but the lowest on adjusted mean Brier score (five), his or her power score would be zero.

For each set of estimates submitted in the first round of this step and of the following step, facilitators will disregard the inputs from all participants whose power score falls below the median power score. This means that, in a team of thirty members, fourteen members would have their estimates put aside for any given rating or estimating question, and the team's median (or mean, for step 3) consensus figure for both the first and second rounds would be calculated using only the inputs from the remaining sixteen members. Also, facilitators should only include rationales from members whose power score equals or exceeds the median power score when providing supporting rationales to the full team at the beginning of the second round.

Facilitators shouldn't inform participants that those whose power scores fall below the group's median will have their inputs discarded in both the first and second rounds. Instead, they should simply tell participants that the results of their forecasting pretests and self-evaluations of confidence and expertise will be used as weighting factors for these steps. For participants' self-evaluations of confidence and expertise to be of any value, they must be honest. If they fear an honest assessment will cause their input to be discarded, participants might be incentivized to exaggerate their self-evaluations. Or if they rate themselves low on confidence and expertise regarding a question, they may then lose motivation to apply their best effort to the estimation or rating task at hand, assuming that their input will not matter; yet the possibility exists that their mean Brier score from the pretest will be strong enough to offset their low confidence and expertise self-rating and put them at or above the group's median power score.

The facilitators calculate the median dollar value of the top scorers' estimates from the second round (those participants whose power scores are at or above the group's median power score). This median dollar value is the consensus value for this deadly dozen scenario, and the facilitators share the consensus value with the participants. Then this process is repeated for each of the remaining scenarios in turn. Participants and facilitators should be able to complete this step for one of the deadly dozen scenarios per workday.

*Step 3—Participants Determine Consensus Values for Each of the Six Probability Factors that Influence the Likelihoods of the Come-to-Market Promethean Technologies Being Used for Malign Purposes*: Consensus Delphi procedures should be used for this step. All the stipulations that apply to phase 5, step 4 also apply to this step except here I recommend giving participants a two-hour window for their first-round submission per retarding factor per scenario and another two-hour window for their second-round submission. All the power score procedures described for phase 7, step 2 pertain to this step as well, with participants conducting self-evaluations on their confidence and expertise for their first-round response *only* for each retarding factor for each scenario and so on.

The facilitators then calculate the mean rating for the retarding factor under review from the top scorers' ratings from the second round (i.e., those participants whose power scores are at or above the group's median power score). This mean rating is the consensus value for this retarding factor for this deadly dozen scenario, and facilitators share it with the participants. This process is repeated for the remaining retarding factors for that particular scenario; then all six retarding factors are estimated for each of the remaining scenarios in turn. Participants and facilitators should be able to complete this sub-step for one deadly dozen scenario per twenty-four hours, or three workdays per scenario.

Team members will only estimate the probability of a scenario becoming actualized after they have already performed consensus Delphi procedures for all six retarding factors for that scenario. At this point, facilitators share with participants the base probability for the scenario under review (the likelihood of the Promethean technology coming to market within a five-to-ten-year window) that is calculated from the TSA results. All the stipulations described for phase 5, step 4 regarding participants' creating models (or not) for the relative effects of the retarding factors and regarding the power scores apply to this sub-step. Facilitators should give participants a two-hour response window for the first-round submission and a two-hour response window for the second-round submission. As was done in phase 5, step 4, facilitators should provide participants with examples of ways that the six retarding factors may be used in conjunction with the independent base probability to estimate a probability of malign use. Additionally, they should provide participants with the group's consensus, an amalgamated mean for each of the six retarding factors, the participants' own second-round scores for each of the six retarding factors, and the summary statistics for each of the six calculated figures. Participants and facilitators should be able to complete this sub-step for one deadly dozen scenario in four hours, or half a workday per scenario, for a total of six workdays for this sub-step.

*Step 4—Facilitators Calculate Estimated Risk Levels for Each of the Deadly Dozen Scenarios and Rank Them in Descending Order of Risk:* Estimated risk levels are all expressed in dollar terms to allow for easy ranking and comparisons. The formula for risk is risk = consensus estimated dollar value of scenario's consequences × consensus estimated probability of the scenario becoming actualized.

Facilitators share with participants the list of scenarios ranked in descending order of risk as well as the risk formula figures for each.

*Step 5—Facilitators Prepare a Promethean Spyglass Analytical Report Including Scenario Narratives, in Ranked Order of Descending Estimated Risk, of the Deadly Dozen Scenarios*: Fortunately for the facilitators, by this point in the process, much of the material they need to prepare a report for the sponsors of the Promethean Spyglass analysis has already been written or tabulated. Far from being a black box procedure, the Promethean Spyglass is entirely transparent, for its participants and facilitators fully document their methods and assumptions as the process unfolds.

Facilitators should share copies of their final report with the participants and welcome their feedback. They should also collect participants' feedback regarding their level of satisfaction with the process and any suggestions for process improvements. If the sponsoring agency's confidentiality requirements allow it, facilitators should ideally keep former participants informed of the progress of various R&D projects initiated by the Promethean Spyglass analysis and perhaps distribute a periodic newsletter highlighting significant project milestones. It will help close the circle for participants and give them a sense of satisfaction that their months of hard thinking and work resulted in concrete actions to prevent the worst of the devil's gestating toys from escaping their box. Since the Promethean Spyglass is an iterative procedure, not a "one-and-done" process, and the participants may be called upon to be members of a future analytical process, showing them generous appreciation and keeping them informed regarding the outcomes of their shared analysis should be an imperative, not merely an afterthought.

# Conclusion

*Buy That Fire Insurance Policy!*

BEFORE DELIVERING THIS BOOK'S closing argument, I want to address some potential criticisms that might be leveled against my proposed Promethean Spyglass procedure. These criticisms revolve around the lack of validation of the retarding factors used in estimating the likelihood of come-to-market Promethean technologies being used malignly as well as the other variable inputs to the analysis. The Promethean Spyglass is not a conventional risk assessment or threat assessment tool. Nor is it meant to be used for a cost-benefit analysis to support a research and development budget request. Instead, it assumes that a budget has already been allocated for as-yet unselected R&D projects intended to counter future-shock threats, and it is intended to guide decision makers in identifying the worst possible plausible threats emanating from over-the-horizon Promethean technologies so that available funding can be better allocated. Thus, the key use of the Promethean Spyglass is to assist decision makers in winnowing the potentially vast number of dire scenarios involving emerging Promethean technologies to a manageable set of scenarios that represent the potential worst of the worst. To do this, managers of the Promethean Spyglass procedure need to ignore 95 percent of the bell-shaped distribution of possible outcomes and concentrate on what might lurk beneath the tapering tail at the right side of the curve—the most severe 5 percent of the distribution.

However, by taking additional validation steps, the Promethean Spyglass could be repurposed to support budget formulations. The first of these validation steps would be for cost estimators, using Monte Carlo simulations, to assign a range of possible dollar values with a 90 percent confidence level to each of the consequences listed for the deadly dozen scenarios: loss of life, property, and productivity; costs of medical care; both prompt and delayed impacts on economic activity; costs of remediation and defensive measures instituted in response to the attack; secondary and tertiary costs stemming from those remediation and defensive measures; and so on. This differs from the basic Promethean Spyglass procedure in that the latter directs participants to assume the worst plausible case for all consequences, pushing the total cost estimate of consequences far out to the right-hand tail of the probability curve.

The second validation step would involve back testing to establish a "best fit" model of the relative weightings of the six retarding factors, insofar as they apply to the base probability of the Promethean technology being brought to market within a five-to-ten-year window. The product of the retarding factors and the time-to-market probability represents the likelihood of a particular Promethean technology being used for the malign purpose envisioned in a scenario.

A reader might ask, "How can somebody use *back testing* to validate a model for an event that has not happened yet?" Even though the Promethean Spyglass is meant to analyze potential future events of an unprecedented nature—namely, the catastrophic malign uses of technologies that have not been invented yet—the notional events being imagined and examined are not entirely unprecedented. Both the 9/11 attacks and the Aum Shinrikyo sarin attack on the Tokyo Metropolitan Subway can be considered as rough analogues to a devil's toy box attack. If one is willing to venture a bit further afield and consider more distant analogues, a huge number of earlier events—successful and unsuccessful terror attacks using conventional technologies and modes of attack—could be used to back test various models of the Promethean Spyglass's probability limiting factors. Various databases can be accessed that describe the sequences of events and operational and environmental factors associated with samplings of both successful and unsuccessful terror attacks. A researcher could retroactively apply each of the notional models that emerge from a standard Promethean Spyglass analysis of the retarding factors (see phase 7, step 3) to a large sample of both successful and unsuccessful terror attacks. In that way, he or she could determine which of the models best correlates with the success or failure of an attack. Each of the notional models would represent a separate hypothesis, which the researcher could test by applying it, in turn, to actual events and seeing how well the model fits. After selecting the model that displays the best fit across the sample of actual events, the researcher could apply the validated model of the weightings of the six retarding factors to the base probability of the Promethean technology of interest coming to market within a five-to-ten-year window, already calculated through a Technology Sequence Analysis. As a last step in the validation process, the probability of the Promethean technology being used for the malign purpose envisioned in the deadly dozen scenario would be multiplied with each of the consequence dollar values estimated through a Monte Carlo procedure. This step formulates a range of possible risk levels for that scenario. Doing the same for all twelve scenarios would establish a broader possible range of risk levels.

A less technical objection to the Promethean Spyglass procedure is that it spends money and expends resources seeking to counter a bunch of notional threats that may never materialize. How does one calculate the bang for the buck when the bang for the buck is the *absence of a bang*? Can the absence of something even be quantified? It *can*, although perhaps not as precisely or with the level of confidence a user would prefer. But more on that in a moment.

It is human nature to focus on already actualized issues or currently pressing problems to the detriment of expending resources to deal with more distant or uncertain threats. This is true even if the latter have far higher potential consequences than the former. If a homeowner's roof leaks and it is raining outside, with more rain projected for the coming week, that homeowner is going to be more concerned about patching the hole in his roof than he is about purchasing a fire insurance policy. This tends to hold true even though the leak may cause, at worst, a couple of thousand dollars' worth of damage, whereas a fire could destroy everything—the entire home and all inside it—potentially costing the homeowner hundreds of thousands of dollars.

It is best to think of the Promethean Spyglass and the R&D projects it facilitates as a fire insurance policy. How much should the insurance policy cost? How much is the policy worth? One way to estimate its worth is to use analogy and look at the costs of the primary, secondary, and tertiary impacts and consequences of an attack that is roughly comparable to one of the envisioned deadly dozen scenarios. I've already suggested two such events—the 9/11 terror attacks and the Aum Shinrikyo Tokyo subway attack.

Setting up the 9/11 attacks cost al Qaeda less than half a million dollars. The resultant costs to the United States? Primary costs included the loss of about three thousand lives (valued at about $4 million apiece), the World Trade Center towers, and the surrounding properties; the repairs to the Pentagon; the four destroyed jetliners; and all the firefighting and police equipment destroyed when the Twin Towers collapsed. Secondary costs were far more varied. They included:

the health care costs incurred by all the persons who were injured but not killed in the attacks, including those who suffered delayed health impacts due to inhalation of the toxic dust resulting from the collapsed and damaged buildings;

the direct costs of the war in Afghanistan;

a portion of the direct costs of the war in Iraq (which was justified, in part, by the U.S. declaration that in the wake of the 9/11 attacks, it could no longer tolerate a hostile regime potentially sharing weapons of mass destruction with terror groups);

the costs of the large-scale federal government reorganization and creation of the Department of Homeland Security;

the costs of the twelve-year hunt for bin Laden;

the costs of armoring cockpit doors on all passenger aircraft;

the costs of additional security measures at U.S. airports;

the costs of shutting down all air traffic for several days following the attacks;

the costs of the economic recession that followed the attacks;

the costs to the travel, tourism, and convention industries of potential customers who opted to avoid air travel following the attacks; and

the psychological and emotional costs of the fear of future terrorism inspired by the attacks (hard as those are to definitize).

Tertiary costs included:

the value of the lives of American servicemen and servicewomen lost to the fighting in Afghanistan, along with the value of the lives of CIA agents, diplomats, and contractors lost;

the value of the lives of Americans lost during the Iraq War and its long aftermath;

the decades-long health cost expenditures for those Americans injured in those two conflicts;

the reduction in Americans' civil liberties and quality of life, taking into account an increase in government surveillance and a degradation in the ease and quality of air travel;

the cost of interest payments that have been and will be made for additional government debt incurred because of increased military and homeland security spending attributable to a reaction to the attacks; and

the opportunity costs of investments and expenditures not made because they were displaced by increased national spending on homeland security efforts and military campaigns and by increased national debt.

These lists should not be considered complete by any means. Add it all up, and the return on investment al Qaeda garnered on its less than half-a-million-dollar investment is staggering: the costs to the United States run into the trillions of dollars, and if lost opportunity costs are added to the total, they perhaps increase to tens of trillions of dollars.

A similar cost tabulation of the consequences of the Aum Shinrikyo sarin attack on the Tokyo subway system can be performed. Unlike the 9/11 attacks, this attack fell far short of its destructive potential due to the cult's primitive, ineffective delivery system for the sarin. Even so, the attackers managed to kill nearly a dozen people and to sicken or injure thousands; however, the secondary and tertiary costs of the attack to the Japanese government and Japanese society far outpaced the primary costs. Yet, if envisioned as one of the Promethean Spyglass scenario stubs, participants would discard the Aum Shinrikyo attack midway through the process given its partial failure to meet its instigators' goals and its falling well short of its lethal potential. It would not survive the culling for the deadly dozen scenarios.

For the sake of argument, let's say the 9/11 and Aum Shinrikyo attacks are two rough analogues for the kind of catastrophic attacks considered by a Promethean Spyglass analysis. Two events are not a lot to work with, but their occurrence since the modern era of terrorism dawned in the late 1960s allows us to estimate the annual chance for a devil's toy box attack. The modern era of terrorism has lasted fifty years thus far. Two devil's toy box attacks in a fifty-year span equates to a 4 percent chance of such an occurrence per year.

Let's (conservatively) estimate the cost of such an attack by (notionally) averaging the consequences of the 9/11 attacks and the far lower consequences of the Aum Shinrikyo attack. We'll use an averaged figure of $1 trillion. Four percent times $1 trillion equals an annual risk level of $40 billion.

Should the homeland security enterprise spend this amount annually on counter-future-shock R&D? Or would it be more accurate to narrow the time span under consideration, perhaps to that between the present and the earlier point of al Qaeda's formation in 1988 and Aum Shinrikyo's turn to terrorism in 1990? Taking this tack would narrow our time span from fifty to thirty years. In this case, two occurrences of a devil's toy box attack in a thirty-year span equates to a 6.7 percent chance of such an occurrence per year. One trillion dollars times 6.7 percent equals an annual risk level of $67 billion.

Should the homeland security enterprise spend *this* amount annually on counter-future-shock R&D efforts?

(For point of comparison, the average allocation annually budgeted for the entirety of the DHS Science and Technology Directorate's R&D efforts from FY 2010 to FY 2014 was $445 million. That represents about 1.1 percent of the lower of the two annual risk levels calculated earlier. Only a small portion of that funding was devoted to what could be characterized as counter-future-shock R&D expenditures.)[1]

Alternatively, budget formulators could perform a series of sensitivity analyses, asking themselves how much they would be willing to spend on an annual basis to avert an attack having combined consequences valued at $1 trillion (or some other amount up to the full tabulation of primary, secondary, and tertiary costs associated with the 9/11 attacks). They could toy with a range of annual likelihoods of occurrence extending perhaps from 0.5 percent to 10 percent likelihood per year. Another method for estimating the value of a devil's toy box insurance policy would be to perform a detailed cost analysis of the consequences set forth in each of the deadly dozen scenarios. They would average the dollar totals for each of the scenarios, then apply one of the preceding formulations for the annual likelihood-of-occurrence figures. To be even more rigorous in their estimations, they could apply the validation procedures I describe at the beginning of this chapter; those validations are needed to use the Promethean Spyglass procedure to support budget formulation efforts.

So are the costs and efforts involved in the Promethean Spyglass procedure and the resultant R&D programs worth it? They may only seem justifiable in hindsight, after we as a society have a dreadful Promethean technology terror attack haunting our shared memories.

The pace of technological development and change is accelerating. Current and near-term developments in nanotechnology, materials science, and machine learning and artificial intelligence promise to bring the impact of Moore's Law to realms of technology far beyond computer chip manufacturing. These developments are paving the way for exponential growth in humanity's abilities to create *and* destroy. Emerging Promethean technologies promise to deliver to average persons, of average skill levels and financial means, capabilities that until the present time have been relegated only to national governments, well-funded military establishments, and research laboratories employing hundreds of highly skilled scientists and technicians.

Prometheus's most significant gift to humanity, the gift of fire, has always offered both life-enhancing capabilities—to cook food; to heat homes in wintertime; to shape bronze, iron, and other metals; and to catalyze chemical reactions that enable the creation of life-saving medicines—and life-extinguishing capabilities, such as the potential to lay waste to entire cities in a single afternoon. The history of technology reflects this dual nature of Prometheus's gift.

Until very recently, the keys to the devil's toy box have been exclusively in the hands of governments. Governments have interests, territory, wealth, and assets to protect. Competing governments have always had the ability to hold each other's interests, territories, wealth, and assets hostage to destruction. Thus, they could often deter one another from acts of aggression, although miscalculations resulted in wars. The big change we are faced with at present is in Prometheus's handing the keys to the devil's toy box to anonymous individuals or small groups. They are not bound by concerns for territory or assets, as governments are. They are not easily detected. Even billion-dollar spy satellites cannot find them. They can hide virtually anywhere while preparing to strike.

While the devil is hard at work on his marvelous, terrifying toys, our shield makers must work just as hard, if not harder. They certainly must work *smarter*. The devil holds the initiative; the shield makers cannot forge enough shields to protect against the nearly infinite variety of terrible toys that could potentially spring forth from the devil's toy box. Yet by making use of their Promethean Spyglass, the shield makers can peer inside the devil's toy box. They can hope to catch glimpses—foggy, flickering glimpses, to be sure—of the toys gestating inside. Then the shield makers can apply their powers of discernment to deciding which of those gestating toys most urgently need to be shoved back inside their box. In the worst circumstances, if the devil's toy box cannot be shut in time, our shield makers at least will not suffer the sort of crippling surprise America's defenders endured on September 11, 2001, for the makers will have had the time and foresight to forge appropriate shields that protect the innocent against the destructive toys that manage to emerge.

# Notes

### 1. Future Shock Visits the Subway

1. Haruki Murakami, *Underground: The Tokyo Gas Attack and the Japanese Psyche* (New York: Vintage International, 2001), vii–viii.

2. Murakami, *Underground*, 10–11.

3. Murakami, *Underground*, 216–19.

4. Murakami, *Underground*, 186.

5. Murakami, *Underground*, 63.

6. Murakami, *Underground*, 32.

7. Murakami, *Underground*, 75.

8. Murakami, *Underground*, 32–37.

9. Murakami, *Underground*, 34.

10. Murakami, *Underground*, 51.

11. Murakami, *Underground*, 96–100.

12. Murakami, *Underground*, 219.

13. Murakami, *Underground*, 136–37.

14. Murakami, *Underground*, 138.

15. Rex A. Hudson, *The Sociology and Psychology of Terrorism: Who Becomes a Terrorist and Why?* (Washington DC: Federal Research Division, Library of Congress, September 1999), 133–39.

16. Hudson, *Sociology and Psychology of Terrorism*, 134–36.

17. Hudson, *Sociology and Psychology of Terrorism*, 134–36.

18. Hudson, *Sociology and Psychology of Terrorism*, 141–51.

### 2. Made in Japan?

1. Hudson, *Sociology and Psychology of Terrorism*, 133–35.

2. Hudson, *Sociology and Psychology of Terrorism*, 133.

3. James Dingley, "The Terrorist—Developing a Profile," *International Journal of Risk, Security and Crime Prevention* 2, no. 1 (January 1997): 29.

4. Dingley, "The Terrorist," 32–34.

5. Hudson, *Sociology and Psychology of Terrorism*, 137.

6. Jaison R. Abel and Richard Deitz, "Are the Job Prospects of Recent College Graduates Improving?" *Liberty Street Economics*, blog of the Federal Reserve Bank of New York,

September 4, 2014, http://libertystreeteconomics.newyorkfed.org/2014/09/are-the
-job-prospects-of-recent-college-graduates-improving.html#.Vko9H6SYVgo.

7. "Up to 30% of Existing UK Jobs Could Be Impacted by Automation by Early 2030s, but This Should Be Offset by Job Gains Elsewhere in Economy," PwC blog, March 24, 2017, http://pwc.blogs.com/press_room/2017/03/up-to-30-of-existing-uk-jobs-could -be-impacted-by-automation-by-early-2030s-but-this-should-be-offse.html.

8. Shona Ghosh, "One of Europe's Most Influential Investors Gave a Brutal Example of How AI Could Wipe Out White-Collar Jobs," *Insider*, June 13, 2017, http://www .businessinsider.com/fred-destin-artificial-intelligence-will-wipe-out-white-collar-jobs -2017-6.

9. Abigail Hess, "This Is the Age Most Americans Pay Off Their Student Loans," *Make It*, CNBC, July 3, 2017, https://www.cnbc.com/2017/07/03/this-is-the-age-most -americans-pay-off-their-student-loans.html.

10. Sarah Jeong, "Social Media and the End of Discourse," *The Verge*, July 10, 2020, https://www.theverge.com/21320338/letter-harpers-writers-free-speech-canceled-social -media-illiberalism.

11. James Lindsay, "The Cult Dynamics of Wokeness," *New Discourses*, June 6, 2020, https://newdiscourses.com/2020/06/cult-dynamics-wokeness/.

12. Lacey Kestecher, "American Pride among Young Americans at All-Time Low," *Campus Reform*, June 15, 2020, https://www.campusreform.org/article?id=15046.

### 3. Promethean Technologies

1. Hudson, *Sociology and Psychology of Terrorism*, 137.

2. Cutler J. Cleveland, "Biophysical Constraints to Economic Growth," in *Encyclopedia of Life Support Systems*, ed. D. Al Gobaisi (Oxford: EOLSS Publishers Co., 2003), 7, https:// www.peakoil.net/files/biophysical%20constraints%20to%20economic%20growth%20by %20Cleveland.pdf.

3. Zachary S. Davis, "Ghosts in the Machine: Defense against Strategic Latency," in *Strategic Latency and World Power: How Technology Is Changing Our Concepts of Security*, ed. Zachary Davis, Ronald Lehman, and Michael Nacht (Livermore CA: Center for Global Security Research at Lawrence Livermore National Laboratory, 2014), ebook edition, 22–23.

4. Davis, "Ghosts in the Machine," 23.

5. Rodrigo Nieto-Gómez, "Power of 'the Few': A Key Strategic Challenge for the Permanently Disrupted High-Tech Homeland Security Environment," *Homeland Security Affairs* 7, no. 18 (December 2011): 5–8, https://www.hsaj.org/articles/50.

6. Daniel M. Gerstein, "Can the Bioweapons Convention Survive Crispr?" *Bulletin of the Atomic Scientists*, July 25, 2016, http://thebulletin.org/can-bioweapons-convention -survive-crispr9679.

7. Gerstein, "Bioweapons Convention."

8. Eben Kirksey, "Who Is Afraid of CRISPR Art?" Somatosphere.net, March 19, 2016, http://somatosphere.net/2016/03/who-is-afraid-of-crispr-art.html.

9. Robert J. Bunker, "Home Made, Printed, and Remote Controlled Firearms— Terrorism and Insurgency Implications," TRENDS Research & Advisory, Terrorism

Futures Series, June 21, 2015, https://scholarship.claremont.edu/cgi/viewcontent.cgi?article=1961&context=cgu_fac_pub.

10. Center on Contemporary Conflict, "Use of 3D Printing to Bypass Nuclear Export Controls" (Monterey CA: Naval Postgraduate School, Center on Contemporary Conflict, CCC-PASCC Research in Progress Ripsheets, October 2016), http://hdl.handle.net/10945/50621.

## 4. Endless Threats

1. The 9/11 Commission, *The 9/11 Commission Report: Final Report of the National Commission on Terrorist Attacks upon the United States, Authorized Edition* (New York: W. W. Norton, 2004), Kindle edition, 9.

2. Rodrigo Nieto-Gómez, "Preventing the Next 9/10: The Homeland Security Challenges of Technological Evolution and Convergence in the Next Ten Years," *Homeland Security Affairs* 7, no. 8 (September 2011).

3. Michael Nacht, "What Is Strategic Latency? An Introduction," in Davis, Lehman, and Nacht, *Strategic Latency and World Power*, 4.

4. Ronald F. Lehman, "Unclear and Present Danger: The Strategic Implications of Latent, Dual-Use Science and Technology," in Davis, Lehman, and Nacht, *Strategic Latency and World Power*, 5.

5. Lehman, "Unclear and Present Danger," in Davis, Lehman, and Nacht, *Strategic Latency and World Power*, 18.

6. The 9/11 Commission, *9/11 Commission Report*, 84–85.

7. Lehman, "Unclear and Present Danger," in Davis, Lehman, and Nacht, *Strategic Latency and World Power*, 6.

8. Daniel Morgan, *Research and Development in the Department of Homeland Security*, CRS Report No. RL31941 (Washington DC: Congressional Research Service, June 20, 2003), 2–10, http://research.policyarchive.org/1741.pdf.

9. Andrew J. Fox, "Putting the Lid on the Devil's Toy Box: How the Homeland Security Enterprise Can Decide Which Emerging Threats to Address" (master's thesis, Naval Postgraduate School, 2018), 326–36, https://www.hsaj.org/articles/14506.

10. Dana A. Shea, *The DHS S&T Directorate: Selected Issues for Congress*, CRS Report No. R43064 (Washington DC: Congressional Research Service, April 14, 2014), 17, https://fas.org/sgp/crs/homesec/R43064.pdf.

11. Science and Technology Directorate, *Strategic Plan 2015–2019* (Washington DC: Department of Homeland Security, 2015), 19, https://www.hsdl.org/?view&did=788584.

12. Nieto-Gómez, "Power of 'the Few,'" 5–8, 10.

13. Nieto-Gómez, "Power of 'the Few,'" 11.

14. Nieto-Gómez, "Power of 'the Few,'" 11.

15. Nieto-Gómez, "Power of 'the Few,'" 13.

16. Christopher Bellavita, "What Is Preventing Homeland Security?" *Homeland Security Affairs* 1 (Summer 2005), https://www.hsaj.org/articles/182.

17. Hon. Jay M. Cohen, Under Secretary, Science and Technology Directorate, U.S. Department of Homeland Security, Testimony before the U.S. House of Representatives,

Appropriations Committee, Subcommittee on Homeland Security, House, 110th Cong., 2 (March 28, 2007), https://www.hsdl.org/?view&did=472664.

18. Cohen, Testimony.

19. Dallas Boyd et al., *Thwarting an Evil Genius: Final Report* (Fort Belvoir VA: Defense Threat Reduction Agency Advanced Systems and Concepts Office and Science Applications International Corporation, April 13, 2009), 7, 9, https://fas.org/irp/agency/dod/dtra/thwart.pdf.

20. Boyd et al., *Thwarting an Evil Genius*, 12–13, 24.

21. Boyd et al., *Thwarting an Evil Genius*, 20, 28–30.

22. Douglas W. Hubbard, "Worse Than Useless: The Most Popular Risk Assessment Method and Why It Doesn't Work," in *The Failure of Risk Management: Why It's Broken and How to Fix It* (Hoboken NJ: John Wiley, 2009), 122–23.

23. Sean Lyngaas, "German Investigators Treating Ransomware Attack as Negligent Homicide, Reports Say," *Cyberscoop*, September 21, 2020, https://www.cyberscoop.com/germany-ransomware-homicide-duesseldorf-hospital/.

## 5. Tools to Build a Promethean Spyglass

1. Alex Roland, "Land Warfare," in *War and Technology: A Very Short Introduction* (New York: Oxford University Press, 2016), 7–41; and Roland, "Naval, Air, Space, and Modern Warfare," in *War and Technology*, 42–83.

2. Olaf Helmer, *Analysis of the Future: The Delphi Method* (P-3558) (Santa Monica: RAND Corporation, March 1967), 2.

3. Juri Pill, "The Delphi Method: Substance, Context, a Critique and an Annotated Bibliography," *Socio-Economic Planning Sciences* 5, no. 1 (February 1971): 58–59.

4. Helmer, *Analysis of the Future*, 4.

5. Norman C. Dalkey, *The Delphi Method: An Experimental Study of Group Opinion* (RM-5888-PR) (Santa Monica: RAND Corporation, 1969), 16–17, https://www.rand.org/pubs/research_memoranda/RM5888.readonline.html.

6. Dalkey, *Delphi Method*, 7.

7. Fred Woudenberg, "An Evaluation of Delphi," *Technological Forecasting and Social Change* 40, no. 2 (1991): 131, https://doi.org/10.1016/0040-1625(91)90002-W.

8. Olaf Helmer, *The Systemic Use of Expert Judgment in Operations Research* (P-2795) (Santa Monica: RAND Corporation, September 1963), 5, https://www.rand.org/pubs/papers/P2795.html.

9. Gene Rowe and George Wright, "The Delphi Technique as a Forecasting Tool: Issues and Analysis," *International Journal of Forecasting* 15, no. 4 (1999): 354.

10. John W. Murry Jr. and James O. Hammons, "Delphi: A Versatile Methodology for Conducting Qualitative Research," *Review of Higher Education* 18, no. 4 (Summer 1995): 423–25, https://doi.org/10.1353/rhe.1995.0008.

11. Kenneth W. Brooks, "Delphi Technique: Expanding Applications," *North Central Association Quarterly* 53, no. 3 (1979): 377–78.

12. Andre L. Delbecq, Andrew H. Van de Ven, and David H. Gustafson, *Group Techniques for Program Planning: A Guide to Nominal Group and Delphi Processes* (Glenview IL: Scott, Foresman, 1975), 7–9.

13. Delbecq, Van de Ven, and Gustafson, *Group Techniques*, 8.

14. Roy Amara, "Views on Futures Research Methodology," *Futures* 23, no. 6 (July–August 1991): 647–48.

15. Nicholas Rescher, *The Future as an Object of Research* (Santa Monica: RAND Corporation, April 1967), 2–4, https://apps.dtic.mil/sti/citations/AD0651425.

16. Theodore J. Gordon, "Technology Sequence Analysis," in *Futures Research Methodology*, Version 3.0, ed. Jerome C. Glenn and Theodore J. Gordon (Washington DC: The Millennium Project, 2009), CD-ROM article 16, 1.

17. Gordon, "Technology Sequence Analysis," in Glenn and Gordon, *Futures Research Methodology*, article 16, 4.

18. Gordon, "Technology Sequence Analysis," in Glenn and Gordon, *Futures Research Methodology*, article 16, 5.

19. Nicole Rijkens-Klomp and Patrick van der Duin, "Evaluating Local and National Public Foresight Studies from a User Perspective," *Futures* 59 (June 2014): 18, http://dx.doi.org/10.1016/j.futures.2014.01.010.

20. Herman Kahn and Anthony J. Wiener, "The Use of Scenarios," in *The Futurists*, ed. Alvin Toffler (New York: Random House, 1972), 161.

21. Kahn and Wiener, "Use of Scenarios," in Toffler, *The Futurists*, 163.

22. Kahn and Wiener, "Use of Scenarios," in Toffler, *The Futurists*, 161.

23. Peter Schwartz, *The Art of the Long View: Planning for the Future in an Uncertain World* (New York: Doubleday, 1996), 241–47.

24. Schwartz, *Art of the Long View*, 247–48.

25. Brett D. Weigle, "Prediction Markets: Another Tool in the Intelligence Kitbag" (master's thesis, U.S. Army War College, 2007), 5.

26. Weigle, "Prediction Markets," 7.

27. Albert E. Mannes, Jack B. Soll, and Richard P. Larrick, "The Wisdom of Select Crowds," *Journal of Personality and Social Psychology* 107, no. 2 (2014): 277–79, https://doi.org/10.1037/a0036677.

28. Mannes, Soll, and Larrick, "Wisdom of Select Crowds," 281–86.

29. Ville A. Satopää et al., "Combining Multiple Probability Predictions Using a Simple Logit Model," *International Journal of Forecasting* 30, no. 2 (2014): 351, https://doi.org/10.1016/j.ijforecast.2013.09.009.

30. Mannes Soll, and Larrick, "The Wisdom of Select Crowds," 281–86.

31. Satopää et al., "Combining Multiple Probability Predictions," 351; and Mannes, Soll, and Larrick, "Wisdom of Select Crowds," 295.

32. George Wright et al., "Coherence, Calibration, and Expertise in Judgmental Probability Forecasting," *Organizational Behavior and Human Decision Processes* 57, no. 1 (1994): 8–10.

33. Nicholas Rescher, *Predicting the Future: An Introduction to the Theory of Forecasting* (Albany: State University of New York Press, 1998), 218–22.

34. Rescher, *Predicting the Future*, 218–22.

35. Don A. Moore et al., "Confidence Calibration in a Multiyear Geopolitical Forecasting Competition," *Management Science*, August 22, 2016, 10, https://doi.org/10.1287/mnsc.2016.2525.

36. Philip E. Tetlock, Barbara A. Mellers, and J. Peter Scoblic, "Bringing Probability Judgments in Policy Debates via Forecasting Tournaments," *Science* 355, no. 6324 (February 3, 2017): 482, https://doi.org/10.1126/science.aal3147.

37. Barbara Mellers et al., "Psychological Strategies for Winning a Geopolitical Forecasting Tournament," *Psychological Science* 25, no. 5 (March 2014): 1107–9, https://doi.org/10.1177/0956797614524255.

38. Gregory Fontenot, "Seeing Red: Creating a Red-Team Capability for the Blue Force," *Military Review* 85, no. 5 (September–October 2005): 4–5.

39. Mark Mateski, "Red Teaming: A Short Introduction (1.0)," *Red Team Journal*, June 2009, 1–7, https://docplayer.net/9857129-Red-teaming-a-short-introduction-1-0-june-2009-dr-mark-mateski-available-at-http-redteamjournal-com-resources.html.

40. Mateski, "Red Teaming," 40–41.

41. Maj. David F. Longbine, *Red Teaming: Past and Present* (Fort Leavenworth KS: School of Advanced Military Studies, U.S. Army Command and General Staff College, 2008), 8–15, http://indianstrategicknowledgeonline.com/web/2286.pdf.

42. Longbine, *Red Teaming*, 67.

43. Brian A. Jackson et al., *Breaching the Fortress Wall: Understanding Terrorist Efforts to Overcome Defensive Technologies* (Santa Monica: RAND Corporation, 2007), xviii–xxii, http://www.rand.org/content/dam/rand/pubs/monographs/2007/RAND_MG481.pdf.

### 6. Core of a Devil's Toy Box Analytical Team?

1. Peter Nicholls, "Prediction," in *The Encyclopedia of Science Fiction*, 2nd ed., ed. John Clute and Peter Nicholls (New York: St. Martin's Press, 1995), 957–58.

2. Allen Steele, "Hard Again," *New York Review of Science Fiction*, June 1992, 1–4.

3. Peter Nicholls, "Golden Age of SF," in Clute and Nicholls, *Encyclopedia of Science Fiction*, 506.

4. Peter Nicholls, "Cyberpunk," in Clute and Nicholls, *Encyclopedia of Science Fiction*, 288–90.

5. "*Blade Runner 2049*," *BoxOfficeMojo*, accessed February 12, 2018, http://www.boxofficemojo.com/movies/?id=bladerunnersequel.htm; and Sam Machkovech, "*Altered Carbon* Somehow Nails the Sci-fi Book-to-TV Landing on Netflix," *ArsTechnica*, February 11, 2018, https://arstechnica.com/gaming/2018/02/altered-carbon-somehow-nails-the-sci-fi-book-to-tv-landing-on-netflix/.

6. Terry Pratchett, back cover material for *Wasp*, by Eric Frank Russell (London: Victor Gollancz, 2000).

7. Arlan Andrews Sr., "SIGMA: Summing Up Speculation," *Analog Science Fiction & Fact* 132, no. 9 (September 2012): 39–40.

8. Andrews, "SIGMA," 39–40.

9. Andrews, "SIGMA," 40–41.

10. Andrews, "SIGMA," 41–43.

11. "Members A–F," *SIGMA Forum*, accessed November 5, 2020, http://www.sigmaforum.org/?page_id=117; "Members G–L," *SIGMA Forum*, accessed November 5, 2020, http://www.sigmaforum.org/?page_id=125; "Members M–S," *SIGMA Forum*, accessed November

5, 2020, http://www.sigmaforum.org/?page_id=134; and "Members T–Z," *SIGMA Forum*, accessed November 5, 2020, http://www.sigmaforum.org/?page_id=140.

12. "SIGMA Members," *SIGMA Forum*, accessed November 5, 2020, http://www .sigmaforum.org/?page_id=107.

### 7. The Promethean Spyglass

1. *Dr. Strangelove, or: How I Learned to Stop Worrying and Love the Bomb*, directed by Stanley Kubrick (1964; Los Angeles CA: Sony Pictures Home Entertainment, 2001), DVD.

2. "Technology Scouting," Quid website, accessed August 10, 2017, https://netbasequid .com/technology-scouting/.

3. Recorded Future website, accessed August 10, 2017, https://www.recordedfuture .com/.

4. "Best-in-Class Client Success Services and Training," Recorded Future website, accessed February 5, 2018, https://www.recordedfuture.com/services/.

5. Mannes, Soll, and Larrick, "Wisdom of Select Crowds," 277–79.

6. Pavel Atanasov et al., "Distilling the Wisdom of Crowds: Prediction Markets vs. Prediction Polls," *Management Science* 63, no. 3 (March 2017): 693–95, https://doi.org /10.1287/mnsc.2015.2374.

7. Philip E. Tetlock and Dan Gardner, *Superforecasting: The Art and Science of Prediction* (New York: Crown, 2015), 16–18.

8. Wright et al., "Coherence, Calibration, and Expertise," 22–23.

9. Delbecq, Van de Ven, and Gustafson, *Group Techniques*, 7–9.

10. Schwartz, *Art of the Long View*, 241–47.

11. William M. Fox, "The Improved Nominal Group Technique (INGT)," *Journal of Management Development* 8, no. 1 (1989): 20–27, https://doi.org/10.1108/eum0000000001331.

12. University of Foreign Military and Cultural Studies (UFMCS), *Red Team Handbook* (version 6.0) (Leavenworth KS: UFMCS, April 2012), https://usacac.army.mil/sites /default/files/documents/RT_Handbook_v6.pdf.

13. Delbecq, Van de Ven, and Gustafson, *Group Techniques*, 7–9.

14. Boyd et al., *Thwarting an Evil Genius*, 24; and Hudson, *Sociology and Psychology of Terrorism*, 134–37.

15. Longbine, *Red Teaming*, 8–15.

16. Michael Abramowicz, "The Politics of Prediction," *Innovations: Technology, Governance & Globalization* 2, no. 3 (Summer 2007): 90–91.

17. UFMCS for Applied Critical Thinking, *The Applied Critical Thinking Handbook* (formerly the *Red Team Handbook*) (version 8.1) (Leavenworth KS: UFMCS, September 2016), 101–2, https://www.benning.army.mil/CFDP_INST_HW/content/2E%20Applied %20Critical%20Thinking%20Handbook%20v8%201_Sep'16.pdf.

18. Rescher, *Predicting the Future*, 218–22.

19. Adapted from UFMCS, *Red Team Handbook* (version 6.0), 189–91.

20. Adapted from UFMCS, *Red Team Handbook* (version 6.0), 210–12.

21. Adapted from UFMCS, *Red Team Handbook* (version 6.0), 210–12.

22. Adapted from Jackson et al., *Breaching the Fortress Wall*, xviii–xxii.

23. Adapted from UFMCS, *Red Team Handbook* (version 6.0), 202–5.

24. Adapted from UFMCS, *Red Team Handbook* (version 6.0), 184–86.

25. Adapted from David P. Duggan et al., *Categorizing Threat: Building and Using a Generic Threat Matrix* (SAND2007-5791) (Albuquerque NM: Sandia National Laboratories, September 2007), 23, https://www.energy.gov/sites/prod/files/oeprod/DocumentsandMedia /14-Categorizing_Threat.pdf.

26. Delbecq, Van de Ven, and Gustafson, *Group Techniques*, 7–9.

27. John Mueller and Mark G. Stewart, *Terror, Security, and Money: Balancing the Risks, Benefits, and Costs of Homeland Security* (New York: Oxford University Press, 2011), 56.

28. Wright et al., "Coherence, Calibration, and Expertise," 22–23.

29. Hubbard, "Appendix: Additional Calibration Tests and Answers," in *Failure of Risk Management*, 262–71.

30. Hubbard, "Worse Than Useless," in *Failure of Risk Management*, 122–34.

31. Tetlock et al., "Bringing Probability Judgments," 481.

## Conclusion

1. Fox, "Putting the Lid," appendix A.

# Index